UNDERSTANDING POVERTY AND WELL-BEING

Research on poverty, inequality and well-being has expanded rapidly throughout the social sciences in recent years and now dominates the international development agenda. However, much of this work remains fragmented and, in particular, the intellectual barriers between economics and other social science disciplines remain strong. The contributions in this volume illustrate the merits of different forms of cross-disciplinary research in facilitating our understanding of poverty and well-being.

Understanding Poverty and Well-Being brings together contributions from economics, sociology, anthropology and politics that transcend the normal boundaries of intellectual disciplines, employ a range of innovative methodologies and are firmly grounded in empirical work with real world relevance.

David Hulme is Joint Director of the ESRC Global Poverty Research Group at the Universities of Manchester and Oxford. He is Professor of Development Studies at the University of Manchester and an Associate Director of the Chronic Poverty Research Centre and the Brooks World Poverty Institute.

John Toye is a former Director of the ESRC Global Poverty Research Group at the Universities of Manchester and Oxford. He is currently Visiting Professor of Economics at the University of Oxford.

UNDERSTANDING POVERTY AND WELL-BEING

Bridging the Disciplines

160901

Edited by
David Hulme and John Toye

Routledge
Taylor & Francis Group

LONDON AND NEW YORK

First published 2007 by Routledge
2 Park Square, Milton Park, Abingdon, Oxon, OX14 4RN

Simultaneously published in the USA and Canada
by Routledge
270 Madison Avenue, New York, NY 10016

Routledge is an imprint of the Taylor & Francis Group, an informa business

Typeset in Times New Roman by KnowledgeWorks Global Limited,
Southampton, UK
Printed and bound in Great Britain by MPG Books Ltd, Bodmin, Cornwall

British Library Cataloguing in Publication Data
A catalogue record for this book is available
from the British Library

Library of Congress Cataloging in Publication Data
A catalog record for this book has been requested

ISBN 10: 0-415-36675-5 (hbk)
ISBN 13: 978-0-415-36675-5 (hbk)

CONTENTS

The Case for Cross-Disciplinary Social Science Research on Poverty, Inequality and Well-Being

DAVID HULME & JOHN TOYE

I. Introduction

> If we ask academics why poor people are poor...different disciplines will
> answer...in their own unique ways; each with certain kinds of data, certain
> methods, certain habits of thinking...in most substantive areas (of the social
> sciences) there is what to outsiders seems like an amazing lack of reciprocal
> knowledge. (Abbott, 2001: 142)

At the end of the nineteenth century, partly as a response to the ebbing of
Christian religious belief, a new secular humanitarianism increasingly coloured
British public opinion. It focused attention on a social phenomenon that had
previously been accepted as natural and inevitable, if unfortunate—the poverty of
those in the lower ranks of society. This new humanitarian feeling of concern for
the poor produced its own scientific analogue. It motivated a new, positivist science
of society, which went well beyond the informational eclecticism and the political

partisanship of Engels' ground breaking *Condition of the Working Class in England* (1973, first published 1845). People now believed that the compassion of concern for the poor should be tempered by a sense of proportion, and that this could be best provided by thorough and intelligent enquiry into numerical information. The aim of social research was to give a sober statistical account of the extent and nature of poverty, and thus to provide the evidence base for a properly measured social policy response (Himmelfarb, 1991: 3–18). Key exponents of this approach were Charles Booth (1892) in London and Seebohm Rowntree (1901) in York.

During the twentieth century, however, research on poverty became increasingly specialized, as the methods of study were gradually refined to make them more penetrating and sophisticated. However, the benefits of specialization brought with them various costs, most particularly an erosion of the overall coherence of the concept of poverty. Those working in different subject areas of social science, such as economics, anthropology, human geography, sociology and political studies, have undoubtedly done much illuminating research into many aspects and dimensions of poverty. However, communications between researchers in different areas have been remarkable largely for their absence: this has particularly been the case between practitioners of economics and of the other social science subjects. Throughout the 1990s, while economists have attempted to define and measure global poverty with increasing precision, researchers taking an anthropological perspective have advised that 'poverty is a myth, a construct and the invention of a particular civilization' (Rahnema, 1992: 158).

There are general reasons, then, arising from the splintering of theoretical and applied knowledge, for believing that the adoption of a more cross-disciplinary research strategy would strengthen the coherence and social relevance of the results that researchers generate. Furthermore, there are reasons to believe that the study of well-being and poverty is a particularly appropriate subject for cross-discipline research. John Knight (1991: 26) put the point well from the economist's perspective.

If we are ultimately concerned with things like poverty, hunger, inequality, 'people's capabilities to be and do things', and so on, and with policies to make improvements, then we must recognise that economics is interdependent and cannot be isolated.

Such recognition leads in the direction of cross-disciplinary research, defined as any analysis or policy recommendation based on questions, concepts or methods of more than one academic discipline. Yet as long as many economists still claim that economics can be 'contaminated' by the 'softer' disciplines of other social sciences and many non-economists dismiss as 'reductionist' economists' analyses of human action, it will require considerable energy, intellectual courage and integrity to design and implement a cross-disciplinary research strategy on poverty and well-being.

When we speak of social science, we have a particular set of subjects in mind, and it is useful at the outset to specify our coverage. Our focus is on economics, sociology, anthropology, politics and human geography. Much of our discussion will contrast economics with sociology, anthropology, politics and human geography (henceforth SAPG).[1] To two potentially important subject areas we pay limited attention. The first is psychology, often formally classified as a science, rather than a social science, in UK universities. Psychology, and even social psychology, has less frequently engaged with development studies or the analysis of well-being, poverty and inequality in the context of developing countries.[2] However, very recently, economists and social psychologists have begun to work together and in future psychology may well demand greater attention. The second is philosophy. Every social science draws on philosophy, in one way or another, in search of answers to its specific ontological, epistemological, methodological and conceptual problems. Yet philosophy can provide them with neither a Platonic method of acquiring knowledge infallibly nor an Aristotelian map of all branches of knowledge. In this introduction (and in the articles that follow), reference is made to the contributions of social scientists who have drawn on philosophy (especially Amartya Sen)[3] and philosophers who have ventured into social science (such as Martha Nussbaum). The large and growing body of work on well-being produced by philosophers is not explored, however.[4]

A generation ago, Michael Lipton (1970) made the classic statement, from the economic viewpoint, of the case for a cross-disciplinary dimension in poverty research. Yet the arguments of 35 years ago may not be persuasive today, and may be in need of revision in the light of recent intellectual developments. With this in mind, we reassess the case for cross-discipline research on poverty and well-being, to see how much validity it retains and where it needs to be supplemented. In the course of this reassessment, we introduce some relevant key ideas from the cross-disciplinary collection of papers that follows.

The next section considers both the reasons why cross-discipline research is essential for future investigation of poverty and well-being, and the incentives that have favoured ever more specialised single-subject research: incentives that at times have generated self-justifying subject stereotypes. The paper then argues in Section III against the application of dichotomous stereotypes to economics, on the one hand, and the SAPG or 'non-economics' subjects on the other.[5] The commonly applied dichotomies are objective versus subjective, quantitative versus qualitative, and positivist versus post-positivist. In Section IV, we explore the meaning of an intellectual discipline and suggest that it is the normative practice of a 'knowledge community', and that it shapes both cohesion within social science subjects and the degree of affinity between researchers in different subject areas. We decompose cross-disciplinary research by distinguishing between multidisciplinary and interdisciplinary approaches. Section V makes a qualified defence of those researchers, and particularly economists, who 'trespass' beyond the assumed boundaries of their disciplines against charges of intellectual imperialism. In Section VI, we examine the ways in which different disciplines do and do not relate to practising professions. This has profound implications for cross-disciplinarity. The conclusion suggests ways in which the benefits of cross-discipline research can be realised.

The paper draws on the existing literature and the cross-disciplinary seminars mounted by the ESRC's Global Poverty Research Group (GPRG) at the universities of Manchester and Oxford. In addition, it makes use of the results of two types of empirical analysis. Content analysis and citation analysis studies, applied to articles in academic journals by economists and other social scientists, are used to give an account of how social sciences differ with respect to quantification, and how they communicate with each other.

II. Why is Cross-Discipline Collaboration Needed?

How does the need for cross-discipline collaboration arise? One reason is that the individual disciplines have, over the years, become increasingly differentiated and refined. In the very process of differentiation and refinement, they have also developed blind spots and methodological limitations that arise from their high degree of specialisation. Within a discipline, its basic working assumptions are accepted uncritically, because they are part of the consensus around its research paradigm. Sophistication has been purchased at the cost of an excessive narrowing of focus. For example, the bulk of econometric research on poverty dynamics still uses a concept of income/consumption poverty (Hulme and McKay, 2005), even though many of the econometricians conducting the work agree that poverty has to be understood as a multidimensional phenomena and that 'non monetary' measures are feasible (see below).

Similarly established paradigms shape the work of sociologists, social anthropologists, political scientists and others who have refined their own conceptual vocabularies, and developed preferred strategies of investigation that are highly specific to themselves. Sociologists and human geographers may have documented fascinating life histories of poor people that reveal important processes (for example Gulati, 1982; Bourdieu et al., 1999; Hulme, 2004), but it is difficult (econometricians would say impossible) to use these to test hypotheses or to make generalisations in the absence of a sampling procedure that can explain the position of respondents in the wider population. The existence of these distinctions in research paradigms means that new efforts are now required in collaboration among disciplines that study well-being, poverty and inequality, to deepen understanding and contribute to more effective policy. Indeed, the recent shift from analysing poverty (deprivation) to well-being favours cross-disciplinary approaches that can capture some or all of the different aspects of well-being.[6]

This insight is by no means new, but it does seem to be something that has to be repeated. It is important to recall that Charles Booth's foundational studies of poverty in late nineteenth century London were based on a mixture of methods of investigation and a multidimensional concept of poverty. Booth believed that 'the statistical method was needed to give bearings to the results of personal observation, and personal observation to give life to statistics' (quoted by Himmelfarb, 1991: 93). He never attempted to define the poor solely as those whose consumption fell below a monetary poverty line. His investigators used figures of apparent weekly earnings as one criterion among several, including information on health status and school attendance recorded by authoritative local observers, to assign households to a number of different social classes (see Booth, 1892). This made it possible to triangulate findings, consider the linkages between different dimensions of poverty and examine some of the underpinning processes.

Later work on poverty has tended to be more methodologically bifurcated. Rowntree, for example, developed much more sharply than Booth the idea of a 'primary poverty line' based on the income required for a diet providing bare physical efficiency. He also produced a social class analysis of the people of York based on observations and judgements about 'obvious want or squalor' or 'secondary poverty', but this could not be reconciled with his income-based analysis.[7] By 1941, Rowntree had abandoned the concept of secondary poverty, and the primary poverty line based on a minimum diet took on a life of its own (Glennerster, 2004: 26). Today this kind of incongruence is most evident between disciplines. Many economists of poverty tend to operate as if the poor could be defined exclusively with reference to a criterion level of consumption or income, and sociologists (and others) often operate as if income and consumption surveys were redundant and all that was needed to identify the poor was oral testimony and qualitative information collected by participant observation.[8] This specialisation in partial approaches to estimating the incidence of poverty has been accompanied by a loss of overall perspective, and particularly a loss of connection with the motivation for poverty research, and the reasons for being concerned about the fate of the poor.

Economists may take it for granted that it is useful to discover that X per cent of the population of Country Y are income or consumption poor, although the use to which their estimate is put falls in someone else's problem area. The government of Country Y may be very keen to employ economists to make such an estimate, not because it is essential for devising anti-poverty policies, but because it wants to prove that the figure has fallen or is lower than in neighbouring Country Z. In this collection, Francis Teal's paper performs two useful functions in this context. It both clarifies the reason for regarding measures of consumption as measures of welfare (essentially because increases in consumption indicate increases in choice), and explains why average measures of consumption are widely distrusted. Using data from Ghana in the 1990s, he shows that while average measures show a decline in poverty, the poorest households headed by farmers experienced falls in their consumption expenditures. He concludes that a decrease in poverty – measured in the standard way – does not at all imply that most people in the economy had greater opportunities. This is a valuable antidote to a superficial reading of the income or consumption poverty line studies that economists produce. At the same time, Teal's paper raises questions about the view, often favoured by anthropologists, that larger families are better off than smaller.

III. The Resort to Intellectual Stereotyping

The current situation provides many professional incentives to stay within disciplinary confines. This has had the effect of reinforcing the fissiparous and centrifugal tendencies in poverty analysis. In 1970, Lipton (1970: 11) remarked: 'the lack of professional prestige in (interdisciplinary development studies) is self-confirming'. Since then, unfortunately, the mechanisms that regulate professional prestige have created even more incentives not to stray across subject boundaries, especially within economics. Professional standards are maintained by a peer review that is done almost exclusively from within each social science subject. University evaluation, and linked funding of research, again often depends on peer review within one subject. People undertaking social science research are nowadays required to be in an academic institution, so they are all engaged in pursuing an academic career, progress in which again depends heavily on single subject peer review. In the

UK they are brigaded into 'units of assessment' that have little motivation to encourage them to explore across subject boundaries and they fear the loss of resources that such encouragement would entail.[9]

Unfortunately, as the incentives for collaboration across subject boundaries are weakened, so the potential for mutual misunderstanding and ill-informed mutual criticism by researchers in different subject areas increases. Much of this is conducted at the individual and anecdotal level, by quoting examples of 'obviously wrong' statements made by those outside of one's own discipline. This will not do. Because the logic of disciplines is normative – that is it maintains standards advising researchers what they ought to do – the critique of disciplines cannot proceed merely by noting that some researchers in a particular discipline have said something absurd. Actual research is often 'undisciplined', and, while to point that out is a valid criticism of the researcher, it is not a valid criticism of the discipline. The critique of a discipline, if it is to succeed, must show that the intellectual procedures that researchers in it are expected to follow are absurd. This is always a harder case to prove.

Ideologies of disciplinary rivalry provide the currency for a debate in which self-justification is a stronger motive than the search for understanding. Examples of such disciplinary ideologies are many and various, but perhaps most familiar are dichotomies that are put into service as stereotypes of entire social science disciplines. Example of such dichotomies include: objective *vs.* subjective; quantitative *vs.* qualitative; positivist *vs.* post-positivist; and generalised *vs.* contextualised.[10] In a further simplification, the terms 'objective', 'quantitative', 'positivist' and 'generalised' are assigned by the stereotype to the whole subject area of economics. By contrast, their opposites are assigned to the other social science subjects.[11] While many SAPG researchers see 'subjective', 'qualitative', 'post-positivist' and 'contextualised' as noble banners to carry (and few would find them objectionable), for economists, scientists and many policy-makers these terms signal 'soft' social science that produces unreliable, anecdotal, and sometimes incomprehensible, accounts of what is happening. Are such stereotypes justified or are they merely unhelpful representations?

Taking the objective–subjective dichotomy as an example, it is not the case that there is a difference between economics and other disciplines in what it is that they analyse, or that economics focuses on concrete phenomena (incomes, exports) while sociology and anthropology study intangible things like beliefs and feelings. Economics, at least in its marginal utility version, is based on the analysis of preferences. It is true that some economists, starting with Hicks and Allen in the 1930s, pioneered an 'objectivist' shortcut for the purposes of demand theory, arguing that the choices people actually make provide all the information necessary to establish the utility of outcomes.[12] This move was dictated by a belief that subjective experience was unobservable, and that the use of reports on it was therefore methodologically problematic. This was a wrong turning, and by the 1970s, economists who, like Lipton, were dissatisfied with this exercise in reductionism, looked to psychology to supply the missing information on the actual motivations of the rural poor.

Since 1970, reliance on the axiomatic revealed preference approach has been challenged by a growing number of economists, who have explored what can be done with data on 'reported subjective well-being'.[13] Concerns about what surveys of such data really tell us remain, but now they are being actively explored rather than being taken as a reason for research passivity. These explorations are opening up a somewhat different avenue of cooperative work between economics and psychology. Psychologists know how to tackle the question of whether, for example, people's reports of their state of happiness are systematically influenced by their personality traits. This and related questions have to be resolved before the relation of reported subjective well-being to economic indicators can be done in a properly critical manner.

To the extent that this proves to be possible, the exciting new, cross-disciplinary field of the economic and other determinants of happiness will be opened up for further research. Some of the perennial questions of well-being studies – under the rubric of poverty, inequality and the quality of life – will then have to be re-examined. At present, this research suggests that, on the one hand, subjective well-being depends, other things being equal, on one's position in the hierarchy of income levels, but that increases in income do not increase well-being proportionately. Kingdon and Knight (in this volume) argue that subjective well-being can be viewed as an encompassing concept that allows the importance of other variables such as income, basic needs, relative position and security to be evaluated. Their originality is to explore the idea of subjective well-being as an encompassing notion, a line of research that has not been attempted for either developed or developing countries. Using South African data, they show that factors such as education, employment, health and personal security all enter, along with income, into subjective well-being. They warn that researchers who adhere to the income approach to poverty run the risk of over-simplifying what is at issue.

In terms of cross-discipline research, the economics and happiness theme opens an opportunity for economists to learn from sociologists about the formation of economic aspirations. If it turns out that it is the fulfilment of a range of economic and social aspirations that makes people happy, what is it that shapes aspirations? How do variations between countries in social mobility affect the way in which income aspirations play into assessments of subjective well-being? Are there significant differences between the income aspirations of those living in rich and poor countries? Here is further fertile ground for disciplinary cooperation in poverty research.

To label economics as a quantitative discipline and other social sciences as qualitative disciplines lacks any fundamental justification. It seems plausible only because people confuse 'quantitative' with 'mathematical'. If by 'quantity' we mean a determinate amount, a sum that has been counted or measured, a quantitative discipline is one that makes use of empirical statistical data. There is nothing about the subject of economics that makes research into it uniquely well suited to using the methods of statistical inference.[14] Economics is not intrinsically more amenable (or less, as many famous economists have argued!) to statistical treatment than politics or sociology or even history. It is worth noting that:

The development of statistical thinking was a truly interdisciplinary phenomenon for which mathematics had no priority of position; new ideas and approaches arose as a result of the application of techniques borrowed from one or more disciplines to the very different subject matter of another. (Porter, 1986: 8)

The urge to co-opt statisticians to the cause of research was driven by the pursuit of objectivity, and the desire to achieve empirical results that are inter-subjectively testable, and tested. That pursuit and that desire can be an aim of any knowledge community or intellectual discipline. Indeed, the decision of very different knowledge communities to co-opt statisticians is perhaps the principal cause of the growing affinities across social science subjects.

The pursuit of objectivity does not, however, require an exclusively quantitative approach. Because of the cost of surveying large numbers of households and firms, questioning in this mode will be both researcher-determined and limited in depth. David Lawson and Andy McKay's paper (in this volume) shows how quantitative and qualitative approaches to the persistence of poverty in Uganda can be complementary. Participatory appraisal inevitably takes a more holistic view and can bring to the surface specific determinants of the persistence of poverty that are unanticipated by the researcher. The importance of excess alcohol consumption, domestic violence and personal insecurity has been brought to the surface by these techniques. These can be complementary with quantitative results, and enrich the causal story that emerges from the statistical analysis of survey data.[15]

Jocelyn de Jong's paper (in this volume) contributes further to this theme. It shows the limitations of a purely statistical approach to women's reproductive health in developing countries. Morbidity associated with poor reproductive health is increasingly recognised as an important diminution of women's well-being, markedly more so than in the case of men. Yet using the disability adjusted life years (DALY) method of accounting for morbidity misses important effects on well-being, such as the social stigma or social approval that is associated with conditions like female circumcision, pregnancy and labour complications. However, these effects can be gauged through anthropological methods. The relevance of this paper to the study of HIV/AIDS need not be underlined.

When examining the qualitative/quantitative 'divide' it is important to note similarities and differences between the evolution of the social sciences in Europe and North America. Economics and anthropology in the two regions have tended to follow similar paths. Economics in both Europe and North America has become increasingly mathematical and/or based on the manipulation of large, quantitative datasets.[16] At the same time, rational choice theory in its many varieties has increasingly provided the analytical framework for the research of economists. Similarly, anthropology in both regions focuses on the application of the ethnographic method to examine the understandings that people have of the social and physical worlds and has been influenced by postmodernism. In marked contrast, sociology and political science in Europe have diverged from North America. While in Europe the disciplines have increasingly focused on qualitative data and shifted towards critical realism and postmodernism, in North America the disciplines have become more positivist, more guided by rational actor models and/or more inclined to analyse large quantitative datasets.[17]

The dichotomy between positivist and post-positivist orientations, at least in Europe, does have considerable substance and has made cross-disciplinary work more difficult. Economists have largely avoided engagement with critical realist and/ or postmodernist analytical frameworks. The critical realism of Tony Lawson (1997) and his associates is an exception that proves the rule, because few mainstream economists engage constructively with his work. For other social scientists, the disciplinary drift has been away from positivism and has focused on whether to align with critical realist/interpretive approaches or to commit to a full-blooded, eclectic postmodernism. An important component of these shifts is that, while SAPG researchers have increasingly highlighted the importance of context to effects (Sayer, 2000: 15), economists tend to assume that contexts are similar, unless there is some specific reason to believe otherwise.[18] While positivist economists and critical realist SAPG researchers may be able to converse and even learn from each other, at the extremes of ontological positions – super positivism and postmodernism in the style of Jacques Derrida – communication is very difficult and the likelihood of descent into mutual disparagement very high.

Postmodernism à la Derrida maintains that the truth content of no discourse may be privileged relative to that of any other. Its scepticism leads to a radically relativist account of truth. Yet if Derrida's argument is applied to itself, the conclusion is that there can be no compelling reason to believe it. As a result, the Derrida version of postmodernism implodes by self-contradiction. Super-positivism, on the other hand, derives from a simplified model of 'science', taken over rather unthinkingly from what is supposed to be true of research in the natural sciences. Without entering further into the epistemological debate on the differences between natural and social science, it is sufficient to note the Duhem–Quine thesis, that what would count as falsification of a given proposition depends on some other beliefs that the researcher accepts as true, but without testing them. As a result, it is hard to argue that individual statistical tests can provide definitive evidence of the falsity or otherwise of hypotheses. This does not imply that such testing should be abandoned. It remains a valuable way of developing logically different 'webs of belief', and disciplining the competition for credence between them (Bevir, 1999). The point here is that the rhetoric of science should not be used to drive a wedge between economics and other social science subjects, with the claim that it is – or is capable of becoming – more 'scientific' than they are.

IV. Knowledge Communities, Intellectual Disciplines and Cross-Disciplinarity

For the natural scientists, the standard view is that they form a single 'republic of science' stretching from astronomy to medicine, and that all are subject to the authority of 'scientific opinion' (Polanyi, 1962: 59). For such a unified republic, the problem of cross-discipline work does not really arise. For social scientists, people studying other people, the issues of intention and meaning are never absent, and differences in methods of researching them strongly divide 'social scientific opinion' in a way that complicates cross-discipline work.

There is an additional problem. Discussion of cross-discipline research in social science is often conducted on the assumption that the social science subjects in which we are interested – economics, sociology, anthropology and so on – should be treated as if each were a separate intellectual discipline. This assumes that each subject constitutes a unitary intellectual endeavour, clearly bounded, and distinguishable by differences in characteristics across a number of common criteria from all the others. Unfortunately for the simplicity of analysis, this is not true of social science subjects. We have to preserve a clear distinction between a social science subject and a social science discipline.

The organisation of subjects in the social sciences is not the result of any clear or logical division of intellectual labour. Rather it is the outcome of complex historical processes. Abbott (2001: 122 ff.) argues that social science subjects, as we recognise them today, largely evolved in the US, as 'social structures' inside universities and as a mechanism across universities to manage the labour market for faculty. The organisation of academics in other countries (England, France, Germany) went through quite different histories (ibid.). Over time, however, the US model has spread globally, so that now 'we find economics, political science, sociology, anthropology, history... and psychology' as a common core of social sciences (ibid: 125).

There are three main reasons why a strategy of taking the conventional list of core social science subjects as co-extensive with intellectual disciplines comes to grief.

(i)   Unlike in the natural sciences, in social science the subject areas have different 'axes of cohesion'. 'In the social sciences... axes of cohesion are not aligned... anthropology is largely organised around a method, political science around a type of relationship, and economics around a theory of action. Sociology – best conceived as organised around an archipelago of particular subject matters – presents yet another axis of cohesion. These axes do not fall in any hierarchical order, a fact that has made interdisciplinarity in the social sciences more complicated than the simpler, linear interpretation of the natural sciences' (ibid: 140).

(ii) There is thus considerable intellectual diversity within subjects (as well as differences in levels of intellectual diversity between subjects).[19] This has important consequences, with some subjects (such as economics) having a relatively high level of intra-subject cohesion, while others (such as sociology) have much less. Some sociologists indeed seem to have greater intellectual affinity with researchers 'outside' their subject area than with others inside it.[20]

(iii) Whereas social science subjects do evolve over time (for example sociology barely existed before the 1930s), they do so relative slowly. By contrast, the composition of intellectual activity within a subject changes relatively rapidly (for example in economics over the last twenty years, agricultural economics and neo-Marxist economics have both waned, while mathematical modelling and econometrics have flourished). Looking only at the evolution of core social science subjects often conceals the fate of intellectual disciplines.

In order to understand the diversity within and between subjects, we need to invoke social network theory, and specifically the idea of 'knowledge communities', sometimes also known as 'epistemic communities'. A knowledge community is defined here as a network of knowledge-based experts who share an interest in a subset of knowledge issues, and who accept common procedural protocols as criteria to judge the success of their knowledge creation activities. What is essential here is not that all members of a knowledge community know or communicate with each other, but that they have common intellectual interests and aims, and a shared understanding and acceptance of the methods by which their sort of knowledge is successfully created. (This is in contrast with the definition used by Haas, who stresses shared faith in the application of knowledge to policy, thus allowing an epistemic community to encompass members from a variety of disciplines; see Haas, 1992: 1–37) In our definition, the legitimate methods or 'procedural protocols' of each knowledge community provides it with its intellectual discipline, determining among other things the content of the training thought to be appropriate for those aspiring to become members.

Disciplines arguably share not just aims, interests and methodological norms, but also a distinctive culture – made up of attitudes, aspirations and social values.[21] While generalising plausibly about these cultural elements is perilous, many poverty researchers claim to recognise such cultural differences as shaping the work that people within a discipline undertake. Arguably, economists (and, to a lesser degree political scientists) mix well with more powerful people and feel relatively confident about explaining the implications of their findings to politicians and high-level bureaucrats. By contrast, anthropologists and sociologists are less ready to mix and empathise with people in power and much less likely to be confident about arguing for the implications of their work for public policy. They are more likely to mix and relate well to the less powerful and even the powerless and marginalized. These characteristic values and attitudes are relatively resistant to change and may be both reinforced and reproduced by the notable gender disparities between the disciplines.[22]

Be that as it may, in the social sciences, actual knowledge communities (in the above sense) correspond highly imperfectly with the boundaries of the core social science subjects, also confusingly often called 'disciplines'. For example, Hickey (2005) challenges the idea that political studies represent a single discipline, highlighting the divide between political science and political sociology as contrasting knowledge communities within political studies. He further argues that political sociology will provide the greater insights into the condition of the poor because its concern with the social bases of power makes it cross-disciplinary from the outset. Thus, within each social science subject are varying numbers of knowledge communities, with different intellectual orientations and norms, that bind them more or less closely to their subject area and which shape the degree of affinity they have with knowledge communities outside their subject boundary. For example, there are strong methodological and conceptual parallels in the analysis of poverty as between micro-economists, political scientists using rational choice theory and quantitative sociologists. By contrast, there is a chasm between applied micro-economists using advanced econometrics and economists pursuing the old institutionalist research programme.

Cross-disciplinary work on poverty and well-being in the social sciences, as in all other fields, involves the active extension of two or more knowledge communities' networks, and the making of a link or junction between them. Junction may provoke some adjustment or widening of the common interests of both communities, but it may also challenge the accepted 'procedural protocols' with which both currently work. Such protocols are not necessarily incommensurable, they are currently often incommensurate, and the way to making them common is not yet clear. The resulting potential for normative dissonance inevitably raises the question of the different forms that successful cross-disciplinary work can take.

Cross-disciplinary research can be seen as having two main variants: inter-disciplinary and multidisciplinary approaches. Although the terms are used interchangeably by many people, we suggest that they are not the same, and that there is a valid distinction to be made, one that is more than just a minor quibble. The term 'interdisciplinary' is the older, dating from the 1920s. It was used then mainly in the context of the natural sciences, although the idea also affected the social sciences. The US Social Science Research Council was actually founded at that time to 'deal only with such problems as involve two or more disciplines'.[23] Interdisciplinary research often implied a belief that those who practised it could create new research fields as a result. This promise was more likely to be fulfilled in the natural sciences than in the social sciences, for the reason already explained – the different axes of cohesion in the latter. The term was slow to gain currency, and it was only from the 1960s that it began to make much impact.[24]

Michael Lipton (1970) advocated 'interdisciplinary development studies', and the adjective 'interdisciplinary' has been the one that has tended to persist in the vocabulary of social science research funding bodies. The precise formulation that Lipton gave to the term 'interdisciplinary' has been largely forgotten in the intervening years. Ravi Kanbur (2002) has recently sought to define the terms 'a little more precisely to indicate different types of mixing of disciplines'. We follow his definitions, so that:

- *Crossdisciplinarity* is a generic term referring to any analysis or policy recommendation based substantively on analysis and methods of more than one discipline.
- *Interdisciplinarity* refers to research that attempts a deep integration of two or more disciplinary approaches from the beginning and throughout an entire research exercise.[25]
- *Multidisciplinarity* refers to work in which individual discipline-based researchers (or teams) do their best, within their disciplinary confines, to examine an issue and subsequently collaborate to develop together an overall analytical synthesis and conclusions (Kanbur, 2002: 483).

We should note, however, that there are a variety of ways in which mixes of interdisciplinarity and multidisciplinarity might be combined.

Cross-disciplinary research has been advocated in a variety of contexts. At the practical level, a developmental task, such as strengthening food security, planning new towns or increasing female school enrolment, is often said to require the cooperation of specialists from different disciplines, and we regard this as uncontroversial. At the academic level, it has been argued at least since the 1940s that a fuller understanding of social phenomena requires the cooperation of specialists in different intellectual disciplines, making use of the light that each can throw on the others' analyses.[26] This could involve either multidisciplinary or interdisciplinary approaches.

The concept of 'multidiscipline research' emphasises that individual researchers (or teams) should continue to conduct research within the discipline or disciplines in which they have been trained. Kanbur's definition of multidiscipline research also usefully emphasises that polymath abilities in individuals, or the learning of a second discipline in which one is as expert as in the first, are not pre-conditions of such research – as Streeten once argued.[27] While some have mastered a second discipline

(Amartya Sen,[28] for example, moved with ease from economics into philosophy) others have been less successful in the attempt.[29] The alternative is by coordination within a group of individuals. Whether it is best to pursue a polymath or group approach will depend on the human and financial resources available, the time scale for any specific piece of research and the preferences of researchers.[30]

Some might object that the concept of 'multidiscipline research' gives excessive credence to the intellectual virtue of 'disciplines'. 'What is a discipline', they might ask, 'that its preservation should be so important?' Others might respond that every discipline has its specific logic, which is a set of norms of reasoning appropriate to the subject matter being analysed (see Bevir, 1999: 8–9). This normative logic has to be learned, and hopefully improved, by each new generation of researchers in the discipline. The normative logic of disciplines can thus be thought of as accumulated distillations of long traditions of enquiry. Cross-disciplinary research would be suspected of lack of rigour if its practice required participants to abandon conceptual and methodological standards that their knowledge communities had previously regarded as essential. Multidisciplinary research does not take that risk.

By contrast, interdisciplinary research is relatively more challenging to social scientists and is more likely to take them out of their intellectual comfort zones. It requires that an individual (or more likely a group drawn from two or more disciplines) seek to integrate the concepts and methodologies of different disciplines from the outset of a research project. This is demanding (intellectually and in terms of finance and researcher time), as each discipline has to learn about the logic of other disciplines and to strive to integrate these logics without compromising the standards of rigour of its own discipline. For some pairings of knowledge communities, for example econometrics and critical realist sociology, this may be impossible as the 'rigour' of each group is seen as fundamentally flawed by the other. While cross-disciplinary criticism can sharpen work it is unlikely to be something that can be built on, if the criticisms are that a collaborator, who is respected within his/her discipline, has produced 'nonsense'.

Fortunately, successful examples of interdisciplinary poverty research are emerging, as illustrated by the work of Adato et al. (2004). In this example, econometrics and sociological life histories are rigorously combined. The econometrics yields statistically representative findings about the correlates and characteristics of poverty dynamics. Then, using the survey results as a sampling frame, sociological life histories provide deep accounts of the processes that are associated with falling into, climbing out of and being trapped in poverty for a subset of households whose position within the larger population is known.

V. The Fallacy of Intellectual Territory

Apart from stereotypes of disciplinary rivalry, another persistent obstacle to cross-discipline research has been a discipline-based territoriality about subject matter. It is often (wrongly) assumed that certain subjects belong within the boundaries of specific disciplines. Anthropologists were thought to have a prior claim to the family and the tribe, sociologists to religions and trade unions, political scientists to governments and elections and economists to money and the market. Therefore, when a researcher in one discipline investigated a subject that was 'beyond his intellectual jurisdiction' something academically improper was thought to have occurred. Researchers who committed this impropriety even paid tribute to the prevailing view by speaking of their activity as 'trespassing' (for example Hirschman, 1981: v).

This territorial view of the subject matter of knowledge has led to economists being accused of intellectual 'imperialism' for their recent willingness to apply economic logic to realms of enquiry that have not been conventionally viewed as part of economics. For example, Jackson (2002: 497) writes of 'an economic imperialism which colonises another discipline, rather than conversing with it'. Criticisms of such 'colonisation' are, on the whole, directed towards economists from SAPG researchers. In recent times these criticisms have focused less on defending a claimed subject matter than on opposing the intrusion of an alien analytic method. Particularly in the line of fire has been the application of 'methodologically individualist, choice-based economic theory' (Harriss, 2002: 488) to issues such as social capital.

Marcel Fafchamps' paper (in this volume) on social capital responds to this charge. He defends economists' preoccupation with individual rationality and choice by reference to the type of policy recommendations that this produces – policies for changing incentives, rather than for propaganda or compulsion. Moreover, his discussion of social capital is set firmly in the context of the theory of public goods and collective action. It stresses that, depending on the level of development of formal institutions, social capital can act either as their substitute or their complement. Fafchamps carefully points out some of the dangers of encouraging social capital to substitute for formal institutions, such as increased inequity and/or damage to generalised trust, and how these dangers might be minimised.

To put up 'no trespassing' signs in the face of arguments like these is surely misguided, as well as ineffective. From its start in the 1980s, the social capital debate was intended to explore how economics and sociology could be brought together intellectually. Rather than denounce or disdain economists' studies of personal and group relations, a critical attempt to build on their insights is required. Which have been fruitful, which unfruitful, and why? Criticism and counter-criticism across disciplines, rather than a blanket prohibition, seem to be called for here.[31] The same is true in reverse. There are sociological and political aspects to subjects that may seem fundamentally economic, such as the operations of markets, the structure of the firm and the forms of economic contracts. Forays in the reverse direction are well established in the sociology, social psychology and social anthropology of economic life, and have proved fruitful fields of study. There is every reason why they should be encouraged rather than discouraged. The junction of sociology and economics can be approached from two directions.

If there is no territoriality of subjects in social science, how are the boundaries of social science disciplines constituted, and why does the need to go beyond them arise? Lipton's (1970) answer was that the cultural and institutional context of developed industrial countries had been decisive in the formation of the dividing lines, which he claimed corresponded 'to the division of variables into sets that can safely be treated as 'nearly independent'' in that rich country context. This definition of boundaries then provided him with the justification for research outside them. In the actual cultural and institutional context of rural poverty in poor countries, near-independence does not hold; in this different reality, the conventional sets of disciplinary variables are much more interdependent, and thus need to be studied together if their analysis is to make sense.

Today the Lipton notion of social science disciplines as sets of variables that are strongly correlated among themselves, but not with other sets, in a given social context, may seem less than fully convincing. We have suggested that disciplines are not just bundles of variables that it is useful to think about together. They are also different ways of thinking about 'variables' – different conceptions of what is the problem with them and different conceptions of what would constitute a solution to it (for example causal explanation or understanding). A disciplinary paradigm comprehends an authoritative protocol of investigation, as well as its characteristic objects of thought. It has typical problematics, axioms, and assumptions, and approved procedures of successful investigation. It is this conceptual logic that helps researchers to select out of the myriad of possibilities the variables whose co-variation – or lack of it – is of interest, and to tell them what interpretation they may give to their results.

Granting that disciplines have distinctive conceptual logics, as well as differences in the variables of analysis, does not weaken the case for cross-discipline research. Rather, it strengthens it. The earlier approach could be seen as a summons by economists to other social scientists to bring them some new and exotic variables to be fitted into their equations and subjected to their idea of rigorous testing. This is a summons that other social scientists are often – perhaps not so very surprisingly – reluctant to obey. Lipton himself, despite deploring the arrogance of economists, might even be read in this sense by an unkind critic.[32] Yet once it is agreed that all disciplines are looking at the same phenomena – that there is an underlying reality, human behaviour, but that it is being viewed through different lenses, focussed differently – does it not become more interesting, for the purposes of one's own research, to know what it is that the others are seeing?

Wendy Olsen's paper (in this volume) argues strongly that it does. Using the example of the debate on land tenancy in India as her example, she makes a strong plea for greater resort to methodological and theoretical pluralism. She sees the placing together of theories that are at odds with each other as a source of intellectual tension, and that tension as a source of creativity, both conceptual and metrical. Recognising from the Duhem-Quine paradox that a pure falsification strategy is incomplete, she advocates the use of additional criteria of truth under the banner of 'scientific realism'.

VI. Disciplines and Practising Professions

Michel Foucault's work has emphasised the links between knowledge creation and power, explaining how that process supports patterns of domination (see Philip, 1985: 67–81). It is surprising, then, given the regularity with which commentators on development and poverty research have distinguished between what economists and other social scientists do, that hardly any literature points out that economics is very different as it is an officially recognised 'practising profession'. In most countries, including the UK and US, governments recognise economists as a profession and recruit significant numbers of them into public service. While anthropologists, human geographers, political scientists and sociologists are recruited into public service this is to take on specific roles for which they are competent and not to join a professional cadre that is recognised across the public services. This difference has profound implications for the ways in which disciplinary based knowledge can influence public policy.

The professional status of economics means that academic and research economists have direct access to a cadre of like-minded and like-trained colleagues in government, in our example to economists engaged in the analysis of poverty and well-being. This creates a channel through which what is happening in the discipline (for example methodological individualism, choice based theory) is directly transmitted to the analytical frameworks and policy recommendations of key advisors to government.

The status of economics as a practising profession stands in stark contrast to the SAPG disciplines. Until relatively recently they had to rely on influencing public debates and policy through 'enlightenment' – letting their knowledge filter through to public agencies and policy makers through the media (lectures, books, newspaper commentaries) and NGOs – rather, than being able to transfer it directly through the 'engineering' approach that is available to economists and scientists (Hulme and Turner, 1990). This situation has contributed to dividing economics from the other social sciences, and weakening the prospects for cross-disciplinary work, in three ways. Firstly, it has left SAPG researchers on the sidelines (in reality and/or in their perceptions), carping about economists dominating analysis and policy. Second, it has meant that economists play a direct role in shaping the research agendas of development agencies and thus development studies. Third, economists have (or are perceived to have) easier access to research funding as academic economists converse regularly with practising economists. An obvious and important example of this is the World Bank, where 'research' often seems synonymous with 'development economics'. Indeed, Clift (2002: 475) points out that the Bank-initiated Global Development Network (GDN) was 'dominated by the economics discipline'. In effect, the initial design of the GDN was basically as a global development economics network! Given the way in which multinational and bilateral agencies have influenced the academic agenda of development studies (and now poverty and poverty reduction), such a single subject orientation has profound implications for knowledge creation.

Maia Green's paper (in this volume) explores these implications. She emphasises that anthropological studies conducted outside the framework of 'development' have consistently demonstrated the social constitution of categories and the importance of social relations as the bedrock of inequality. The anthropological perspective thus illumines the constitution of poverty, both as a category of development thinking and as a label applied to particular social categories. From this understanding, she draws out the role of the national and international development agencies in reifying and homogenising the concept of poverty and guiding its research priorities.[33]

The recent emergence of the sub-professions of 'social development' and 'governance' may have begun to create mechanisms by which the SAPG disciplines can more easily relate the knowledge they create to public agencies. However, it would be quite incorrect to see these sub-professions as having the status of a practising profession, similar to economics.[34] Social development and governance are not recognised civil service professions in any country; the links between academic training, a specified disciplinary knowledge base and professional standing in these sub-professions is unclear; and, these sub-professions are largely based in multilateral and bilateral development agencies – they barely exist in the public service in developing countries. For the foreseeable future, the status of economics as both a discipline and a practising profession seems likely to encourage economists to envision their contribution to the understanding of poverty and well-being as a mono-discipline, rather than a cross-discipline, activity.

VII. How to Gain the Benefits of Cross-Discipline Research?

How might it be possible, in a prevailing atmosphere of disciplinary inversion and rivalry, to bring about greater collaboration and fruitful cross-discipline social science research? An examination of the existing patterns of cross-disciplinary exchanges is an obvious starting point. In this we are assisted by recent analysis of the pattern of citation between economics and other disciplines. Twenty years ago, little such analysis had been attempted. Such work as there was seemed to show that economics drew little from any other social science discipline, but that it was drawn on modestly but significantly by political science and sociology (Rigney and Barnes, 1980: 114–27). Now a more extensive study of 42 economics and 20 'non-economics' journals has been conducted, and an analysis of disciplinary cross-citation for the years 1995–97 has been reported. In general, it does not contradict the findings of the earlier study. The picture of economics that emerges is as a discipline that 'builds only slightly on knowledge from its sister disciplines' (anthropology, political science, psychology and sociology), and as one that is a 'modest but significant source of scholarly knowledge for political science and sociology' (Pieters and Baumgartner, 2002: 504). Cross-citation between economics, anthropology and psychology was reported as nil.

This study cannot tell the whole story of cross-disciplinary communication. In the first place, it relates only to journal articles, and a selection of those. Books remain an important, though declining source of citations. Second, people cite for different reasons, and not always to refer to a source of knowledge that is regarded as valuable – often it is to criticise a high-profile but controversial author's work. Third, their citation behaviour also changes over time, so that the most influential contributors to a discipline tend to get taken for granted rather than cited (Stigler, 1982: 173–91). Having made these necessary caveats, it would still be an exaggeration to claim that much cross-disciplinary communication is taking place, or that no more could be achieved.

To look forward to greater cross-disciplinary cooperation might, in the face of this evidence, seem to be the triumph of hope over experience. Yet, if one were inclined to be hopeful, what would it be necessary to do? First, it is necessary to encourage groups or teams to take on such activity. While we also welcome 'renaissance people' with two or more disciplinary trainings it is unlikely that there are enough of them around to make a difference within the next few years. Out of such group work an essential ingredient for effective collaboration, 'mutual professional respect' (White, 2002: 519), can be developed as researchers recognise that 'rigor is the proper application of techniques' (ibid: 512) and not something on which any discipline has a monopoly.

Next, it is necessary to find agreement among a group of social scientists of different disciplines that there indeed are social problems of a multi-faceted character, which it is important to investigate, and to the investigation of which any one discipline cannot make a wholly conclusive contribution. There has to be a set of social phenomena that provide an agreed common ground. Fortunately, the awareness is gradually increasing that the study of poverty and well-being does provide such a common ground.[35] Economists may still use income and consumption measures of poverty and inequality extensively, but they recognise that 'non-monetary indicators' (Baulch and Masset, 2003) and 'multidimensional' measures (Barrientos, 2003) now have great relevance to their work. Recently SAPG researchers have begun to work more closely with economists on poverty research. And there are increasingly numerous examples of the contribution that cross-disciplinary research can make to the understanding of poverty on topics such as labour exchange, household economies of scale and child survival (White, 2002). However, cross-disciplinarity has to be striven for. As Booth et al. (1999) point out, much of the proclaimed 'multidisciplinary' approach to national poverty assessments has been 'twin track'. The specialists concerned have focused on their own products and have rarely made the effort to try to synthesize findings or interrogate disparities.

Then there must be agreement that, if one discipline cannot provide a wholly conclusive contribution, it is worthwhile to monitor what is being done by other disciplines in this field, conceptually and empirically. This may be hard to achieve. At a minimum, the ideologies of disciplinary rivalry must be abandoned. However, even when they can be set aside, the individual researcher will see that monitoring other disciplines has a certain cost in time and uncertain benefits in intellectual stimulation and career development. As Lipton (1970: 6) foresaw, such research is 'expert-intensive, especially since yet more time is needed for inter-expert communication'. At the start, therefore, there must be some way of breaking through this impasse, and regular group cross-discipline seminars could provide it. Yet there is nothing inevitable about success; thought processes will not be dragooned. It is individuals bent on the creation of knowledge through their personal efforts, supported and constrained by the social structures of disciplines, knowledge communities and professional practices, who must 'make the difference'.

One more hopeful inference can be drawn from today's clearer picture of cross-disciplinary communication. Lipton feared that the lack of professional prestige of cross-disciplinary studies would be self-confirming, but it is now possible to argue that this is not the case, at least as far as the central act of publication is concerned. It turns out that most of the existing cross-disciplinary communication (at least in terms of citing and being cited in journals) occurs through the top-ranking 'core' journals of the economics profession. This is a disappointment for those of us who have devoted much effort to 'peripheral' journals expressly designed for cross-disciplinary communication. However, it implies that those willing to look across disciplinary boundaries for their inspiration need not fear exclusion on those grounds from the most favoured journals of the economics profession.[36] One often-mentioned disincentive for economists to engage across a broader scholarly range looks increasingly like a paper tiger.

How will the benefits of greater collaboration between disciplines make themselves felt? The changes in understanding that this collaboration – if successful – will bring are changes not only for those engaging in cross-disciplinary research but also for those who see themselves as working only within their own discipline. In other words, by attending to the poverty research of anthropologists, economists may produce more imaginative and searching economic analyses; by sharing the understandings of economists of poverty, political scientists or social psychologists may be led to new questions, or to better elaborated answers to old questions. The approach taken to cross-disciplinarity is likely to change over time as researchers get to know each other more. Initial cross-disciplinary contacts (seminars, meetings, critiques of each others work) can serve as a base to design multidisciplinary work from which systematic interdisciplinary research may evolve over time.

Acknowledgements

Hulme and Toye wrote this paper and edited this collection when serving as Joint Directors of the ESRC's Global Poverty Research Group (GPRG). The authors would like to thank colleagues in the Global Poverty Research Group at the Universities of Manchester and Oxford for discussions on these subjects and comments on the draft paper and David Clark for research assistance. The constructive criticisms of the earlier drafts by two anonymous referees were extremely helpful. The support of the UK Economic and Social Research Council is gratefully acknowledged. The work was part of the programme of the ESRC Global Poverty Research Group (grant no. M571255001).

Notes

1. This is Jackson's (2002) SAP with human geography added. We have added human geography as in the UK, parts of Northern Europe and US geographers of development studies have played an increasingly active role in research on poverty, inequality and well-being over the last 10–15 years.
2. A notable exception is the World Health Organisation's WHO-QOL project, which developed and applied an instrument for assessing the quality of life in one hundred different fieldwork sites. The abridged version of this measure, which draws on work in 32 localities, covers more second and third world countries than first world countries (see WHOQOL Group, 1998: Table 2).
3. See Sen (1987, 1999). Also see the work of researchers focusing on development ethics such as Crocker (1991), Gasper (2004), Goulet (1971, 1995), Nussbaum (2000), Qizilbash (1996) and Clark (2002a, b), inter alia. There is also a vast literature in mainstream philosophy on the subject of well-being. One of the most notable contributions is Jim Griffin's (1986) book, *Well-Being: Its Meaning, Measurement and Moral Importance*. For further references to the well-being literature see Clark (2002b).
4. Interestingly, Clark (2002b) proposes that an 'empirical philosophy' of well-being might advance the understanding of well-being by detaching from social science disciplines and engaging with the views and experiences of 'ordinary people' in a logically rigorous manner.
5. The term 'non-economics' is sometimes used to refer to the social sciences other than economics. However, such a label may not be helpful as many 'non economists' point out that their research is focused on the social, political and cultural understanding of economic issues such as markets, financial institutions, access to resources and accumulation.
6. While the concept of income poverty remains very powerful, aspects of well-being and human development are increasingly on both practical and theoretical agenda. The MDGs are headed by income poverty but vast attention is also focused on the educational, health, equality and other goals that are set. In the world of theory, leading economists are striving to make their research multidimensional (Atkinson, 2003; Bourguignon and Chakravarity, 2003).

7. See the fuller discussion of this problem in Himmelfarb (1991: 171–73).
8. Bourdieu's (1999) study of 'social suffering' in France provides a classic example: Of the 629 pages in the text 565 are direct transcripts of interviews and little attempt is made to indicate levels of income or the specific forms of consumption deprivation that interviewees experience.
9. In the 2001 UK research assessment exercise (RAE) groups who submitted to the development studies sub unit of assessment received grades well below the average for social sciences. No group received a grading above 4, indicating that none of them were judged to have achieved 'international' standing for their research.
10. Abbott (2001) argues that the 'chaos of disciplines' can be understood as fractal distinctions – these are dichotomies in which each dichotomy then fractures into a further dichotomy. This may provide a framework for a more detailed interrogation of the dichotomies listed here than we have space to provide.
11. Lipton (1970), Hill (1986), Bardhan (1989), Harriss (2002), Kanbur (2002), Jackson (2002), White (2002) and Ruttan (2001).
12. The formalisation of the revealed preference approach in demand theory is attributable to Paul Samuelson (1948: 107–17).
13. An early example was Tibor Scitovsky's 1973 lecture on 'The place of economic welfare in human welfare' (Scitovsky, 1986: 13–25).
14. But note that while anthropology and 'qualitative' sociology sometimes use numerical information they commonly prioritise non-numerical information that does not lend itself to statistical inference and which requires a separate process of numerical transformation, such as scaling or counting, if it is to be subjected to numerical scrutiny.
15. Also see McGee (2004) for a detailed examination of the complementarity of statistical surveys and participatory poverty assessments in Uganda.
16. See the next paragraph for a discussion of the 'super-positivism' that is driving much economic research.
17. For a startling contrast see *Sociologia Ruralis*, the Journal of the European Society for Rural Sociology and *Rural Sociology*, the Journal of the (North American) Rural Sociology Society. While the journals focus on similar issues, their approaches and preferred methodologies are very different.
18. This was one of Polly Hill's (1986) most trenchant criticisms in her classic attack on development economics, *Development Economics on Trial*.
19. This can be illustrated by the comments that leading figures make about their disciplines in the same highly reputed, cross-disciplinary encyclopaedia: 'an important achievement of economics has been its internal intellectual coherence'; 'it is questionable whether there remains any coherence in the term anthropology at all'; 'a pervasive dissatisfaction with the continuing divisions and fragmentation [in sociology]...it remains an open question whether a more unified and intellectually coherent discipline will eventually emerge'; 'political science has still not acquired fully independent status (as a discipline) in many parts of the world' (Outhwaite and Bottomore, 1992: 20, 184, 483, 636).
20. As an illustration, positivist and critical realist sociologists working (in the same department) on social capital and poverty may find they rarely communicate. The positivists may, however, find their work is closely related to econometricians researching social networks, while the critical realists will find a close affinity to researchers within human geography (see Sayer, 2000: 106–107 for a discussion of the latter).
21. We are indebted to an anonymous reviewer for helping us develop this point.
22. Over the last 10 years this may have started to moderate with gradually increasing numbers of female economists (and even econometricians) and through the influence of feminist economics on development economics. However, we suspect that, at any meeting of poverty/well-being researchers, the probability of an economist being female is still significantly less than of an anthropologist or sociologist being female.
23. Evans (2003, p. 10) citing Charles Merriam in the *American Political Science Review* (Volume 20, 1926: 186).
24. Historically, development studies has played a major role within Anglophone social sciences in promoting cross-disciplinary research. Abbott (2001: 133) observes that 'the 1960s, by contrast (to earlier decades) proved an interdisciplinary bonanza, as the modernization paradigm swept development studies in anthropology, sociology, economics and political science. Enormous multidisciplinary teams took on major problems...population, area studies, agriculture, development'.

25. This might be through an individual who personally integrates disciplinary perspectives and methods or by a team (two or more) people coming from different disciplines and producing a unified design for research.
26. See, for example, Julian Huxley's (1946) discussion of the social sciences in *UNESCO: Its Purpose and its Philosophy*.
27. Paul Streeten (1974: 26) claimed that 'the only forum where interdisciplinary studies in depth can be conducted successfully is under one skull'.
28. Sen holds positions as Professor of Economics and Professor of Philosophy at Harvard along with other positions.
29. Lipton (1970, p. 11) cited the case of Everett Hagen, when remarking that 'attempts by first-rate (single discipline) specialists to work in other disciplines...often produce results that are not highly regarded by the new discipline and not understood in the old'.
30. An excellent recent example of effective multidisciplinary research is Hickey and Bracking's (2005) multi-authored collection on the politics of poverty reduction.
31. Cooperation within a cross-disciplinary research programme does not have to mean agreement amongst partners: it can be highly productive when a partner in one discipline puts time and effort into explaining to someone from another discipline their precise criticisms of the concepts, assumptions and methods that have been utilised.
32. 'To be brutal, economists are forced by the realities to seek to impose their own quantitative and testable hypotheses...so long as other [disciplines] do not put such hypotheses forward' (Lipton, 1970: 12).
33. Also see Green and Hulme (2005) for a discussion of moving beyond a measurement led conceptualisation of poverty.
34. The UK's Department for International Development (DFID) has recently merged its social development and governance advisors into a single group that seems likely to function as issue specific 'generalist' policy advisors rather than the 'disciplined' professional role of economists.
35. Most obviously in the UK through the support of the ESRC which has financed an interdisciplinary research centre (the Well-being and Development Research Centre, see www.welldev.org.uk) and a multidisciplinary research centre (the Global Poverty Research Group, see www.gprg.org). DFID has also supported the cross-disciplinary (that is multidisciplinary and interdisciplinary) Chronic Poverty Research Centre (www.chronicpoverty.org).
36. Similar data are not available for other social science disciplines, but one can argue that the 'high rating' placed on 'premier division' cross-disciplinary journals such as the *Journal of Development Studies, World Development, Economic Development and Cultural Change, Economy and Society* and *Development and Change* by the SAPG disciplines and economics in the UK's research assessment exercise augurs well for the future. In the UK the recent establishment of a development studies unit of assessment for the 2008 research assessment exercise (RAE), which allocates research income across departments, creates a potentially favourable context for cross-disciplinary work.

References

Abbott, A. (2001) *Chaos of Disciplines* (Chicago: University of Chicago Press).

Adato, M., Carter, M. and May, J. (2004) Sense and sociability: social exclusion and persistent poverty in South Africa, BASIS background paper for the conference on *Combating Persistent Poverty in Africa*, 15–16 November, University of Wisconsin-Madison, accessed at: http://www.basis.wisc.edu/persistentpoverty_papers.html

Atkinson, A. B. (2003) Multidimensional deprivation: contrasting social welfare and counting approaches, *Journal of Economic Inequality*, 1(1), pp. 51–65.

Bardhan, P. (1989) *Conversations between Economists and Anthropologists* (Delhi: Oxford University Press).

Barrientos, A. (2003) What is the impact of non-contributory pensions on poverty? Estimates from Brazil and South Africa, *CPRC Working Paper 33*, Institute for Development Policy and Management, University of Manchester, accessed http://www.chronicpoverty.org/pdfs/Armando%20Barrientos No33.pdf

Baulch, B. and Masset, E. (2003) Do monetary and non-monetary indicators tell the same story about poverty? A study of Vietnam in the 1990s, *World Development*, 31(3), pp. 441–54.

Bevir, M. (1999) *The Logic of the History of Ideas* (Cambridge: Cambridge University Press).

Booth, C. (1892) *Life and Labour of the People in London* (London: Macmillan).

Booth, D., Leach, M. and Tierney, A. (1999) Experiencing poverty in Africa: perspectives from anthropology, *Background Paper 1(b)* for the World Bank Poverty Status Report 1999, Washington, DC: World Bank.

Bourdieu, P. and Accardo, A. (eds) (1999) *The Weight of the World: Social Suffering in Contemporary Society* (London: Polity Press).

Bourguignon, F. and Chakravarty, S. R. (2003) The measurement of multidimensional poverty, *Journal of Economic Inequality*, 1(1), pp. 25–49.

Clark, D. A. (2002a) *Visions of Development: A Study of Human Values* (Cheltenham: Edward Elgar).

Clark, D. A. (2002b) Development ethics: a research agenda, *International Journal of Social Economics*, 29(11), pp. 830–48.

Clift, C. (2002) Foreword to cross-disciplinarity in development research, *World Development*, 30(3), p. 475.

Crocker, D. (1991) Toward development ethics, *World Development*, 19(5), pp. 457–83.

Engels, F. (1973) *The Condition of the Working Class in England: From Personal Observation and Authentic Sources* (Moscow: Progress Publishers).

Evans, G. R. (2003) The scholarly misfits, *Oxford Magazine*, 211, pp. 10–2.

Gasper, D. (2004) *The Ethics of Development* (Edinburgh: Edinburgh University Press).

Glennerster, H. (2004) The context of Rowntree's contribution, in Glennerster, H., Hills, J., Piachaud, D. and Webb, J. (eds), *One Hundred Years of Poverty and Policy* (York: Joseph Rowntree Foundation).

Goulet, D. A. (1971) *The Cruel Choice: A New Concept in the Theory of Development* (New York: Atheneum).

Goulet, D. A. (1995) *Development Ethics: A Guide to Theory and Practice* (London: Zed Books).

Green, M. and Hulme, D. (2005) From correlates and characteristics to causes: thinking about poverty from a chronic poverty perspective, *World Development*, 33(6), pp. 867–80.

Griffin, J. (1986) *Well-Being: Its Meaning, Measurement and Moral Importance* (Oxford: Oxford University Press).

Gulati, L. (1982) *Profiles in Female Poverty: A Study of Five Working Women in Kerala* (Oxford: Pergamon Press).

Haas, P. M. (1992) Introduction: epistemic communities and international policy coordination, *International Organization*, 46(1), pp. 1–35.

Harriss, J. (2002) The case for cross-disciplinary approaches in international development, *World Development*, 30(3), pp. 487–96.

Hickey, S. (2005) Capturing the political? The role of political analysis in the multi-disciplining of development, *GPRG Working Paper 6*, Universities of Manchester and Oxford, UK, accessed www.gprg.org/pubs/workingpapers/pdfs/gprg-wps-006.pdf

Hickey, S. and Bracking, S. (eds) (2005) Special issue: exploring the politics of poverty reduction: how are the poorest represented?, *World Development*, 33(6), pp. 851–1024.

Hill, P. (1986) *Development Economics on Trial: the Anthropological Case for a Prosecution* (Cambridge: Cambridge University Press).

Himmelfarb, G. (1991) *Poverty and Compassion: The Moral Imagination of the Late Victorians* (New York: Vintage Books).

Hirschman, A. O. (1981) *Essays in Trespassing: Economics to Politics and Beyond* (Cambridge: Cambridge University Press).

Hulme, D. (2004) Thinking "small" and the understanding of poverty: Maymana and Mofizul's story, *Journal of Human Development*, 5(2), pp. 161–76.

Hulme, D. and McKay, A. (2005) Identifying and understanding chronic poverty: beyond monetary measures, paper presented at the *WIDER Conference on The Future of Development Economics*, Helsinki, 17–18 June 2005, accessed at http://www.wider.unu.edu

Hulme, D. and Turner, M. (1990) *Sociology and Development: Theory, Policy and Practice* (London: Harvester-Wheatsheaf).

Huxley, J. (1946) *Outline of a Philosophy for UNESCO* (Paris: UNESCO).

Jackson, C. (2002) Disciplining gender? *World Development*, 30(3), pp. 497–510.

Kanbur, R. (2002) Economics, social science and development, *World Development*, 30(3), pp. 477–86.

Knight, J. B. (1991) The evolution of development economics, in V. N. Balasubramanyam and S. Lall (eds), *Current Issues in Development Economics*, pp. 10–1 (Basingstoke: Macmillan Education).

Lawson, T. (1997) *Economics and Reality* (London: Routledge).

Lipton, M. (1970) Interdisciplinary studies in less developed countries, *Journal of Development Studies*, 7(1), pp. 5–18.

McGee, R. (2004) Constructing poverty trends in Uganda: a multidisciplinary perspective, *Development and Change*, 35(3), pp. 499–524.

Nussbaum, M. C. (2000) *Women and Human Development: The Capabilities Approach* (Cambridge: Cambridge University Press).

Outhwaite, W. and Bottomore, T. (1992) *The Blackwell Dictionary of Twentieth Century Social Thought* (Oxford: Blackwell).

Pieters, R. and Baumgartner, H. (2002) Who talks to whom? Intra- and interdisciplinary communication of economics journals, *Journal of Economic Literature*, 40(2), pp. 483–509.

Philip, M. (1985) Michel Foucault, in Q. Skinner (ed.), *The Return of Grand Theory in the Human Sciences*, pp. 67–81 (Cambridge: Cambridge University Press).

Polanyi, M. (1962) The republic of science: its political and economic theory, *Minerva*, 1(1), pp. 54–73.

Porter, T. M. (1986) *The Rise of Statistical Thinking 1820–1900* (Princeton: Princeton University Press).

Qizilbash, M. (1996) Capabilities, well-being and human development: a survey, *Journal of Development Studies*, 33(2), pp. 143–62.

Rahnema, M. (1992) Poverty, in W. Sachs (ed.), *The Development Dictionary*, pp. 158–76 (London: Zed Books).

Rigney P. and Barnes, D. (1980) Patterns of interdisciplinary citation in the social sciences, *Social Science Quarterly*, 61, pp. 114–27.

Rowntree, B. S. (1901) *Poverty: A Study of Town Life* (London: MacMillan).

Ruttan, V. (2001) Imperialism and competition in anthropology, sociology, political science and economics: a perspective from development economics, *Journal of Socio-Economics*, 30, pp. 15–29.

Samuelson, P. A. (1948) *Foundations of Economic Analysis* (Cambridge, MA: Harvard University Press).

Sayer, A. (2000) *Realism and Social Science* (London: Sage).

Scitovsky, T. (1986) *Human Desire and Economic Satisfaction* (Brighton: Wheatsheaf Books).

Sen, A. K. (1987) *On Ethics and Economics* (Oxford: Basil Blackwell).

Sen, A. K. (1999) *Development as Freedom* (Oxford: Oxford University Press).

Stigler, G. J. (1982) *The Economist as Preacher and Other Essays* (Oxford: Basil Blackwell).

Streeten, P. (1974) Some problems in the use and transfer of an intellectual technology, *The Social Sciences and Development*, pp. 3–54 (Washington, DC: The World Bank).

White, H. (2002) Combining quantitative and qualitative approaches in poverty analysis, *World Development*, 30(3), pp. 511–22.

WHOQOL Group (1998) Development of the World Health Organization WHOQOL-BREF quality of life assessment, *Psychological Medicine*, 28, pp. 551–8.

Representing Poverty and Attacking Representations: Perspectives on Poverty from Social Anthropology

MAIA GREEN

I. Introduction

This article considers the potential contribution of social anthropology to the study of poverty in development. Despite increasing anthropological attention to the social and institutional relations of international development (Ferguson, 1990; Bornstein, 2003; Haugerud and Edelman, 2004; Mosse, 2004) social anthropology has remained to some extent outside the formal apparatus of development studies (Cernea, 1995; De L'Estoile, 1997; Green, 2005) to the extent that development studies has been viewed at least partially in some recent ethnographies of development as part of the research problematic (for example Ferguson, 1990; Escobar, 1991). The ambivalent relationship between anthropology and international development has contributed to an apparent paradox in development studies, that despite the longstanding association of social anthropology with research in communities and countries where the effects of poverty are pronounced, social and cultural anthropology has not yet prioritised poverty as an object of study (Ferguson, 1997; Booth et al., 1999).[1]

The apparent silence of anthropology on the subject of poverty should not be interpreted as indicative of that discipline's irrelevance to or disengagement from the study of poverty. Anthropological research offers important insights into the causes of poverty and can reveal the diversity of experience among those classified as poor. I argue that an anthropological perspective throws considerable light on the constitution of poverty, as both a category of development thinking and as a label applied to particular social categories. The application of these categories and the political implications of such classifications are explored through an examination of some recent ethnographies of poverty as a process of classification. Anthropological perspectives on poverty prioritise poverty not as an absolute measurable condition but as a qualitative social relation. Anthropological accounts of poverty examine how the groups categorised as poor come to be so classified and by whom. This process of classification is of course essential to an international development effort which orients itself around the elimination of poverty. The final part of this article explores the social processes involved in attempting to establish the necessary systems for measuring and classifying poverty as the target of development through a brief analysis of the ongoing attempt to institutionalise internationally promoted definitions of poverty as the target of development interventions in Zanzibar.

II. Introducing Poverty

The concept of poverty has been central to the international development agenda for more than a quarter of a century. During this period the constitution of poverty, how it is conceptualised as a problem and the kinds of solutions promoted to address it, have shifted along with transformations in policy thinking, in political relationships after the Cold War and in the social sciences. Contemporary policy discourses promoting political inclusion, the participation of the poor in policy dialogues and the recognition of the need for national ownership of strategies to reduce poverty are consequences of the paradigm shift which has sought to situate poverty reduction at the focal point of the international development effort. Economic growth in the current paradigm, as set out in the Millennium Development Targets, is not conceptualised as an end in itself but as a means through which poverty reduction can be achieved.

The World Bank as the principal agency in international development has assumed leadership in the attack on poverty.[2] The Bank has also lead the way in establishing systematic ways of representing, analysing and theorising poverty. These have become internationally significant through the publication of the highly influential annual World Development Report; the promotion of academic research around poverty issues (Mehta, 2001) and, in the past five years, the introduction of the national poverty reduction strategies (PRS) which increasingly form the contractual basis of the relationship between donor agencies and developing country governments for countries having fulfilled the macroeconomic and regulatory requirements that are prerequisites to the new development partnerships. As the impacts of development efforts are tracked through global and national monitoring systems, the measurement and assessment of poverty has become institutionalised as a responsibility of government within aid recipient countries, as well as a specialist function within development agencies.[3]

Increased alignment between donors around PRS and the use of direct budgetary support as the aid instrument to effect harmonization implies not only shared instruments of international aid, but shared conceptual frameworks. Reducing poverty has become not merely the stated priority of international development agencies and the target of the international development effort but certainly, within the social universe of international development at least, a total social fact. Poverty as a category of analysis, as the object of policies and as the frame through which countries, programmes and people are brought into the project of development unites seemingly disparate practices and institutions in a manner analogous to Mauss's (1990: 3) perception of the totalising institution of the gift in non-monetised economies. More narrowly, the facticity of poverty is attested through the numerous studies and research institutions devoted to the empirical analysis of its scale and dimensions. The various poverty departments, research centres and systems for monitoring poverty nationally and internationally all point to the tangibility of poverty, its existence as an objective subject about which facts can be determined and known.

As development knowledge is first and foremost instrumental knowledge that can be made to work in realising particular policy priorities, topics for development research tend to be determined by particular interpretations of current policy agendas. The agencies and agents with a vested interest in poverty as a policy objective determine the content of the agenda for the study of poverty in development and what issues are deemed central for the poor.[4] This agenda is not determined by those people subject to categorisation as poor. Nor is it determined by the findings of other studies which have addressed poverty tangentially, although evidence from these studies feeds into the knowledge production cycle. The constitution of poverty as a research focus is predetermined by the current policy agendas of international development institutions, and the World Bank in particular (Escobar, 1995: 21–44; Finnemore, 1997: 208). The discourse on poverty only began to be hegemonic after the World Bank under Robert McNamara vigorously promoted it in the 1970s. Prior to this poverty, viewed simply as the inevitable accompaniment of failure to develop economically, was rarely the explicit focus of development initiatives, or of academic study. James Wolfensohn's Presidency in the 1990s reinvigorated the commitment to making poverty the central focus of the Bank's endeavours. It was only once the Bank realigned its policy priorities to the elimination of poverty that poverty assessments became central (Finnemore, 1997: 204–07). The Bank set about trying to understand its enemy better through developing methodologies for poverty assessment and promoting the study of different aspects and dimensions of poverty. Quantitative and qualitative approaches to poverty were incorporated into Bank poverty assessments, at the same time as the Bank's policies increasingly assimilated civil society and activist policy positions.

Conceptualisations of poverty have altered radically during this period, from the biologically informed basic needs approach of the 1970s to today's more sophisticated understanding of poverty as multi-dimensional deprivation, not merely of income, but of capabilities, entitlements and rights (Sen, 1981; Rist, 1997; Carvahlo and White, 1997; Kanbur and Squire, 2001; Gordon et al., 2003; Ruggeri

Laderchi et al., 2003). While current definitions of poverty represent a significant advance on the more restricted conceptualisations which preceded them, their widespread acceptance in policy-making circles and in academia derives more from the multilateral framework of policy and institutions subscribing to the Millennium Development Goals (MDGs) than their ability to capture the experience of those categorised as poor, or from their explanatory potential in accounting for the state they set out to define (c.f. Ruggeri Laderchi et al., 2003). Poverty as defined through MDG targets and consumption measures is a construct of international development organisations. We do not know what such categorisations mean for diverse individuals within diverse social and economic contexts. What poverty as a scale provides for development organisations is a justification for intervention and a means of ranking units, countries or regions, on a poverty index. Arguably, what the current emphasis on poverty assessment reveals is not so much the scale and magnitude of poverty in the world, as the power of development institutions to make it visible (Escobar, 1991: 664). Poverty as an entity is brought into being through the institutions established to describe, quantify and locate it (Escobar, 1995: 21–2).

III. Representing Poverty

Against this background of evolving policy it is not surprising that definitions of poverty, and thus proposed strategies for reducing it, differ significantly between the two *World Development Reports* at either end of the past decade (World Bank, 1990, 2001). Whereas the 1990 report viewed poverty primarily in monetary terms, the 2001 report sees poverty as multifaceted deprivation not only of income but of the capabilities to achieve full human potential. Poverty from this perspective is not merely a matter of reduced income or consumption, but amounts to a state of relative powerlessness and exclusion from decision-making processes. Being in a state of poverty is manifested in low levels of education, high rates of mortality and poor health, factors which also contribute to poverty (World Bank, 2001: 31). Although the diversity of the experience of poverty globally is reiterated, through the 'voices of the poor' (Narayan et al., 2000), the 2001 World Development Report, in constructing poverty as an object, serves to homogenise attributes of poverty and the situation of those categorised as poor. Marginal, excluded, vulnerable, unwell, illiterate and often indigenous and female, the poor predominantly live in remote rural areas and urban shanties, with few assets and weak social networks. Their relative powerlessness is emphasised, and by implication, the power of various groups over them, not only of local and national elites and governments, but the power of development institutions to recognise and define them, and to determine when poverty matters. The poor have much in common in this representation and the proximate causes of their poverty, and hence policies for addressing poverty, are represented as being remarkably similar across geographical regions and national boundaries (Green and Hulme, 2005).

If the experience of poverty appears relatively homogenous, its quantitative dimensions seem equally striking. One fifth of the world's population is represented as being in poverty; defined as living on less that $1 a day (World Bank, 2001: 3). Graduations of poverty and the huge qualitative differences between extreme poverty and destitution on the one hand and, on the other, poverty as development policy informed by neoliberal leanings defines it are obscured in a projection of the problem, and hence the required interventions, which is made to seem amenable to economic rather than social policy prescriptions (Elson, 2000; Gledhill, 2000). As the anthropologist Arjun Appadurai has shown in relation to the effects of the census in colonial India, technologies of representation have important consequences for the kinds of truths they reveal. Similar statistics can create an impression of the similarity of experience (Geertz, 1984; Appadurai, 1993: 321) and of the processes which contribute to poverty in diverse settings. An identity of form rather than content justifies the grouping together of countries and populations that may be quite different, with different histories and different causes of poverty.

Quantitative methodologies and poverty lines help to create poverty as a tangible entity, a thing in itself, the scale of which can be captured through measurement. Assessing poverty, locating the poor and trying to measure comparatively the incidence and depth of poverty assumes that poverty is a state universally accessible to these technologies of representation. It is these devices that make poverty generalisable, as a state that shares commonalities across diverse settings (cf. Hastrup, 1993: 720). Quantitative methodologies for assessing poverty allow magnitude to be addressed. Poverty can be seen to be increasing or decreasing, and the scale of poverty assessed. Quantitative indices also enable the calculation of measures to address poverty, the cost benefit analyses that are the basis of economic appraisals, and which, in the case of income and consumption, validate the models of growth needed to raise incomes and 'lift the poor' out of poverty. The language used in the *World Development Report 2001*, but which recurs elsewhere in other anti-poverty documentation from other agencies, reinforces this notion. Not only is poverty ascribed agency to impact on the lives of people who 'fall into' it. It is represented as an evolving entity that must be 'attacked' rather than as a consequence of social relations (World Bank, 2001: 21). Size matters. The growth in poverty, its sheer scale, prompts a response. Poverty in these development writings is represented as inherently problematic, not only for the poor themselves, whose suffering is graphically documented, but for the wider society which is threatened by it.

IV. Attacking Poverty

At first sight these representations of poverty seem relatively straightforward, even obvious. Their acceptance comes partly from the fact that they are so familiar and partly because they have become a necessary and expected preamble to virtually any kind of development policy or programme documentation. In practice, such accounts are far from being unproblematic statements about the incidence of poverty in particular places, and are not intended to be.[5] The kind of poverty they present is both highly subjective, depending on the perspective of the perceiver, and highly political, that is related to the wider context in which such rankings and accounts become important for justifying proposed interventions (Apthorpe, 1997: 24; Pansters and de Ruijter, 2000: 5). Moreover, such descriptions are part of a long established intellectual tradition of perceiving poverty in ways which, in making *poverty* the object of analysis abstracts poverty from people and obscures the social processes that make certain people subject to its effects (O'Connor, 2001: 15).

The rich and processes of wealth creation are rarely the focus of these accounts.[6] This is not because wealth and poverty are unconnected, far from it, but because such approaches are essentially concerned with a normalising vision of society that is premised on the elimination of what is socially accorded the status of the deviant or pathological (cf. Douglas, 1991; O'Connor, 2001). Representations of society as functional and holistic characterised social theory for much of the twentieth century. These assumptions were not confined to the theoretical models developed by the founding fathers of sociology such as Emile Durkheim (1960). They had significant practical implications in a period when knowledge about the social was beginning to be used as the basis of a scientific understanding of society, with implications of prediction and control (Rabinow, 1989: 171; de L'Estoile, 1997). Michel Foucault has delineated the intellectual genealogy of this perspective in the context of the history of social policy in nineteenth century France. An evidence base concerning the spread of cholera associated the disease with the poor. Surveillance and social control were the imposed solutions, not only to epidemics, but to the potential social disruption that the poor presented. Poor victims of disease were to be treated in public hospitals not only for humanitarian reasons, but in order to generate the knowledge about the disease that was necessary to develop treatments for those with sufficient wealth to pay for it. Foucault (1976: 84) remarks, 'What is benevolence towards the poor is transformed into knowledge that is applicable to the rich'.

Although the present day institutionalisation of knowledge about poverty in other countries is not directly comparable to the situation of medical knowledge in nineteenth century France, the parallels are striking. Scientific, evidence based policies which adopt planning modalities based on the calculation of outcomes are not merely the accepted basis of development and wider policy practices, they are of course constitutive of the modern government with which such rational practices are associated (Rabinow, 2003: 65). As with the medical profession's capacity to define sickness and, backed by the state, to cordon infectivity, what constitutes knowledge about poverty and the demarcation of the poor is a consequence of the power of international development organisations and of the national governments with whom they work. With poverty as a subject the poor, who by definition lack the resources and entitlements to reframe the terms of this engagement, become objects of study.

To assert the social construction of poverty as a category within international development is not to deny that the phenomena grouped today in its classificatory frame exist or have always existed in some shape or form. Social and economic opportunities in all societies have always been inequitably distributed and large numbers have suffered the negative health and capability outcomes deriving from such exclusion. Many at the extreme end of the deprivation spectrum are destitute. Societies have always acknowledged the problem of destitution and social isolation, and distinguished this from idiosyncratic transient poverty (cf. Iliffe, 1987: 4; Hulme and Shepherd, 2003). What has not been so usual is the encompassing classification of substantial proportions of a population as suffering from poverty, moreover a poverty determined largely through the application of internationally defined criteria. The social construction of poverty as the target of international development assistance means that what constitutes poverty changes depending on the perspective of those charged with its assessment. Shrestha (1995) has written about the impact of development agents' categories of 'poverty' and 'development' on Nepalese rural communities, and the social consequences of being defined as lacking what outsiders think they should have. Similarly, Goldman (2001: 208), describing the introduction of donor driven development planning in Laos, quotes a government official poised to write his first concept paper on 'poverty' who remarked that it was not until Bank involvement that their government had 'ever used the term 'poverty'. The content of the category of 'poverty' is neither self-evident nor universally pervasive. Indeed if it were it would surely have come to the attention of other empirical social sciences outside development, notably anthropology.

V. Anthropological Approaches to Poverty

The focus on poverty within international development institutions has fostered the emergence of a new sub profession of anti-poverty specialists and a burgeoning literature on its constitution and definition. Poverty as the object of the international development effort has become the overriding problematic in development studies, and especially in development economics, disciplines which have a symbiotic relationship with the international development institutions that provide much of their financing. Development research and policy documentation represents poverty as an overwhelming problem of global proportions. However, despite the apparent scale and depth of poverty in the world, poverty as a research focus outside the industrialised countries of the west has yet to capture the attention of the qualitative social sciences to the same extent. This is particularly the case for social and cultural anthropology.

Social anthropology as it has evolved in the UK and cultural anthropology in the US have been marginal to the policy discourses and funding steams associated with international development, at the same time as anthropological knowledge has pursued a trajectory of highly abstract knowledge influenced by deconstructionist tendencies which, is not readily adaptable to the requirements of policy-makers (Little and Painter, 1995; Horowitz, 1996). Of course, not all anthropologists have opted for deconstructionism. Applied anthropology as a distinct branch of the discipline specialising in policy relevant research, social appraisal and programming remains strong in the US. The sub-discipline is less autonomous in the UK setting, where it operates in practice under the interdisciplinary umbrella of development studies where some of the areas initially associated with anthropology have become mainstreamed into wider development practice through the adoption of participatory approaches. Although large numbers of anthropology graduates and postgraduates are employed within development agencies in the US and across EU states, social and cultural anthropology as practiced within academic departments has effectively maintained a distinct separation from development, in recent years, except as an object of inquiry, and with it from research on and into poverty (Cernea, 1995: 340–341; Little and Painter, 1995: 603; Horowitz, 1996; Green, 2005).

The lack of engagement of anthropologists with poverty as an explicit research focus, albeit with notable exceptions (for example Scheper Hughes, 1992; Passaro, 1996; Farmer, 2003), is not simply a matter of the institutional context in which social and cultural anthropology operate in the US and UK. Nor is the reluctance of anthropologists to confront the topic explained by the continuing discomfort evoked by recollections of the discredited culture of poverty theorizing exemplified in the work of Oscar Lewis (O'Connor, 2001: 117–21). More fundamentally, a qualitative analytical perspective from anthropology or sociology would start from a position of interrogating the assumed categories of analysis and the assumed object of study Accounts of 'poverty' from this perspective would not seek to refine globally applicable definitions, nor assume that the experiential dimensions of what was locally categorised as 'poverty' across time and space were similar, although there may well be similarities.[7] Ethnographic research takes the categories through which people think their worlds and act upon them as the starting point for an analysis of the significance of social practice. Such approaches at their best can challenge the imposition of apparently universal priorities on the social values of others. Ethnographic accounts of the constitution of social worlds, whether those of Western laboratory scientists (Latour, 1987) or of Ilongot head hunters (Rosaldo, 1980), expose the social processes of categorisation through which such worlds are constructed conceptually through practice (for example Bourdieu, 1977; Douglas, 1996; Wenger, 1998).

From this perspective, the anthropologist cannot be so much concerned with her own idea of poverty or with concepts of poverty derived from development documentation as with what concepts of poverty do or do not exist in particular places and at particular times. Where do these ideas come from? Who do these categories include? What does it mean to be labelled as 'poor', or as 'destitute' in these different settings? How do these categories relate to other social categories? Moreover, researchers in anthropology, in starting with human beings, as opposed to ideal types read off survey data, perceives poverty as a consequence of relations between people. For researchers in anthropology, as for our informants, poverty is a social relation, not an absolute condition (Sahlins, 1972: 37). Ethnographic studies of communities and the social relations through which they are structured have yielded numerous insights into poverty and inequality. These include studies of rural society, and on caste, social exclusion, and the structural transformations brought about by rapid economic growth (Gudeman, 1978; Nash, 1979). Displacement, dispossession, the social construction of property relations and how people have rights over other people are long standing anthropological themes. Anthropological studies have consistently demonstrated the social constitution of categories and the importance of social relations as the bedrock of inequality (Dumont, 1970; Douglas, 1991; Hart, 2001). Such accounts point to the distortions inherent in viewing poverty in absolute and ahistorical terms and, in presenting poverty as a wholly subject position, of denying the agency of those so categorised.[8]

As the gaze of anthropological researchers adjusts to accommodate postcolonial landscapes, anthropologists have looked inwards and upwards at their objects of study. Anthropologists now concern themselves not with local societies as self-reproducing social universes (for example Evans Pritchard, 1940), or with the articulation of these into metropolitan or capitalist relations of production as in the Marxist derived visions of the unequal economic integration of third world local communities and first world industrial centres of the 1970s (for example Meillassoux, 1981), but with the entire span of social relations that comprise the contemporary world. No longer focusing solely on small-scale rural communities mostly in non-Western countries, anthropologists today conduct research into diverse social worlds in all social contexts and across all continents. Recent works by anthropologists explore the social relations around new fertility practices in the UK (Franklin, 1997), how 'ordinary'[9] North Americans think about mathematics in their daily numerical practices (Lave, 1988) and the implementation of education policy on Kilimanjaro (Stambach, 2000). Anthropologists are also exploring the institutions through which contemporary international society is constituted. Examples include Richard Wilson's (2001) study of the South African Truth and Reconciliation Commission, Laura Nader's work on the social processes through which special kinds of knowledge come to have status as 'science', with all the claims to truth that this category implies (Nader et al., 1996), and Ian Harper's (1997) ethnography of the IMF.[10]

As well as globalisation and the changing nature of contemporary life in all societies, anthropological research has become more concerned with larger issues of human suffering and how these are brought about by the conjuncture of specific social and political relations (Das et al., 1998; Farmer, 2003). Pertinent examples include Malkki's (1995) account of the relation between refugee status and the emergence of a politicised ethnicity amongst Hutu exiles in Tanzanian refugee camps during the 1980s, Harrell Bond's (1986) classic ethnography of life for the recipients of humanitarian assistance in a refugee camp in Sudan, and Paul Richard's (1996) empathetic analysis of the meaning and motivation behind an atrocity filled guerrilla war in Sierra Leone. Away from the aftermath of war, anthropologists have acknowledged ill-being in the unavoidable 'violence of everyday life' brought about by appalling social conditions in some very poor communities. Nancy Scheper Hughes' (1992) description of the normalisation of infant mortality in a chronically low-income *favela* in Brazil shows how because poor mothers expect that weaker children will die as a matter of course, they do little to save them. Dying infants and those perceived as having minimal chances of survival are treated as little 'angels' who are merely visiting the living and are not expected to be anything other than the most transient of guests. Scheper Hughes (2002) has since turned her attention to the transnational social relations of inequality that promote and sustain the trade in human flesh between first and third worlds – not slavery or prostitution, but the buying and selling of body parts, blood, kidneys and corneas.

If poverty as a state and status is the manifestation of social relations it is also a category of representation through which social agents classify and act upon the world. An anthropological approach explores the content of this category and its genealogy in relation to the specific historical and social contexts in which it has salience for different categories of persons. These approaches reveal the continuity between current notions of poverty in development and social policy, and the assumptions that inform them. As we have seen, these centre on normative ideas of social order and a perception of poverty as an inherent threat to this order. Poverty is not represented as the outcome of historical and social relations but as a problem that must be eliminated to maintain social functionality. Where social relations are described as contributing to poverty these are represented as flawed in terms of quality, rather than content, as in the policy discourse about social capital where the low quality of local social relations is deemed to contribute to poverty, rather than the terms on which a community is embedded within wider regional, national and international economies (cf. Bracking, 2003). The ahistoricism of such visions is also echoed in some contemporary development representations of poverty in which poverty is presented as a state in the present with causal relations similarly present-focused, as exemplified in 'livelihoods' frameworks and some PPAs, rather than as the outcome of longer historical processes.

VI. Marginality as Social Process

Historically informed perspectives on poverty reveal not only the social construction of the category within specific historical and institutional settings, and the key role of powerful institutions in globalising the poverty agenda, but also the fact that the constitution of the kind of poverty that development practitioners aspire to reduce is itself a product of the socio economic relations of modernity. If poverty is measured in terms of access to services and levels of income or consumption, those seemingly excluded from market participation and services require integration into state and market systems for poverty to be addressed (Green and Hulme, 2005). This integration, or rather the terms on which the certain social groups are integrated, can be a point of transition from sustainable community to social exclusion, from locally enfranchised to disenfranchised and destitute.[11] The San of Botswana, an ethnic and cultural group associated with a semi- peripatetic lifestyle and a mode of subsistence based on the gathering of wild foods, hunting and casual labour on cattle ranches, provide a case in point. Land reforms have restricted their rights of access to game and wild resources, forcing an increased reliance on low wages in the ranching sector. Those without paid employment have been made dependant on meagre state handouts, which do not compensate for the loss of the hunting resources now claimed by the national elite. Although the San had previously been poor, occupying a kind of vassal position in relation to herding landlords, they had been able to mitigate this with access to game and the possibility of foraging (Wilmsen, 1989). Their present situation of destitution is a direct consequence of the terms of their integration into the contemporary state (Good, 1999).

Marginality is not always perceived as wholly negative by those communities wishing to limit such engagement. Indeed, some groups strive to maintain their autonomy through marginal relations to mainstream society and the state, relations characterised by Roma and traveller communities in eastern and western Europe and by some contemporary hunting and gathering communities in Africa and Asia. Such groups may strive to evade entrapment into the economic relations that characterise the society they wish not to be subject to. This is achieved through the adoption of livelihood strategies involving nomadism, economic activities that yield immediate economic returns (for example foraging) (Woodburn, 1981), and an emphasis on the redistribution of resources through gambling and sharing, rather than accumulation and saving. Such strategies are an important aspect of identity and self-definition for these communities, but the ideological emphasis on freedom is limited in practice by the very real powerlessness they face in relation to other social groups and the state. Subject to discrimination, often excluded from education and denied inclusion on anything other than the terms set by the majority, such groups become encapsulated within highly restricted economic and cultural niches (Day et al., 1999). Marginality in relation to place is equally an artefact of social and historical processes, namely historical decisions to situate the centre elsewhere, rather than an inherent attribute of people or places. Anna Tsing's (1993) account of a remote forest community in Indonesia reveals how they see themselves as fortunate to live in an 'out of the way' place, far from the parasitical state. The ethnography demonstrates how 'out of the wayness', and marginality, are socially, historically and *intentionally* constructed (ibid., 1993: 41–71), by those defined as marginal as well as by those with the power to enforce it.[12]

VII. The Moral Basis of Marginality

Marginality and social exclusion, once established, are often reinforcing. While deliberate processes of discrimination are rarely admitted, they are clearly evident in the kinds of mutually reinforcing policies applied to many marginal communities and which serve to ensure that the odds against their integration into mainstream society are often insurmountable. Extreme examples of this kind of strategy are the policies pursued by the Australian government against Aboriginal communities (McKnight, 2002), the Botswana state's policies on the San and the systemic institutionalisation of discrimination against Black citizens in the US. Mortality rates for Black citizens of some US cities are higher than those in some of the world's poorest countries (Sen, 1999) and a significant proportion of young Black American men are in prison.[13] Discourses legitimating differential treatment for communities on the basis of differences in lifestyle and livelihoods accompany these exclusionary strategies, informing not merely the negative stereotyping of minority cultural groups but providing the rationalisation for a perception of exclusion as a problem of the excluded categories. Poverty becomes not only a problem of the poor, but also their responsibility.

The notion that certain individuals and social groups are undeserving of assistance because they somehow cause their own poverty is pervasive in the US, where it informs racist discourse about non-White low income groups (Adair, 2002: 464). The anthropologists Felipe Bourgois (2003) has written about the problems faced by young male Puerto Ricans in a run down district of New York City who find their access to even low income jobs restricted through a combination of institutional racism and the feminisation of the unskilled sector. One of the few options for young men to earn good money in the neighbourhood is through the illegal drugs trade, selling highly profitable crack cocaine to a client group consisting of addicts from outside the Puerto Rican community. Only a minority of men in the neighbourhood earn their living in this way, but the high rewards and glamour of the big dealer lifestyle make an appealing, and rational, career option for those men willing to practice sufficient violence to gain 'respect' and ensure that their supply networks are protected.

Involvement in violence, drugs and crime perpetuate the stereotypical images of the neighbourhood, effectively a 'no go' zone for those who see themselves as law abiding and for the better off who can afford to live elsewhere. Ghetto dwellers working in the legal economic sector of the city become daily commuters out of poverty, only to commute back in once their working day is finished. Outsiders blame ghetto poverty on what they categorise as the drugs and guns culture of the ghetto. Bourgois shows how the ghetto and its poverty are best viewed in social and historical context, as the products of and reaction to particular social and economic configurations in the US and the ongoing colonial subjugation of Puerto Rico. Puerto Rican poverty has very little to do with the cultural practices and attitudes of Puerto Ricans but rather serves US interests, both within Manhattan, where Puerto Rican migrants provide a source of cheap labour and in Puerto Rico where industrial production can take place for US firms free of the constraints for the firm and protection for the labourer provided by US labour laws. Interestingly, the cultural values of the men that Bourgois worked with were not very different from those of mainstream American society – a desire to get on, make some money, a belief in the free market and individual freedom, and the belief that poverty is both an individual responsibility and an index of moral failure.[14]

The US approach to welfare is informed by an ideology of individual economic responsibility in which failure to achieve, and hence poverty, is viewed as a failure and thus as the responsibility of the individual, a kind of rational choice. The perception of poverty as a moral failure justifies punitive welfare interventions (Adair, 2002: 460–62). Welfare regimes based on an assumption that the majority of the poor are undeserving and need to be closely monitored are oriented towards making public assistance hard to obtain and unpleasant to survive on. Various schemes aimed at getting people to work, often for very low wages, aim to make the poor more deserving of assistance through labour, hence the concept of 'workfare'. Claimants must permit state scrutiny of their homes and private lives over their consumption and spending. These attitudes are not confined to the US. They inform recent attempts at welfare reform in European countries, including the UK, and underlie the promotion of conditional transfer programmes more generally. These programmes, of which *Progresa* (now called *Opportunidades*) in Mexico is the best known, make access to support dependant on the recipient's compliance with the objectives of other social programming, notably in health and education (Lazar, 2004), that is on being able to demonstrate that they are not merely in need but are morally deserving.

Ideas about the responsibility of the poor for their own poverty have a long history in Western society.[15] They were the basis of discourses about poverty and social responsibility for the destitute in England until the mid twentieth century, hence the intentionally punitive welfare regimes in workhouses where the destitute could go to seek food and shelter in return for hard labour in conditions that were explicitly designed to replicate the prison.[16] Related attitudes live on in popular perceptions of poverty even within poor communities (Woodhouse, 2003) and within the international development community (Hossain and Moore, 1999). Donor preoccupations with accounting for even trivial amounts of cash when spent in villages reflect similar concerns whereas central spending of hundreds or thousands attracts little audit attention within country and head quarters offices where the emphasis is on millions. There is no doubt that the idea of giving cash as opposed to food aid in famine situations is still widely resisted because of a belief that this would benefit the undeserving poor, despite evidence to suggest that this is cheaper and more effective in supporting local grain markets and empowering local people than food aid (de Waal, 1989; Devereux, 2002). Food for work programmes also promote this way of thinking, the idea that the work should be so menial and unpleasant and lowly paid that a person would have to be virtually starving to want to do it (what is referred to as 'Self-targeting') rather than simply allocate funds to those in need of support which it is feared would create 'dependency'.[17] The labour intensive public work schemes for minimal pay to provide relief for the very poor are similar. Such schemes may provide some people with some income but they will never alter the unequal structure of social relations nor address the macroeconomic conditions that keep people in poverty (McCord, 2003).

VIII. Social Critique and Social Transformation

The social critique of the society of the poor, rather than the society that produces poverty, is equally present in development thinking, even in the very paradigm of international development as a moral imperative itself. Certainly, where the development paradigm is premised on an explicit desire to transform societies deemed as poor and therefore as somehow dysfunctional, a moral judgement implying social failure is never far away. Although small scale sanitation and latrine projects may seem very different on the surface from the recent drive to foster strong social networks and relationships of trust through civil society support programmes thought to build social capital, both types of interventions depend on shared assumptions about the inappropriateness of certain kinds of social organisation and social practices for achieving development or conversely on an association between poverty and particular social and institutional forms. This kind of thinking is most evident in ambitious social modernization programmes carried out by governments (Scott, 1998) and in some colonial social policy (Lewis, 2000). It also informed the strategies of colonial Christian missions which strove to associate their ideas of desirable society with what was termed 'civilization', implying a wholesale devaluation of the societies that were the targets of conversion (Comaroff and Comaroff, 1991; Green, 2003). Similarly, the sanitation policies so vigorously pursued in colonial Fiji (Thomas, 1994), the mass campaigns for the eradication of sleeping sickness (Lyons, 1992) and tsetse fly which involved large scale reorganisation of rural communities into new and more governable social forms were premised on the notion of the inappropriateness of certain kinds of social organisation and social practices for what was defined as positive change (Chachage, 1988).

Although accounts of the one sidedness of developer–developee relationships are no longer an accurate reflection of development partnerships in which poverty reduction strategies are created nationally and in collaboration with those deemed to be stakeholders, the scope for equal partnerships is clearly limited by the political considerations of aid and the economic influence of donors (Lewis, 1998; Crewe and Harrison, 1999). Opportunities for local and national initiatives are also constrained by the dominance of particular visions of development problems and solutions which attain legitimacy at particular times. This explains why the content of development strategies and plans, even when these are prepared under substantial national or local ownership and where participatory modalities have been encouraged, reveal remarkable similarities across countries and continents. This uniformity comes about through the effects of a variety of mechanisms, including the policy influence of a limited number of organisations, the standardisation of development planning and analytical practices across many organisations in development from NGOs to multilaterals, and the relatively restricted pool within which the same professionals circulate from agency to agency (Green, 2003). Also significant is the production of what comes to be constituted as authoritative knowledge about development, and with poverty as the central problematic, about poverty itself (Cooper and Packard, 1997: 24; Goldman, 2001; Moore, 2001). Current claims to authoritative knowledge are dispersed through the development satellite agencies universities, development research institutes and NGOs as part of the World Bank's strategy to become, as 'knowledge Bank', the centre of knowledge about development (Mehta, 2001). The Bank not only conducts research on development but assimilates different knowledge on development into its understanding of development to present a unitary but evolving vision. This perspective informs the increasing complexity of the Bank's accounts of development and of the factors which may be significant for its realization.

This power to know is also, inevitably, the power to judge. Just as notions of the deserving poor and the culture of poverty seem natural to apply at the level of individuals within wealthy societies, so the same moral judgements are implicitly made when advocating mass social transformation or cultural change as precursors to 'development'. And, as with the intrusive state's power to invade the domestic space of welfare mothers in the US to assess whether they have spent their rations wisely or have cheated the system (Adair, 2002: 460), so the inequalities of power mean that the benefactor also claims the power not only to judge the moral claims of the poor to assistance, and to police them, but to set the terms of the assessment. Participatory poverty assessments permit, at least formally, the poor themselves to engage in framing the terms by which poverty in particular places is recognised. They do not radically shift the relations of power through which the non-poor and the outside determines when and how poverty is to be recognised and assessed. New modalities for facilitating local ownership of development strategies through the PRSP process potentially offer space for local definitions of poverty and strategies for action to emerge within the global discourse of poverty reduction (Booth, 2003). The extent to which such mechanisms provide an opportunity to address inequality and poverty must remain open to question (Weber, 2004). Given that poverty is neither an absolute condition, nor a readily identifiable entity, and that the content of the category is ultimately politically determined, it is not surprising that the new institutional structures for perceiving poverty become politicised contexts where poverty can be claimed not so much as a problem for some social categories, but as a potential asset by others who stand to gain from the inputs associated with the development relationship.[18]

This process works itself out in different ways depending on the power relations involved in the construction of poverty. In South Africa under Apartheid for example, what was in effect a participatory poverty study although termed a 'commission of inquiry' financed by the Carnegie Foundation, a US charitable entity, became a forum where the politics of apartheid could be publicly critiqued, within and outside South Africa. Local ownership and involvement in the design of the study created credibility and ensured that the product was viewed as an indigenous, rather than an outsider, vision (Bell, 2002). In contrast, the weight attached to development rankings in relation to determining priorities for spending makes the positioning in rankings critical for governments or regions seeking to maximise their credibility as deserving recipients of international assistance, even where these rankings are determined by outsiders. It is in the interests of some countries to be categorised as poor and to be ranked as amongst the poorest in order to justify claims for development support just as it is in the interests of donors to represent them this way. Development rankings, including poverty, are differently interpreted and assessed depending on the policy priorities of different donors and different governments (Viopio, 2000: 189). These rankings and indicators are never just perceived as data (nor are they intended to be), but as:

> ... message, meaning and judgement ... the most strongly identified and perhaps contested messages ... [are] ... official social and cultural values and open or hidden policy agendas seen to be *driving*, not driven by, numerical scores and rankings. (Apthorpe, 1997: 24, my emphasis)

IX. Institutionalising Poverty: The Example of Zanzibar

The centrality of poverty reduction to the national strategies of aid recipient governments has promoted the new institutionalisation of poverty outside the research centres and outside the Bank itself. While the Bank relied on consultants and its national offices to work with local research institutes and governments to provide data for assessments, UNDP were working with developing country partners to establish national systems for monitoring poverty that would provide indicators for progress in the implementation of National Poverty Reduction Strategies and Development Visions. The introduction of Poverty Reduction Strategy papers as vehicles for the formalisation of what are in effect national development strategies based on the development visions and poverty reduction plans legitimated the institutionalisation of poverty monitoring within governments as a state function. With the institutionalisation of poverty came the need to formally integrate poverty into policy and planning. This entails making *all* policies relate to the overarching policy objective of poverty reduction.

In practice the linking of anti-poverty polices with an evidence base about poverty is difficult. Not only are national statistical and information systems under resourced and weak, but also the indicators selected to represent for poverty do not necessarily capture its multifaceted dimensions and may not be responsive to the proposed interventions (Lucas, 2000: 100). In addition, it is far from clear in poor countries where the line should be drawn, if at all, between degrees of poverty, resulting in a tendency to categorise virtually all policies as poverty reducing and in the imposition of poverty as a blanket label justifying a broad brush approach to resource allocation within and between countries, perpetuating vast inequalities in the allocation of development resources (Baulch, 2003; Minujin and Delamonica, 2003).

An east African example clearly illustrates the way in which poverty is institutionalised at the national level as an object of assessment and the target of policy. These processes are evident in the ongoing drive to create a poverty focus in Tanzania and Zanzibar, the outcome of an initiative spearheaded by multi lateral agencies, notably UNDP.[19] What emerges from a brief comparison of the establishment of poverty as a development priority in these two settings is the politically constructed content of the category poverty and the ways in which poverty, once defined as the main development problem, comes to assume status as an analytical device which is used to account for other problems development policy seeks to address, ranging from agriculture to governance. Zanzibar is formally part of the United Republic of Tanzania, although it exists as a separate country within the Union, with its own parliament and own spheres of responsibility. Excluded from access to EU aid for much of the past decade, as a consequence of political conditionalities over the management of elections (amongst other things), Zanzibar is in the process of seeking readmission into the ambit of western development assistance. Excluded from the HIPC initiative (and hence from the necessity to produce a PRSP) due to the aid boycott and the fact that development assistance is a responsibility, formally at least, of the union government, in 2002 Zanzibar was nevertheless striving to demonstrate its commitment to the core aims of international development in a bid to rebuild its relationships with aid donors. As a result Zanzibar has adopted the poverty reduction model piloted on the mainland, and was seeking to frame its development policies in terms of a Zanzibar Poverty Reduction Plan (ZPRP).

The poverty reduction plan approach was promoted by the United Nations Development Programme (UNDP), whose staff provided the technical assistance to adapt approaches developed elsewhere to the new setting. The ZPRP represented the situation in Zanzibar as defined by poverty which is equated, in background studies, to the extent and intensity of poverty on the mainland. Poverty on Zanzibar was attributed to various causes, and assigned various solutions, most advocating economic investment and industrial expansion. The ZPRP analysis at that time omitted reference to the political conflicts which have disrupted governance and public services since the 1960s and contributed to asymmetrical subsidisation of the islands' population of less than one million from the United Republic's coffers. Indeed, according to some estimates Zanzibar received subsidies from the United Republic of Tanzania in excess of $870 million US dollars between 1983 and 1999, an amount greater than the eleven years of Tanzania's development expenditure from 1986–97 (Maliyamkono, 2000: 214). During this time Zanizbar was not starved of funds. It derived substantial wealth from its foreign exchange and tariff regimes that made its ports a channel through which international goods could be easily imported (ibid: 213, 187). Against this background, poverty as an effect emerges as a result of significantly more complex relations and processes than represented in the ZPRP documentation with its emphasis on feeder roads and access to markets.

The analysis of poverty and equation of Zanzibar poverty with mainland poverty creates the impression that we are dealing with a phenomenon which is fundamentally similar in the islands and on the Tanzania mainland. While this may be the case at the level of manifestation, that is of *effect* in terms of poverty headcounts, poor nutrition and infant mortality for example, the *causes* of poverty, and hence realistic solutions to it, are radically different in the two countries which have radically different economies, different histories and, in all likelihood, different trajectories of development. As both cause and effect of the respective problems of Zanzibar and Tanzania the ZPRP says virtually nothing about the very different economic and social profiles of the two countries, nor about the very different historical and contemporary political relations which have contributed to the way they are today.

X. The Poverty of Representations

If poverty as a category in development is the outcome of politically contested processes of negotiation, with variable content, what then does it mean to assert that so many people live in poverty or that poverty needs to be attacked? As we have seen, the content of the category of poverty is not specific. It conveys a range of associations, including consumption measures and access to basic services, aggregated at rather crude levels with an emphasis on magnitude and scale. The quantification of poverty permits the homogenisation of poverty across time and space. This drive to generalise permits the construction of poverty rankings which aim to compare the amount and depth of poverty, rather than its causes and consequences. The tendency to generalise equally informs qualitative approaches – especially the participatory poverty assessments (PPAs) – to apprehending poverty which have concentrated on how poverty is similarly manifested in different places rather than on the historical and social factors which differentially contribute to poverty in different places. Such accounts tell us that people are hungry because of lack of access to food or that infant mortality is high because of poor health services. They do not however tell us why food cannot be accessed or why health services are inadequate, but this is essential if effective action is to be taken.

The emphasis on poverty as the problem and the locus of analysis diverts attention from the social relations, local, national and international, which produce poverty as an attribute of people. Very often it is not among the poor that we should be looking for those relations which have contributed most to the poverty of others. The reification of poverty deflects from the issue of agency. Poverty is not a 'thing' to be attacked, but the outcome of specific social relations that require investigation and transformation. Focusing on social relations highlights the centrality of the actions and strategies of rich and poor alike in determining poverty outcomes, and the quality of the embodied experience of deprivation. Robert Chambers (2001: 303) reminds us that for the most marginal the only asset they have is their bodies. While the able bodied can sell their labour as long as they are able, inadequate access to health services and high risk of accidents renders many destitute. Some are forced to transact this asset in other ways. Prostitution, bondage, slavery and the sale of human organs are the ultimate reminders that wealth buys life, literally, and other people. It is not so much the threat posed by the poor but the threats to the poor that should concern us. Quantification can capture the extent of the incidence of such practices. It cannot capture the nexus of desperation which forces people to consider them as choices. As well as encouraging us to be more reflexive about our categories and labelling, anthropology can make an important contribution here.

Acknowledgements

The support of the UK Economic and Social Research Council is gratefully acknowledged. The work was part of the programme of the ESRC Global Poverty Research Group (grant M571255001). This paper was originally presented as part of a session on methodologies for addressing poverty organised by GPRG at the International Conference on Chronic Poverty in Manchester in April 2003.

I am grateful to colleagues in GPRG and to the anonymous reviewers at JDS whose critical insights have informed the revisions of this paper.

Notes

1. But there are exceptions. See for example Farmer (2003), Passaro (1996) and Scheper Hughes (1992).
2. See the Bank's website for the full mission statement and accounts of how the Bank works with the poorest people in the poorest countries and its aspirations to be the primary source of knowledge about development (http://www.worldbank.org).
3. Once poverty reduction becomes a goal for public policy then poverty must be turned into something tangible that can be measured and about which correlates can be identified.
4. For a comparative example in the west see O'Connor (2001), who shows that while early poverty studies in the UK and US were influenced by an activist agenda poverty knowledge since the 1960s, certainly in the US, has been largely policy determined.
5. James Ferguson (1990: 27) remarks of such statements apparently based on empirical research which find their way into development documentation and which are contradicted by more academic studies, which are not cited, that 'It must be recognized that which is being done here is not some sort of strangely bad scholarship, but something else entirely.'
6. Hence Chambers' (2001: 306) rhetorical suggestion that the *World Development Report* 2010 be titled 'Challenging wealth and power'.
7. See for example Baumann's (1998) description of the new 'poor' in consumer societies whose poverty is manifested through inability to share in the purchase of the consumer items through which identity is articulated.
8. For a discussion of the relation between subjection and agency in academic representations of the 'Other' see Prakash (1994).
9. The book is concerned with averagely educated adults in urban communities in the US, who have not had anything other than elementary education in mathematics. Lave shows how most think of themselves as unable to 'do math', but in practice are adept at managing essential calculations in daily life, a kind of popular mathematics.
10. Riles' (2001) ethnography of transnational activist networks leading in up to a UN summit is another pertinent example.
11. Devereux's (2003) distinction between poverty and destitution is pertinent here, in highlighting the social nature of destitution as a situation where people are rendered dependent on others through social and economic constraints which render their livelihoods unsustainable.
12. Similarly, the economic stagnation of much of southern Tanzania, and its ensuing 'poverty', owes much to game protection policies of successive colonial and postcolonial governments which have created and maintained one of the largest game reserves in Africa right in the middle of what was until the early twentieth century the economic heartland of the region (Seppala, 1998; Green, 2003).
13. According to the 2001 *World Development Report*, 'the life expectancy of African Americans is about the same as that in China and in some states in India' (World Bank, 2001: 46).
14. 'Like most other people in the US, drug dealers and street criminals are scrambling to obtain their piece of the pie as fast as possible. In fact, in their pursuit of success they are even following the minute details of the classical Yankee model for upward mobility. They are aggressively pursuing careers as private entrepreneurs; they take risks; work hard and pray for good luck' (Bourgois, 2003: 326).
15. Prior to the introduction of the workhouse, parish relief in England was quite generous towards the destitute and was unconditional (Fogel, 2004).
16. For a contemporary account of the conditions inside workhouses at the start of the twentieth century, and for insights into Victorian attitudes towards poverty, see the novelist Jack London's *The People of the Abyss*, originally published in 1903 (1998).
17. Aid, Mary Anderson (1999: 55) points out, and the way in which it is delivered conveys implicit and explicit ethical messages.
18. In the form of contracts, large scale, resource transfers, opportunities for employment, travel and study tours, capacity and institution building, seating allowances and so on.
19. For an overview of poverty in Tanzania in the context of PRS see Ellis and Ntengua (2003).

References

Adair, V. (2002) Branded with infamy: Inscriptions of poverty and class in the US, *Signs*, 27(2), pp. 451–71.

Anderson, M. B. (1999) *Do No Harm: How Aid Can Support Peace – or War* (Boulder: Lynne Rienner).

Appadurai, A. (1993) Number in the colonial imagination, in C. Breckenridge and P. van der Veer (eds), *Orientalism and the Postcolonial Predicament: Perspectives on South Asia*, pp. 314–39 (Philadelphia: University of Pennsylvania Press).

Apthorpe, R. (1997) Human development reporting and social anthropology, *Social Anthropology*, 5(1), pp. 21–34.

Baulch, B. (2003) Aid for the poorest? The distribution and maldistribution of development assistance, *CPRC Working Paper 35*, Manchester: Institute for Development Policy and Management, University of Manchester.

Bauman, Z. (1998) *Work, Consumerism and the New Poor* (Buckingham: Open University Press).

Bell, M. (2002) Inquiring minds and postcolonial devices: examining poverty at a distance, *Annals of the Association of American Geographers*, 92(3), pp. 507–23.

Booth, D., Leach, M. and Tierney, A. (1999) Experiencing poverty in Africa: perspectives from anthropology, background paper 1(b) for the World Bank Poverty Status report 1999.

Booth, D. (2003) Are PRSPs making a difference? The African experience, *Development Policy Review*, 21(2), pp. 131–87.

Bornstein, E. (2003) *The Spirit of Development: Religious NGOs, Morality and Economics in Zimbabwe* (New York: Routledge).

Bourdieu, P. (1977) *Outline of a Theory of Practice* (Cambridge: Cambridge University Press).

Bourgois, P. (2003) *In Search of Respect. Selling Crack in El Barrio* (Cambridge: Cambridge University Press).

Bracking, S. (2003) The political economy of chronic poverty, *CPRC Working Paper 23*, Manchester: Institute for Development Policy and Management, University of Manchester.

Carvalho, S. and White, H. (1997) Combining the quantitative and qualitative approaches to poverty measurement and analysis: the practice and the potential, *World Bank Technical Paper No 36*, Washington DC: World Bank.

Cernea, M. (1995) Social organisation and development anthropology, *Human Organisation*, 54(3), pp. 340–52.

Chachage, C. S. L. (1988) British rule and African civilization in Tanganyika, *Journal of Historical Sociology*, 1(2), pp. 199–223.

Chambers, R. (2001) The world development report: concepts, content and a chapter 12, *Journal of International Development*, 13, pp. 299–306.

Comaroff, J. and Comaroff, J. L. (1991) *Of Revelation and Revolution: Christianity, Colonialism and Consciousness in South Africa* (Chicago: University of Chicago Press).

Cooper, F. and Packard, R. (1997) Introduction, in F. Cooper and R. Packard (eds), *International Development and the Social Sciences: Essays on the History and Politics of Knowledge*, pp. 1–41 (Berkeley: University of California Press).

Crewe, E. and Harrison, E. (1999) *Whose Development? An Ethnography of Aid* (London: Zed Books).

Das, V., Kleinman, A. and Lock, M. (eds) (1998) *Social Suffering* (Berkeley: University of California Press).

Day, S., Papataxiarchis, E. and Stewart, M. (1999) Consider the lilies of the field, in S. Day, E. Papataxiarchis and M. Stewart (eds), *Lilies of the Field, Marginal People Who Live for the Moment*, pp. 1–24 (Boulder: Westview Press).

De L'Estoile, B. (1997) The natural preserve of anthropologists: social, scientific planning and development, *Social Science Information*, 36(2), 343–76.

De Waal, A. (1989) *Famine That Kills: Darfur, Sudan, 1984–85* (Oxford: Clarendon Press).

Devereux, S. (2002) Can social safety nets reduce chronic poverty? *Development Policy Review*, 20(5), pp. 657–75.

Devereux, S. (2003) Conceptualizing destitution, *IDS Working Paper 217*, Brighton: Institute of Development Studies.

Douglas, M. (1991) Witchcraft and leprosy: two strategies of exclusion, *Journal of the Royal Anthropological Institute, Man*, 26(4), pp. 723–35.

Douglas, M. (1996) *Natural Symbols: Explorations in Cosmology* (London: Routledge).

Dumont, L. (1970) *Homo Hierarchicus: An Essay on the Caste System* (Chicago: University of Chicago Press).

Durkheim, E. (1960) *The Division of Labour in Society* (Glencoe: Free Press).

Ellis, F. and Ntengua, M. (2003) Livelihoods and rural poverty reduction in Tanzania, *World Development*, 31(8), pp. 1367–84.

Escobar, A. (1991) Anthropology and the development encounter: the making and marketing of development anthropology, *American Ethnologist*, 18(4), pp. 658–82.

Escobar, A. (1995) *Encountering Development. The Making and Unmaking of the Third World* (Princeton: Princeton University Press).

Elson, D. (2000) The social content of macroeconomic policies, *World Development*, 28(7), pp. 1347–64.

Evans Pritchard, E. E. (1940) *The Nuer* (Oxford: Clarendon).

Farmer, P. (2003) *Pathologies of Power: Health, Human Rights, and the New War on the Poor* (Berkeley: University of California Press).

Ferguson, J. (1990) *The Anti-Politics Machine: 'Development', Depoliticization and Bureaucratic Power in Lesotho* (Cambridge: Cambridge University Press).

Ferguson, J. (1997) Anthropology and its evil twin: the constitution of a discipline, in F. Cooper and R. Packard (eds), *International Development and the Social Sciences: Essays on the History and Politics of Knowledge*, pp. 150–75 (Berkeley: University of California Press).

Finnemore, M. (1997) Redefining development at the World Bank, in F. Cooper and R. Packard (eds), *International Development and the Social Sciences: Essays on the History and Politics of Knowledge*, pp. 203–27 (Berkeley: University of California Press).

Fogel, R. W. (2004) *The Escape from Hunger and Premature Death, 1700–2100. Europe, America and the Third World* (Cambridge, Cambridge University Press).

Foucault, M. (1976) *The Birth of the Clinic: An Archaeology of Medical Perception* (London: Tavistock).

Franklin, S. (1997) *Embodied Progress: A Cultural Account of Assisted Conception* (London: Routledge).

Geertz, C. (1984) Culture and social change: the Indonesian case, *Man* (NS), 19(3), pp. 511–32.

Gledhill, J. (2000) Disappearing the poor? A critique of the new wisdoms of social democracy in an age of globalization, *Urban Anthropology*, 30(2/3), pp. 123–56.

Goldman, M. (2001) The birth of a discipline. Producing authoritative green knowledge, World Bank style, *Ethnography*, 2(2), pp. 191–217.

Good, K. (1999) The state and extreme poverty in Botswana: the San and destitutes, *Journal of Modern African Studies*, 37(2), pp. 185–205.

Gordon, D., Nandy, S., Pantazis, C., Pemberton, S. and Townsend, P. (2003) *Child Poverty in the Developing World* (Bristol: Policy Press).

Green, M. and Hulme, D. (2005) From correlates and characteristics to causes: thinking about poverty from a chronic poverty perspective, *World Development*, 31(3), pp. 867–79.

Green, M. (2003) Globalizing development in Tanzania. Policy franchising through participatory project management, *Critique of Anthropology*, 23(2), pp. 123–43.

Green, M. (2005) International development, social analysis . . . and anthropology? Applying anthropology in and to development, in S. Pink (ed.), *Applications of Anthropology* (Oxford: Berghahn).

Gudeman, S. (1978) *The Demise of a Rural Economy: From Subsistence to Capitalism in a Latin American Village* (Boston: Routledge).

Harper, R. H. R. (1997) *Inside the IMF: Documents, Technology, and Organisational Action* (London: Academic Press).

Harrell-Bond, B. (1986) *Imposing Aid: Emergency Assistance to Refugees* (Oxford: Oxford University Press).

Hart, K. (2001) *Money in an Unequal World. Keith Hart and His Memory Bank* (London, Texere).

Hastrup, K. (1993) Hunger and the hardness of facts, *Man* (NS), 28(4), pp. 727–39.

Haugerud, A. and Edelman, M. (eds) (2004) *Development Anthropology: A Reader* (Oxford: Blackwell).

Horowitz, M. (1996) On not offending the borrower: (self?)-ghettoization of anthropology at the World Bank, *Development Anthropologist*, 14(1/2), pp. 1–12.

Hossain, N. and Moore, M. (1999) Elite perceptions of poverty: Bangladesh, *IDS Bulletin*, 30(2), pp. 106–16.

Hulme, D. and Shepherd, A. (2003) Conceptualising chronic poverty, *World Development*, 31(3), pp. 403–24.

Iliffe, J. (1987) *The African Poor* (Cambridge: Cambridge University Press).

Kanbur, R. and Squire, L. (2001) The evolution of thinking about poverty: exploring the interactions, Revised version published in G. Meier and J. Stiglitz (eds), *Frontiers of Development Economics: The Future in Perspective* (Oxford: Oxford University Press).

Latour, B. (1987) *Science in Action: How to Follow Scientists and Engineers Through Society* (Milton Keynes: Open University Press).

Lave, J. (1998) *Cognition in Practice: Mind, Mathematics and Culture in Everyday Life* (Cambridge: Cambridge University Press).

Lazar, S. (2004) Education for credit: development as citizenship project in Bolivia, *Critique of Anthropology*, 24, pp. 301–19.

Lewis, D. (1998) Development NGOs and the challenge of partnership: changing relations between north and south, *Social Policy and Administration*, 32(5), pp. 501–12.

Lewis, J. (2000) *Empire State–building: War and Welfare in Kenya, 1925–52* (Oxford: James Currey).

Little, P. and Painter, M. (1995) Discourse, politics, and the development process: reflections on escobar's 'anthropology and the development encounter', *American Ethnologist*, 22(3), pp. 602–16.

London, J. (1998) *The People of the Abyss* (London: Pluto).

Lucas, H. (2000) What do you mean, 'social policy analysis'? Reflections on concepts and methodology, *IDS Bulletin*, 31(4), pp. 98–109.

Lyons, M. (1992) *The Colonial Disease: A Social History of Sleeping Sickness in Northern Zaire* (Cambridge: Cambridge University Press).

Maliyamkono, T. (2000) Zanzibar's financial benefits from the union, in T. Maliyamkono (ed.), *The Political Plight of Zanzibar*, pp. 213–44 (Dar es Salaam: TEMA Publishers).

Malkki, L. (1995) *Purity and Exile: Violence, Memory, and National Cosmology among Hutu Refugees in Tanzania* (Chicago: University of Chicago Press).

Mauss, M. (1990) *The Gift: Form and Reason for Exchange in Archaic Societies* (London, Routledge).

McCord, A. (2003) *An Overview of the Performance and Potential of Public Works Programmes in South Africa* (Cape Town: SALDRU, Department of Economics, University of Cape Town).

McKnight, D. (2002) *From Hunting to Drinking: The Devastating Effects of Alcohol on an Australian Aboriginal Community* (London: Routledge).

Mehta, L. (2001) The World Bank and its emerging knowledge empire, *Human Organization*, 60(2), pp. 189–96.

Meillassoux, C. (1981) *Maidens, Meal and Money: Capitalism and the Domestic Community* (Cambridge: Cambridge University Press).

Minujin, A. and Delamonica, E. (2003) *Equality Matters for a World Fit for Children: Lessons from the 1990s* (New York: UNICEF).

Moore, S. F. (2001) The international production of authoritative knowledge: The case of drought stricken West Africa', *Ethnography*, 2(2), pp. 161–89.

Mosse, D. (2004) *Cultivating Development: An Ethnography of Aid Policy and Practice* (London: Pluto).

Nader, L. (ed.) (1996) *Naked Science: Anthropological Inquiry into Boundaries, Power, and Knowledge* (London: Routledge).

Narayan, D., Patel, R., Schafft, K., Rademacher A. and Koch-Schulte, S. (2000) *Voices of the Poor: Can Anyone Hear Us* (New York: Oxford University Press).

Nash, J. (1979) *We Eat the Mines and the Mines Eat Us: Dependency and Exploitation in Bolivia* (New York: Columbia University Press).

O'Connor, A. (2001) *Poverty Knowledge: Social Science, Social Policy and the Poor in Twentieth Century U.S. History* (Princeton: Princeton University Press).

Pansters, W. G. and de Ruijter, A. (2000) Poverty and social exclusion in a comparative perspective, in G. W. Pansters, G. Dijkstra, P. Hoebink and E. Snel (eds), *Rethinking Poverty: Comparative Perspectives from Below*, pp. 1–11 (Assen: Van Gorcum).

Passaro, J. (1996) *The Unequal Homeless: Men on the Streets, Women in Their Place* (New York: Routledge).

Prakash, G. (1994) Subaltern studies as postcolonial criticism, *American Historical Review*, 99(5), pp. 1475–90.

Rabinow, P. (1989) *French Modern: Norms and Forms of the Social Environment* (Chicago: University of Chicago Press).

Rabinow, P. (2003) *Anthropos Today: Reflections on Modern Equipment* (Princeton: Princeton University Press).

Richards, P. (1996) *Fighting for the Rain Forest: War, Youth and Resources in Sierra Leone* (London: James Currey).

Riles, A. (2001) *The Network Inside Out* (Ann Arbor: University of Michigan Press).

Rist, G. (1997) *The History of Development: From Western Origins to Global Faith* (London: Zed Books).

Rosaldo, M. (1980) *Knowledge and Passion: Ilongot Notions of Self and Social Life* (Cambridge: Cambridge University Press).

Ruggeri Laderchi, C., Saith, R. and Stewart, F. (2003) Does it matter that we do not agree on the definition of poverty? A comparison of four approaches, *Oxford Development Studies*, 31(3), pp. 243–74.

Sahlins, M. (1972) *Stone Age Economics* (New York: Aldine).

Scheper Hughes, N. (1992) *Death Without Weeping: The Violence of Everyday Life in Brazil* (Berkeley: University of California Press).

Scheper Hughes, N. (2002) Min(d)ing the body: on the trail of organ stealing rumours, in J. McLancy (ed.), *Exotic No More: Anthropology on the Front Lines*, pp. 33–63 (Chicago: University of Chicago Press).

Scott, J. (1998) *Seeing Like A State: How Certain Schemes to Improve the Human Condition Have Failed* (Newhaven: Yale University Press).

Sen, A. K. (1981) *Poverty and Famines: An Essay on Entitlement and Deprivation* (Oxford: Clarendon Press).

Sen, A. K. (1999) *Development as Freedom* (Oxford: Oxford University Press).

Seppala, P. (ed.) (1998) *The Making of a Periphery. Economic Development and Cultural Encounters in Southern Tanzania* (Dar es Salaam: Mkuki na Nyota).

Shrestha, N. (1995) Becoming a development category, in J. Crush (ed.), *Power of Development*, pp. 266–77 (London: Routledge).

Stambach, A., 2000, *Lessons from Mount Kilimanjaro: Schooling, Community and Gender in East Africa* (New York: Routledge).

Thomas, N. (1994) *Colonialism's Culture: Anthropology, Travel and Governance* (Cambridge: Polity Press).

Tsing, A. L. (1993) *In the Realm of the Diamond Queen: Marginality in an out-of-the-way place* (Princeton, NJ: Princeton University Press).

Voipio, T. (2000) Poverty narratives: linking theory, policy and praxis. The case of Tanzania, in G. W. Pansters, G. Dijkstra, P. Hoebink and E. Snel (eds), *Rethinking Poverty: Comparative Perspectives from Below*, pp. 187–209 (Assen: Van Gorcum).

Weber, H. (2004) Reconstituting the "third world"? Poverty reduction and territoriality in the global politics of development, *Third World Quarterly*, 25(1), pp. 187–206.

Wenger, E. (1998) *Communities of Practice: Learning, Meaning and Identity* (Cambridge: Cambridge University Press).

Wilmsen, E. (1989) *Land Filled with Flies: A Political Economy of the Kalahari* (Chicago: University of Chicago Press).

Wilson, R. (2001) *The Politics of Truth and Reconciliation in South Africa: Legitimising the Post-Apartheid State* (Cambridge: Cambridge University Press).

Woodburn, J. (1981) Egalitarian societies, *Man* NS, 17(1), pp. 31–51.

Woodhouse, P. (2003) *Local Elite Perceptions of the Poor in Uganda*, mimeo, Manchester, Institute for Development Policy and Management.

World Bank (1990) *World Development Report* (Oxford: Oxford University Press).

World Bank (2001) *World Development Report 2000/2001: Attacking Poverty* (Oxford: Oxford University Press).

Pluralism, Poverty and Sharecropping: Cultivating Open-Mindedness in Development Studies

I. Introduction

Renting land is a multi-dimensional, multi-market transaction which fascinates scholars. The act of renting land in or out is both an intentional act of agency, and a fluctuating part of the class structure which distributes resources. In this paper deep divisions among theorists will be shown to have implications for poverty studies. In particular, the neoclassical and new institutionalist economists, who theorise tenancy differently from political economy, find that they have to build bridges with political economy before they can embark on linking their research to the anti-poverty agenda. The specific bridges built in this paper relate to measuring the productivity of tenants; the ethics of challenging poverty in the sharecropping literature; discussing landlords' power explicitly; relating government regulation to the empowerment of tenants; and using a relational approach to poverty rather than a residual approach. The paper arrives at these substantive points through a methodological lens. The assumptions associated with realism are described in this initial section. In development studies, the sharecropping literature proves a good sowing-ground for cultivating a theoretically pluralist approach to poverty research.

In the rest of this introduction, I will introduce the realist approach that illuminates the pluralist method. The paper then moves into the specific area of Indian tenancy debates. Section II reviews the literature on tenancy and specific empirical claims made in that literature. Is tenancy an important way for landlords to exploit labour more efficiently? Is share-cropping on the wane in favour of commercial renting? The reasons for these trends (and their interpretation) forms the material in Section II. Section III examines the comparability of theories in the study of tenancy. Section IV relates the tenancy studies to the themes of poverty and inequality. A discussion of the moral content of theories is a highlight of Section IV. I conclude in Section V.

Methodological pluralism[1]

Critical realists like Sayer (1992) claim that it is possible to have knowledge of social structures even though that knowledge is both fallible and limited. Social knowledge claims are fallible because of the complex interrelation of the real structures with the diverse meanings of those structures to today's society. Knowledge is also likely to be limited in scope, since human knowledge cannot simply mirror or correspond to reality. According to Sayer, false claims can be challenged through the use of empirical evidence, but there will remain a range of claims whose validity is contestable. Each of these latter has some evidence in its support (ibid., 1992: 242–48). In examining these competing claims, a pluralist comparative approach can be useful because there is no single 'truth' that perfectly describes the complexity of the social world.[2] The meta-theoretical approach taken here, which is scientific realist, argues that the comparison of competing claims is a useful project that helps to discern which interpretations are most worthy (Smith, 1994). Realists normally argue that there is no 'pure' stance on the world that is not mediated by the social context of the narrator (Patomaki and Wight, 2000: 226). 'There is no 'neutral' metalanguage with which to compare competing theories.... However, this does not mean that communication/translation across theories/paradigms is impossible' (ibid.). For this reason the phrase 'critical realism', which highlights the critical stance taken by the narrator to the language used to interpret the world, is often used as a synonym for scientific realism (Sayer, 2000a).

In debates about realism, scientific realism is characterised by a depth ontology – the assumption that the world contains structures which interact with each other in complex ways. Structures are defined as sets of related objects, whose relationships show patterns which cannot be reduced to their atomistic components. The depth ontology recognises agents who try to interpret the structures (Archer et al., 1998). This paper will presume that a depth ontology offers a useful foundation for the study of society, and that knowledge about society is necessarily embedded in its historical and spatial context (that is in languages, cultures, and their trajectories). Structure, culture and agency are widely recognised to be interacting dialectically in society (ibid.), but realist approaches to social reality oppose the stronger forms of postmodernism as well as challenging the methodological individualism that is found at times in economics (surveyed by Sayer, 2000a).

Critical realism does not simply attempt to essentialise 'the real', but recognises that its existence has implications for knowledge. Specifically, the real tendencies of social objects can have effects (and hence can be causal) even if actors in a given scene do not recognise these causal mechanisms. Thus some explanatory claims can be false. In addition, that which can be considered to be true is likely to be subject to contestation – particularly when we are trying to know about the social world – because of the multiplicity of viewpoints that any society holds.

In the debate over peasant studies and 'peasant essentialism', for instance, Bernstein and Byres (2001) took a scientific realist viewpoint. They argued that whilst 'peasants' really exist, it is important not to oversimplify their situation by merely essentialising peasants. Realists look for evidence about the world, but carefully distinguish that evidence from the world itself, that is from reality. Claims based on evidence are subject to further refinement and improvement.

In summary, realists usually describe the world as consisting of three levels, which are linked: structures; events; and empirical evidence. The evidence can give hints as to the nature of the underlying structure. Evidence is simultaneously shaped by its concrete historical context and origin, including the aims of the agents who try to describe society. The problem of the possibility of false (or badly phrased) empirical evidence is a profound one for social scientists.

Realists focus upon the essential attributes of a named thing, as well as the act of naming. Scientific realism is the specific form of realism which questions the naming of things since names cannot easily make direct reference (by correspondence) to the thing-in-the-world that one wants to refer to (Sayer, 2000a). Things like tenancy institutions are more differentiated and nuanced than words can say. Of course essentialism would simplify analysis. In a sense words always essentialise or reify 'things'. So do mathematical symbols in social theory. A number of realists have argued that mathematical 'models', like ideal types, tend toward being irrealist (Lawson, 1997). This paper aims to make explicit several ways to avoid irrealist social science, and thus to improve research on poverty.[3]

The most obvious way is to avoid atomism. Atomism is the assumption that society can be reduced to a set of homogeneous objects.[4] Many social scientists from a range of disciplines agree on rejecting methodological individualism, but realists go further in exploring the implications of a depth ontology. (See Figure 1 for short definitions of the terms used here from the philosophy of science.) For instance, is the 'tenant' a person, or a household? Obviously households have the emergent property of being contracted to rent land, but persons are also involved. Individuals agree to pay the rent to another household; individuals do the work on the land. The interactions of persons with households are complex. There is both nesting and layering between the set of households and the set of persons. The 'depth' of a realist ontology also allows for other institutions, macro regulatory systems, social norms and other entities to exist. All the entities interact.

Depth ontology: A set of assumptions that allows for the existence of inter-penetrating entities including people, households, institutions, regulatory systems, conceptual frameworks, and the inter-dependence of all of these entities.

Interdisciplinarity: The use of conceptual frameworks from different academic disciplines such as sociology and economics.

Methodological pluralism: An approach to social science in which theories are examined using a meta-review, so that neither theory nor empirical evidence can be taken as 'given' or as factual (see Danermark, 2001, for details).

Neoclassical theory: An economic theory which typically sees markets as the essential basis for social interaction, sees individuals (or proto-individuals, such as profit-maximising firms) as the basic units of society, is atomistic in its ontology, and uses marginal movements along functions – such as utility functions or production functions – as well as demand-and-supply to analyse economic decision-making.

New institutionalist: An economic theory which allows for the existence of social institutions as well as markets. Social institutions include the system of property rights, contracts which are normatively constructed (and hence include implicit contracts and unwritten agreements), social norms about marriage, and others. To distinguish old institutionalism from new institutionalism, see Chang (2003).

Ontology: A theory of what exists; or, a discussion of competing assumptions about the existence of things such as social structures.

Political economy: The study of the provisioning of societies through a variety of market and non-market mechanisms, firmly grounded in the study of social relations and of the various aspects of power which permeate them. See Lukes (2005).

Realism: A theory of existence which allows for the possible reality of each 'thing' in society and in nature, for example 'cells', 'classes', and 'patriarchy'. Realism has different branches such as naïve realism, scientific realism and critical realism (see Williams, 2000).

Relational approach: An approach to poverty and social relations in which poor and rich are seen to be in continual relationship with each other. Social class analysis is the typical example of a relational approach (see Allen and Thomas, 2000).

Residual approach: An approach to poverty which isolates the poor as one element of society. Their living conditions are examined separately, and appear to be conceived as a residual or leftover compared with the main bulk of society.

Pluralism: A stance that accepts the co-existence of competing ways of conceptualising the same things.

Social structures: Patterned relations between objects in society, such as the social classes or the genders, which consist of more than merely the objects themselves. Structures are thought to have emergent properties that arise from the synergy between the elements within the structures. See Sayer (2000a); for the history of the debate about structuralism see Outhwaite and Bottomore (1993).

Structuralism: The analysis of social structures, assuming that they exist, allowing for the factors which cause them to change over time.

Figure 1. Summary of key terms

Several social scientists' works (Berger and Luckmann, 1966; Roth, 1987; Sayer, 1992, 2000a; Harré, 1998) help to illustrate this realist view of the complex social system. Berger and Luckmann, writing in 1966, noted that:

> It is important to bear in mind that most modern societies are pluralistic. This means that they have a shared core (symbolic) universe taken for granted as such, and different partial (symbolic) universes coexisting in a state of mutual accommodation. (Berger and Luckmann, 1966: 142)

Berger and Luckmann took a critical realist position[5] which recognised the existence of structures in society. A standard realist formulation of the role of social science, given this sort of complex ontic assumption, is offered by Patomaki and Wight:

> A significant part of what constitutes science is the attempt to identify the relatively enduring structures, powers, and tendencies, and to understand their characteristic ways of acting. Explanation entails providing an account of those structures, powers and tendencies that have contributed to, or facilitated, some already identified phenomenon of interest ... Science is seen to proceed through a constant spiral of discovery and understanding, further discovery, and revision, and hopefully more adequate understanding. (Patomaki and Wight, 2000: 223–24)

Roth (1987) in a detailed study of how social science can come to grips with a pluralist approach to knowing about society (that is a pluralist epistemology), argued the case that all hypotheses in science are coloured by prior theoretical frameworks.[6] Theoretical frameworks reflect the inherent social, historical and local grounding of the researcher. Habit, established discourses, and research traditions colour our choice of theory (Kuhn, 1970). Roth argued that the social groundedness of theories does not demolish the possibility of rational choice between theories. In this he opposed the relativism of some postmodern methodologists.[7] He argued in favour of a conscious approach to theory.

Roth's work supports meta-theorising (assessing competing theories), as does the work of Bhaskar on meta-critique (see Olsen, 2003a, for a summary; extract from Bhaskar in Archer et al., 1998). Meta-critique is the critique of theory, and of the underlying society, aimed at choosing theories that contribute to the improvement of that society, whilst challenging weak or inappropriate theories (Olsen, 2003a). Meta-theoretical work is part of meta-critique. Meta-theoretical work, like the pluralist approach described in this paper, involves attempting to view several theories' character, and their strengths and weaknesses, from a vantage point that takes into account both empirical evidence and the nature of the different available theories. Meta-theoretical analysis is currently conducted by heterodox economists when they compare heterodox theories with orthodox theories (see Dow, 2002, for a survey). For development studies it is a useful technique.

Harré's (1998) essay 'When the knower is also the known', argues that the expert social scientist is embedded in society and is part of a system which includes the 'object' or subject of their enquiries (see also Bryman, 1998; Layder, 1998).

By being part of the social system, Harré argues, the observer cannot avoid using a self-reflexive consideration of the political impact of their social science. In Harré's view the observer is not neutral. The value-neutrality of theory is one of the tenets of empiricist social science which realists have carefully questioned (Sayer, 2000b).

In an earlier work I explored the epistemological values that arise in social science, arguing that there are at least ten valued dimensions of knowledge – such as validity and replicability – of which value-neutrality is one of the most contested dimensions (Olsen, 2003b). It is contested because value stances are often woven into theoretical discourses in a taken-for-granted way. For instance, poverty research has an underlying value-orientation which gives poverty a negative connotation. Some causes of poverty, for example excessive inequality or coercion, may also be judged undesirable. In poverty studies, part of each explanation has a normative resonance or makes explicit a value judgement. Far from value neutrality, then, research may need to be value-relevant.

One useful position on values and research was offered by Harding (1995). Harding argued that researchers can attempt 'strong objectivity', by which she refers to the uncovering of ethical stances and making deliberate attempts to compare and contrast the implicit or explicit values of different theoretical discourses. Harding contrasted strong objectivity with the 'weak objectivity' of using survey measurement procedures to create impersonal, replicable indicators of social phenomena. Strong objectivity, as Harding called it, makes moral assessments explicit, as seen in some political economy writings and in most anti-poverty literature. Theories' ethical stances will be explored here (see Section IV), but the issues raised are large ones which have also had lengthy treatments elsewhere (for instance, see Athreya et al., 1990).

Realists have also advocated the combination of qualitative data with other types of data. Bryman, for instance, argues that deliberate sequencing of quantitative and qualitative research can usefully improve upon mono-method studies (Bryman, 1996). Analogous arguments were made by Harriss (2002), Jackson (2002), Kanbur (2002), and Hulme and Shepherd (2003). Jackson, for instance, argues that social and anthropological research should not be separated from economic research (Jackson, 2002: 488–89). The idea of synergy between disciplines, particularly when aiming for policy-relevant findings, underlies the whole 'development studies' project (Hulme and Toye, this volume).

However several realists have expressed doubts about the feasibility of triangulation when it includes survey data. Lawson (1997: 221) argues that nothing more than descriptive statistics can be useful, since anything more sophisticated or analytical rests too heavily on the categories into which people, cases, and variables have been coded. Sayer (1992) argued that extensive research was not very worthwhile, having made a biting critique of survey data (ibid., chapter 8). Sayer also argued against combining qualitative (intensive) and quantitative (extensive) research in one study. In his view the two techniques were too different to mix easily. A revised realist position argues that survey data are inherently qualitative (Olsen, 2003b; also argued by Bryman, 1996), and that therefore methods are always being mixed when survey data are used. The main difficulty then is in making sense of survey data results given that their categories may be relatively crude, or too homogenous across a large population domain. An illustration of methodological pluralism in an Indian context is given in Olsen (2003a). Qualitative and quantitative techniques were used in an Indian field research context (ibid.).

Under a revised epistemology, the qualitative and quantitative findings can be reconciled. The two types of methods can be part of one larger project. A team may be needed, rather than a single researcher. Whole disciplines, where peers review and integrate findings across different research techniques, also reflect methodological pluralism writ large. Sociology and political science each have a longer tradition of mixing methods than does economics at present (Manicas, 1987).

Methodological pluralism refers to a mixing of qualitative methods (for understanding things in depth) along with other methods for studying the nature of structures. Mixing qualitative and quantitative methods illustrates methodological pluralism. Realists advocate methodological pluralism because two types of theoretical claim can be found in social science: (1) causal claims which have explanatory content; and (2) interpretive claims which focus on what actions mean to agents (Sayer, 2000a). With methodological pluralism a deeper, richer content is offered to causal explanations.

Theoretical Pluralism

In combining theoretical with interpretive claims, one is likely to draw upon at least two disciplines, as well as the two data types, for example when combining history and economics one might use documents and survey data. Theoretical pluralism involves looking closely at possible explanations of puzzling outcomes using a range of claims from at least two social-science disciplines, or two theories. Since some theories cut across disciplines (as Marxism is both political and economic), theoretical pluralism is inherently multidisciplinary.

Pluralism in general has been advocated by a number of authors, who however warn against relativism. Most authors refer explicitly only to methodological pluralism. Roth, for instance, argues that: 'methodological pluralism is not tantamount to saying 'anything goes'. We should be methodological pluralists in the social sciences' (Roth, 1987). It would be consistent with Roth's argument to also encourage theoretical pluralism.

Hacking, a methodologist specialising in the areas of induction and social representation, argues that:

> Systematic and institutionalized social sciences have their retinues of statistical data and computer analyses that work with classifications of people. It is taken for granted that these classifications work in the same way as those in the natural sciences. In fact the classifications in the social sciences aim at moving targets, namely people and groups of people who may change in part because they are aware of how they are classified. (Hacking, 2002: 10)

It may be difficult for social scientists to avoid ethical implications arising out of their self-reflective research. Meta-critique helps to enable well-informed choice of theories. Methodological pluralism aids in the analysis and utilisation of competing theories, and involves meta-critique. The rest of this paper will illustrate these points.

Avoiding Essentialism

According to realists there are core mechanisms in each social system which researchers try to grasp and describe. These core mechanisms might include social structures like class and caste. These structures, however, also have meaning to people and they can only be interpreted through a transitive (that is interactive) process. According to critical realists, each social situation has a mixture of linked transitive and intransitive elements. The deeper structures are mainly intransitive, since they are not affected by how we describe them. (They are, however, subject to social change.) The transitive domain refers to the things which exist in a fluid relationship with human descriptions. The transitive domain is even more complex than the intransitive domain and has mainly been studied using qualitative methodology. The transitive domain includes the current construal of agents, such as tenants and poor people. Should they be perceived in class terms? In caste terms? Clearly there is scope for interpretive differences of opinion. Differences of opinion among social scientists today must be added onto the differences of viewpoint of the actual participants in these systems. Sayer (1992) argued that the communicability of scientists' discoveries today implies a need to bridge the discursive differences not only among the participants, and among experts, but also between 'lay' and expert understandings of a system. Thus instead of simply essentialising the poor as poor, realists would recognise the inherent complexity of the task of description.

Sayer argued that social science's complex object itself implies considerable hermeneutic complexity and difficulty (Sayer, 1992). Sayer therefore took a pragmatic view of epistemology, and in this he is followed by numerous other supporters of qualitative research and of mixed methods (Kvale, 1996; Lawson, 1997; Harding, 1999). Sayer's view is called 'realist' because he nevertheless admits a prior, partly intransitive existence of the systems which are being studied (Sayer, 1997). A system is a set of structures and agents which interact, generating complexity and emergent properties (ibid.). The systems are real.

To illustrate the relevance of this theoretical framework for the study of poverty, I now turn to the analysis of land rental and poverty in India in recent decades (see Figure 2).

II. An Exemplar: Indian Tenancy Research

In this section a review of literature is organised around four main schools (that is groups of researchers). Some authors don't fit in to a single school and they are discussed later.

Tenancy Literature

In India, renting in land for a cash rent is on the rise and sharecropping is on the wane, but 8 per cent of arable land is still rented in (Sharma, 2000). Fifteen per cent of rural households are renting in land.[8] Evidence from recent national datasets shows convincingly a shift away from sharecropping and toward fixed-rent tenancy (Shankar, 1999; Ramakumar, 2000). Many observers have noted that this kind of rural commercialisation has not mitigated rural poverty (for example Swain, 1999).

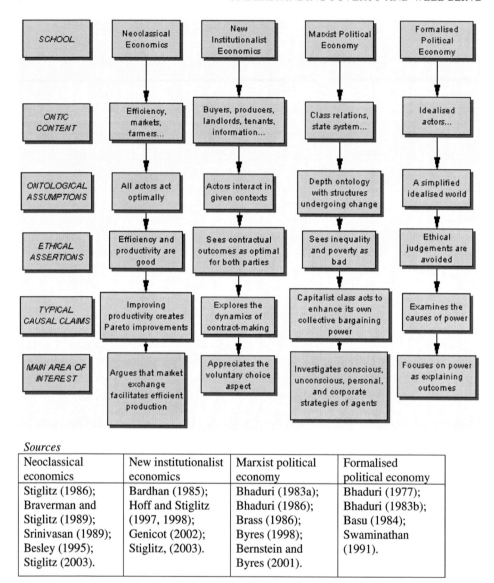

Sources

Neoclassical economics	New institutionalist economics	Marxist political economy	Formalised political economy
Stiglitz (1986); Braverman and Stiglitz (1989); Srinivasan (1989); Besley (1995); Stiglitz (2003).	Bardhan (1985); Hoff and Stiglitz (1997, 1998); Genicot (2002); Stiglitz, (2003).	Bhaduri (1983a); Bhaduri (1986); Brass (1986); Byres (1998); Bernstein and Byres (2001).	Bhaduri (1977); Bhaduri (1983b); Basu (1984); Swaminathan (1991).

Figure 2. Key theories of tenancy

On the one hand contemporary tenancy transactions are seen by some economists as optimal choices which avoid the use of standard labour-market contracts (for example, Bardhan et al., 1984; Skoufias, 1995). For a competing school of economic thought, the indirect management of labour by landlords is part of a pattern of control and manipulation which may have perpetuated the poverty of large numbers of households in India (Bhaduri, 1983a; Singh, 1995; Brass and van der Linden, 1998). According to the Marxist political economy analyses, renting land out is done by powerful households who prefer to arrange (some) cheap labour this way rather than through the casual or permanent labouring contract. The overlap in the substantive interests of these two schools of thought (neoclassical and political economy) is considerable.

The regulation of land markets has long been a major concern of policy-makers. It has been argued that making the tenure of tenants more secure would assist in the growth of agriculture, and that policy in this area could be anti-poverty and pro-growth whilst promoting tenancy itself. Is tenancy an anti-poverty strategy of landless families? Or does tenancy reflect a desperate attempt to avoid unemployment by poor people whose returns are implicitly below subsistence, and who face discrimination against them in other markets: the market for their produce; the market for credit for production; the market for their labour? In particular, is it possible that the tenants are exploited in a masked way, as the political economy school has suggested? The debate has raged since the 1950s, with slightly changing foci: in the 1950s land reform was central to the debate; in the 1960s aggregate productivity of different farm sizes; in the 1970s the freeing of bonded labourers and reduction of usury through state banking were prioritised; in the 1980s the effect of interlinked markets upon market equilibria were explored, and efficiency of markets was central to the debate at that time; and in the 1990s tenancy institutions were deconstructed both through principal-agent models and through historical analysis to reveal their changing nature and their heavy impact upon economic outcomes.

The differences between the main schools of thought on the subject of tenancy are striking (Figure 2). Debates on tenancy within each theoretical school tend to be somewhat narrow and intra-discursive, referencing other work within that school. However there are also studies which cross boundaries and refer to work of two or more schools.

If we take a focused look at debates about tenancy and poverty within India from 1960 to 2004, we find that research has taken place in numerous disciplines. For the sake of highlighting the difficulties with reconciling quantitative and qualititative research, I will focus on the main schools of thought summarised in Figure 2. My focus here is on political economy and economics, although valuable mixed-methods research has been emerging from sociology and anthropology, too.[9] The mixing of methods in the latter disciplines tends to stay within the realm of qualitative analysis, whilst greater difficulties arise when trying to combine extensive survey data with qualitative analysis (Kanbur, 2001).

The four schools compared here are neoclassical economics (involving market equilibrium with given sets of rational agents operating under constraints), new institutional economics, marxist political economy, and formalised political economy. It may be useful to refer to these schools as NCE, NIE, MPE, and FPE respectively, although it is important to note that only some specific *works* can be identified as fitting mainly within one school.

Each school can be described briefly. NCE arose with the Marshallian marginalist framework (circa 1870; Dow, 2002) and is oriented toward modelling the market-wide implications of rational individual choice. Prices, interest rates, productivity are the main outcomes of interest to this school. The NIE school has arisen since about 1980 as a more in-depth analysis of choice under conditions of uncertainty, limited information, and transactions costs. Most NIE studies are grounded on concepts familiar from NCE: demand, supply, income, profit, and utility in particular.

However the NIE recognises that demand–supply models appear rather simplistic and determinist compared with the underlying institutional complexity. An institution, according to NIE, is a set of rules or norms for contracting in a specific area of human life, for example marriage. These institutions were not explicitly or empirically central to NCE.

Marxist political economy arose, too, from works written in the late nineteenth century. MPE begins from a conceptual framework centred upon class, and proceeds to analyse the trajectory of capitalist development. Its sweep is broad so that prices become an explanatory factor rather than an outcome. Outcomes of interest to MPE are the political power of certain classes, a changing class structure, and the interrelations of regions or nations with each other and with their working classes.

Formalised political economy, here labelled FPE, takes a modelling approach to the class actors, placing ideal types into a mathematical model and manipulating that model. FPE has drawn from both NCE and MPE resources. An example of FPE in the poverty literature is Braverman and Kanbur's analysis of urban bias (Braverman and Kanbur, 1987). They provided a mathematical appendix following a detailed argument on the causes of rural poverty in a context where rural and urban classes interacted with government policy and with market outcomes.

Each school has a different ontology. An ontology is a theoretical schema of the types of object that exist in society (ontic content). Within the NIE ontology, tenants and landlords make decisions and influence each other as well as influencing major economic outcomes. The politics and social aspects of the underlying society are more prominent in the political economy writings, whilst the numerical measurement of outcomes such as average productivity, labour's real wage and the degree of risk are more prominent in the NCE and NIE writings. Behind the overt ontic content there are also implicit or explicit ontological assumptions. Ontology refers to the theory of being, or in other words to the study of the existence of things.

In the NCE ontology, structures are ignored by assuming that only agents matter. This is an example of an ontological assumption. MPE and FPE, too, have characteristic ontological assumptions. As Figure 2 indicates, these lead toward particular types of causal claim for each school.

The four main schools of thought described in Figure 2 have detailed explanatory claims which are (pairwise) complementary, competing, or incommensurate. For instance:

- *Claim 1 from NCE:* Tenancy contracts can be explained in terms of landlords' attempts to better utilise their land resources, and tenants' attempts to better utilise their labour resources and bullocks (NCE; Sen, 1964; Sen, 1966; Skoufias, 1995).
- *Claim 2 from NIE:* Tenancy contracts represent an optimal solution to a game-theoretic problem of simultaneous rational choice of landlords and workers. (NIE; Srinivasan, 1989; Majid, 1994; Genicot, 2002).

Claim 2 is primarily a different phrasing of what is argued in Claim 1, and NIE often overlaps with NCE in this way. In Figure 2 the main areas of emphasis and typical causal claims show partial commensurability and overlap for NIE and NCE.

There is overlap between the substance of NIE and NCE's claims which extends toward the substantive interests of marxist political economy. An interesting example is Majid (1994). Majid reviews the declining role of sharecropping in Sindh, Pakistan using NCE and NIE theory. However, he finds that landholding structures which underlie the decisions of landlord and tenant are critical influences upon whether and how sharecropping takes place. His study makes connections with the marxist interest in the relations of production. Both labour relations and operational land holding distributions are looked at closely by Majid. However, because Majid's main interest is in tenancy contracts, not in the dynamics of landholding, the underlying class relationships remain merely background (Majid, 1994: chapter 10).

- *Claim 3 from MPE:* Tenants are used by landlords who try to efficiently extract surplus labour and to realize its value in the crop market (Olsen, 1996); therefore one explanation of blocked technical progress is landlords' preference for retaining attached labour using usurious credit (Bhaduri, 1977, 1983b, 1986).
- *Claim 4 from MPE:* Capitalism has a capacity for uneven development, including different levels of technology and labour productivity even within pockets of a single locale; these pockets of uneven development are best seen in class terms; they are explained in terms of the profit motive of the landowning class (Singh, 1995; Brass and van der Linden, 1998).
- *Claim 5 from MPE:* Tied labour including tied tenants in North India reflects the tendency in capitalism toward deproletarianisation (Brass, 1986); deproletarianisation is a proximate cause of poverty of labourers amidst plenty; antagonistic social class relations are the root cause (see Bhaduri, 1986; Singh, 1995; DaCorta and Venkateswarlu, 1999).

All three above claims from MPE tend to be incommensurate with NCE and NIE. However authors within MPE try to explain and integrate concepts from NCE into their research (for example Athreya et al. (1990) who are MPE in the assumptions examined productivity, returns to scale, and profitability in their research).

Among the MPE writers, not all agree with claims 3–5. For example, Athreya et al. (1990: 308–11) used the methodology of MPE but arrived at empirical claims for south Indian agriculture that contrast with Claim 5 above. No constraints on growth or productivity were found, so Athreya et al. challenged the model put forward by Bhaduri (1983b). Athreya et al. used methodological pluralism. They measured farm-level productivity using statistical analysis whilst underpinning their study with a qualitative and quantitative class analysis, including the study of exploitation (Athreya, et al., 1990).

Formalised political economy has gone further than MPE, but built bridges with NIE, by exploring multiple interest rate equilibria, antagonistic contracting, and differential collateral valuation (Bhaduri, 1977; Basu, 1984; Swaminathan, 1991).

In general, in empirical studies of the NCE and NIE schools, social relations and inequality are little mentioned but they do shape the contracts and the market opportunities which in turn affect the shifts in contractual forms and market outcomes. Whilst MPE would phrase these changes in social terms, NIE and NCE have tended to phrase them in methodological individualist terms. (They portray households as if they were individuals.) Given that both approaches have much to offer, a depth ontology may help researchers to unite and link these diverse theories.

Having reviewed four competing theoretical schools and their cleavages, I will now consider two substantive areas where they overlap: productivity and power.

Measuring Productivity

Productivity concepts in general refer to the aggregate output of joint production. The labour of workers is combined with capital and land to create a joint product. Researchers attribute the value of the product, as realised in a market, to inputs of labour, land, capital, or 'total factor productivity'. The measurement of productivity is more contested than one might think.

In the tenancy literature the crop yields were the focus of early paradoxes: Sen (1964, 1966) showed that small farmers had higher yields than large farmers in India. However in terms of labour productivity, these farmers worked until their marginal product had fallen below the local wage. Sen's model was neoclassical and assumed a diminishing return to labour at the margin. Later research decomposed productivity into the productivity of land, returns on capital investment, and the productivity of labour. However for tenants, records are rarely kept of either the produce of their rented plot separate from other plots they own, or of the returns to individual workers (whose time is not recorded, since they are not doing waged labour) who cultivate the rented plot. Indeed the returns to unpaid household labour are an untold story in the context of tenancy (Agarwal, 1994). Calculations of productivity in the aggregate tend to mask important details.

Walker and Ryan, for instance, showed that certain villages in the ICRISAT panel study had more tenancy than the others, and that the tenant farms had lower aggregate productivity (Walker and Ryan, 1990; see also Skoufias, 1995). However Walker and Ryan did not distinguish the productivity of the owned-land plots from the rented-land plots. In India, well-irrigated land is more likely to have tenants on it and therefore we might find a higher productivity of land among tenants if disaggregated data were available (Chaudhuri and Maitra, 2002). However that does not tell us the distribution of the proceeds of that production. In Punjab, recent micro studies show that immigrant workers who rent land from farmers have low yields. They use manual power rather than diesel-driven plows and receive extremely low returns (Singh, 1995). For poverty studies, analysis of productivity, disaggregated plotwise, and of the returns to labour, disaggregated by the type of worker, are needed. Few studies of tenants have this level of detail (for example see Jain and Singh, 2000; Kaul and Pandey, 2000; Sharma, 2000). Given improved data, both political economy research and neoclassical approaches could contribute to the interpretation of plot-level productivity and the distribution of the returns to sharecroppers.

Choice and Power in the Tenancy Literature

The research in the 1980s was bifurcated into studies of choice versus studies of power. The choice theorists often had demand-supply models of each market in the background of their research, even when these models had elsewhere turned the corner toward analysis of institutions under imperfect information. Srinivasan's (1989) model can illustrate the choice orientation of such models in the NCE and NIE schools. I will then contrast such models with the political economy analysis of power. Srinivasan (1989) developed a mathematical model to simulate the actions of a sharecropper toward their landlord once a bank or other alternative credit source enters the scene. Srinivasan wrote:

> If sharecroppers are otherwise identical, then the extent of the incidence of bonded labour contracts will be determined by the distribution of non-agricultural income.... By closely monitoring the sharecropper's activities and enforcing a bonded labour contract, the landlord avoids default by the sharecropper.... The sharecropper obviously will choose the creditor and the amount of credit so as to maximize his lifetime expected welfare... (Srinivasan, 1989: 204, 208, 211)

In this model, inequality arises in the distribution of non-agricultural income, but otherwise worker households are homogeneous. They have no caste or other social attributes, such as the capacity for shame. Bonded labour arises voluntarily in the context of inequality; bondage is a free choice to which sharecroppers adhere (if they are poor) even in the context of competing lenders. Srinivasan's model was a response to other models of the rural credit market (Bhaduri, 1983b).

Srinivasan draws an interesting policy implication:

> Since, in the above model, the choice of a bonded labour contract is voluntary, it will be chosen by the sharecropper only if it yields him a higher lifetime welfare compared with borrowing from the lending institution. Under such circumstances, the policy of banning bonded labour will be unenforceable or, if forcibly implemented, will *reduce* the welfare of the sharecropper. (Srinivasan, 1989: 215)

The interesting assumption here is that the distribution of income is fixed. It acts as a determinant of outcomes but is not affected by outcomes. In such models, which are static models, there is no feedback; the world is seen as a closed system. Deterministic choice models are idealised and do not adequately reflect the real world.

The models seen in political economy, by contrast, always have a specific locale and time-period underlying their details. Instead of the universal 'landlord' caricature, political economy authors tend to show a competition for power between specific classes. Each class is seen as a social object, rather than being anthropomorphised. Bhaduri (who formalised his model) had classes acting in their own collective interest, affecting other classes, and being reacted upon by those classes. The four classes mentioned were landlords, merchants, farmers, and workers. Thus Bhaduri's (1983b) model was more complex than the bilateral game theory models of new institutionalist economics. However in Bhaduri's model, landlords loaned money, reflecting the northeastern region's economic structure. In other parts of India, landlords are less specialised in lending money. Tenant farmers in the south are more likely to borrow from merchants than from landlords (Olsen,

1996). The complexity of class structures can be taken into account in non-mathematised approaches to the study of interacting market behaviours (Olsen, 1993). Credit markets, land markets, labour markets and crop markets have all been seen as linked in this literature.

But there has been a polarisation of pairs of schools (NCE and NIE versus the MPE and FPE schools). Many studies of choice omit all mention of power, are methodological individualist, and deny the existence of social classes. Studies of power in a few cases also deny the possibility of free choice. Brass's (1986) work on the deproletarianisation thesis perhaps illustrates the determinism of a Marxist structuralist approach to causation. This approach to unfreedom is the polar opposite of the choice theories. A dualism has emerged: choice *vs.* power-over; voluntary choice *vs.* unfreedom. Brass would argue that even if they vouched for making free choices, workers might still be (really) unfree. A problem arises if a deterministic structuralist model is seen as an *alternative* to a choice model. Deterministic models have little scope for empirical testing. Bhaduri's (1986) and Brass's (1993) Marxist models run the risk of being as idealised, as closed-system, and as untestable as the models they wish to criticise.

This polarisation by itself is not helpful. Numerous pieces of excellent empirical research have focused upon *both* power and choice, to good effect (Athreya et al., 1990). The contribution of these studies is to make each of these mechanisms an operationalisable topic for empirical study. Power: how to measure it? Would we examine outcomes or the ongoing social relations? Should we look at static patterns of resources or at wealth trajectories? Even more difficulties arise when studying choice empirically. However it is possible to ask people to describe their choices, strategies, and habits. This may be a good area for further research.

An improved approach to the linkages between choice and power is also desirable. Research like that of Genicot (2002), which *models* choice, leaves us tantalised but no closer to an empirical research programme linking cognitive frameworks, explicit choices, subjective preferences, and actions. Genicot showed that a paradox of unfree labour arises when specific types of worker, such as poor tenants, choose to be bonded. It is promising that new institutionalist economists like Genicot take such an interest in the limitations to freedom that arise from 'mutually advantageous labor-tying agreements' (Genicot, 2002: 105). Choice is one proximate cause of outcomes. Choices are in turn motivated consciously by reasons. Outcomes are also mediated and caused through structured social relations. The real causes are more extensive than choice alone, as all agree.

Thus productivity, power, and choice are common themes about which an empirically grounded debate has occurred. The debate is highly relevant for poverty reduction.

A theoretical pluralist would add commensurability (that is reference to common things) to the criteria for choosing between theories. A methodological pluralist would add the further suggestion that the objects referred to in each theory need to be operationalisable. I return to this point in Section IV. There is a danger of verificationism if each theory is permitted to construct its own criteria for validity. Without some form of operationalisation across theories – either qualitative or quantitative – it is difficult to make rational judgements about the competing schools.

In the rest of this paper reference will be made to specific themes from the tenancy literature. These claims illustrate the theoretical pluralism that is found among some of the best research in this area (for example Lanjouw and Stern, 1998; Banerjee et al., 2002; Genicot, 2002).

III. Commensurability Theories

In this section I describe ways of increasing commensurability of theories. Three ways to do so are described: using bridging discourses; avoiding verification-ism in measurement; and improving the observability of apparently unobservable phenomena.

Complementarity of Explanations

In this sub-section I focus on the complementarities that are evident, even when comparing opposed schools. Complementaries in the language used often reflect the way different theories approach the same (real) thing. Bargaining power in NIE and class power in MPE, for instance, are competing ways to refer to interpersonal or inter-household power relations. Another example of a bridge between these competing theories is their approach to state action, governmental action and, more generally, collective action. In NCE the state was present primarily as an agent intervening in markets (setting land-holding ceilings, offering credit to landlords) but in MPE the state also acts to protect certain classes' vested interests. The 'state' can be found in both theories, although it is seen differently in each. As NIE develops, it too refers to state and collective action. For instance, some new institutionalist authors and most political economy authors agree that the role of the state can be probed for positive synergies with civil society. Institutionalists argue positively that regulation and norms shape all markets. State regulation, even if carried out under federalism as in India, inherently underpins all market action (Harriss-White, 1999). State regulation may provide benefits to poor people. This position has been put by Stiglitz thus:

> Many of the items that were not on the Washington Consensus[10] might bring both higher growth and greater equality. Land reform itself illustrates the choices at stake in many countries.... The sharecropping system itself weakens incentives.... Land reform, done properly, peacefully, and legally, ensuring that workers get not only land but access to credit, and the extension services that teach them about new seeds and planting techniques, could provide an enormous boost to output. But land reform represents a fundamental change in the structure of society. (Stiglitz, 2003: 81)

Stiglitz's focus on the state here marks a divergence from his earlier neoclassical work.

Other research in India also led toward an empirical finding that the state plays a role in empowering people through good governance or legal changes. For instance, Banerjee et al. have shown that the West Bengal state government was able to improve productivity as well as distributive equity by giving tenants more secure access to their plots (Banerjee et al., 2002). Their study used a theoretical model along with empirical data from West Bengal.

To see the actions of government and other state or quasi-state actors as socially grounded in concrete structures, and as historically place-specific, but as being relevant to the economic outcomes of tenancy is to construct a theory that mediates between NCE, NIE and MPE. In this sense the work by Banerjee et al. (2002) is theoretical pluralist.

Thus power and the state are common concepts in NIE and MPE, whilst they bear different meanings and are investigated in different ways in the two schools. NIE often use a survey method and detailed household financial data, whilst MPE often uses a historical comparative method with evidence from government documents, historical records and interviews. The two schools do broach related questions about the same reality.

This example illustrates the bridging that is done by researchers who know their competitors' work well. Each school has a standard discourse in which theories and falsification tests are couched. A discourse is a set of norms or assumptions for speech and other communicative acts. A discourse usually consists of a tendency to combine metaphors, analogies, assumptions, dualisms, and category labels in specific ways. One school might set up a model and test its implications, whilst another might take a more inductive approach and may mimic the descriptive patterns found in historical documents. In general, discourses are the norms for how a school's authors refer to events, examine things, collect data, and analyse or interpret data. There are discursive rules for how data should or should not be manipulated. Statistical manipulation is common in NCE and NIE, whilst reinterpretation and a hermeneutic angle are common in MPE.

Bridging discourses are a special type of discourse, deliberately chosen by authors who have reviewed or used two contrasting theories. They break the rules or boundaries of Theory A in order to make headway into the realm of Theory B. In doing so, the bridging discourse creatively changes or challenges Theory B. The Stiglitz/Bhaduri debate and the Banerjee paper both illustrate discursive bridging. They are temporary moments of contact between disparate academic schools. At times, the political economy school may use the survey method to broach questions of interest to the neoclassical economists (Bardhan and Rudra, 1984), whilst economists at times use a historical method to broach questions of political economy (Banerjee et al., 2002). Mixing research methods, in turn, appears to make more pluralistic theory testing possible.

Idealist Models and the Weaknesses of Testing

Some of the new institutionalist modeling tends to be self-verifying. Whilst testing of predictions is potentially possible, it is rarely done. Instead there is a process of estimating parameters, given the assumption that the model fits. Such models are known as deductivist (Lawson, 1997) or idealist models. They exist only on paper. There is a danger, common to all theories, that empirical tests will verify their hypotheses precisely because the tests work within their own terminology. Some researchers use surveys whose measurements rest within their theoretical discourse (for example surveys of household finance which record the household's total production and not plot-wise production), and the weaknesses of the theory are duplicated in the limitations of the empirical testing.

In order to test theories across a range of disciplines, or two schools, it may be necessary to use innovative instruments (fresh surveys; less structured interviews; and re-interpretation of documents) with a view to competing theories. Open-mindedness at an early stage is helpful here, as seen also in the grounded theory literature (Lee, 2002). Grounded theory approaches attempt a relatively unbiased induction from empirical qualitative data.

Operationalising the Unobservables

In the theories found in Figure 2, some objects are difficult to observe, and some are unobservables (for example utility). Actually these 'things', such as power or choices, can be evidenced by outcomes or events which contingently result from them. Many unobservables are thus indirectly recordable. The difficulties with observability are two. Firstly, to look for the thing one presumes it exists. This presumption brings with it the danger of essentialism. Secondly, most mechanisms work contingently, not necessarily. For instance, choice outcomes can be observed, but records of the unselected alternatives are harder to create. Therefore outcomes are only sometimes evidence of a given cause.

Fleetwood summarises a realist position on unobservables in economics as follows:

> Economics...aims to provide powerful explanations and adequate theory-laden 'descriptions' of the observable and unobservable socio-economic structures and causal mechanisms that govern the flux of events observable in the real world. (Fleetwood, 2002: 44)

This quote usefully highlights the observability of *events*, in principle, versus the difficulties with observing underlying social structures and institutions. Fleetwood's constructive engagement with the empiricists Boylan and O'Gorman (1995) provides the groundwork for distinguishing good description from good observation. Descriptions, according to realists, may include abstractions which refer to structures even though the underlying observations are only indirect reflections of the structures. Clearly a programme of careful operationalisation is called for.

IV. Advantages and Limitations of Pluralism

So far this paper has shown that commensurability and discursive bridging help to make pluralist research possible. A suspension of judgement is needed as a temporary way to make two theories commensurate in some areas. Careful operationalisation is then needed. The pluralist is then in a position to compare two theories without tending to validate their a priori preferred theory. In this section a few comments are made on the advantages and disadvantages of this form of pluralism. The first is that poverty reduction becomes part of the discourse of research work.

Poverty and Tenancy

Methodological pluralist studies such as Dreze et al. (1998), or Athreya et al. (1990), illustrate the linkages between the study of tenancy and poverty alleviation research. A meta-analysis of theories of tenancy, which crosses schools and explicitly draws out comparisons, can develop the ethical implications of changing tenancy relations. There are two steps in the way a theoretical pluralist might develop these implications. First, they would examine the explicit or implicit ethical stance of competing theories (as hinted at, necessarily briefly, in row four of Figure 2). Secondly, their research could contribute toward the construction of a value stance and policy implications related to both tenancy and improvements in people's lives. These improvements may well be classified as poverty reduction either in economic, political or social terms.

The content of the moral stances in neoclassical economics and in marxist political economy (see Figure 2) are strongly differentiated, so I will focus on this contrast. In NCE, productivity increases are perceived as good, and waste as bad. In MPE, equality is seen as good and inequality as bad. Furthermore exploitation is recognised as harmful. Both these latter claims are not accepted by NCE authors. The MPE school tend to make stronger moral claims than NCE, and to have substantive value stances, whereas the writers in the NCE school tend to restrict themselves to procedural evaluations of marginal changes.

To grasp why there are such striking differences in the content of the moral stances, we can examine the *rationale* that is given for having a moral stance at all. In NCE this is usually an argument about Pareto optimality. If there are net economic gains, then a consensus can perhaps be obtained about the distribution of marginal gains without threatening anyone's existing resources. This argument of Pareto optimality has its roots in liberal economics. It appears regularly in western neoliberal thinking, as described by Hussain (1991) with respect to Asia, and by Dow (2002) for economics in general. By contrast, the arguments underlying MPE moral stances comprise a substantive claim that the reduction of inequality and suffering, and the removal of exploitation, offer social good. The confidence underlying this sort of moral statement arises from both the historical roots of Marxist Political Economy in the notion of social science having an emancipatory role (as described by Lawson, 1997), and in the philosophical assumptions of MPE authors which tend to be realist and collectivist. The realist strand in such thinking may lead the authors to think of moral stances as moral facts – a position described by Smith (1994) as 'realist' but not accepted by all realists. Sayer (2000a) for instance, argues that moral debate is a welcome topic for realists but will tend to lead to contested values and not to facts about values (Sayer, 2000a: 170–85; see also Sayer, 2000b).

The authors of the MPE school also have an ontological reason why their stance is so different from that of the neoclassical authors. Their statements relate to collectivities, not just to individuals. Because the MPE authors recognise the existence of society as a corporate entity, which can have a social good and social ills, it is possible to imagine making claims about that which is good for society. For those NCE authors who are methodological individualist, it is much easier to resist notions of the social good and to pay attention to differentiated, individual, subjective notions of what would be good. In philosophy the terms 'holism' and 'atomism' are used to describe the two extremes of ontology here: MPE authors recognise wholes, and use holism, whereas NCE authors have traditionally stressed individuals and not social wholes. The value stances of the two schools necessarily reflect, and arise from, these underlying ontological commitments.

In the confines of this paper I cannot extend the discussion of these ethical stances far, but a growing literature on moral political economy questions the possibility of separating moral pronouncements from factual statements. One author who makes reasoned arguments linking facts with values, and values with facts, was Bhaskar (1979). A scientific realist who discusses the fact-value relation is Williams (2000). Another realist vision of political economy was offered by the historian and philosopher MacIntyre (1998). He reviewed the norms of science and how they have changed over the period since 1900, compared with Greek ethical systems. MacIntyre argues that Aristotelian ethics are substantive and focus upon the good of collectivities (chapter 7), but such ethical claims are rarely found in the twentieth century. In the modern era since the Reformation, he argues, ethical statements have tended to be more individual-oriented, less substantive, and more subjective (also argued in MacIntyre, 1985). Modern ethical precepts often recognise a differentiated society (as does NCE), use notions of free choice, and keep proposed changes within the legal and regulatory context of a capitalist market framework. Ray and Sayer have argued that the moral issues raised by contemporary Aristotelians, such as MacIntyre, Amartya Sen and Martha Nussbaum, have not been explored thoroughly yet (Ray and Sayer, 1999; Sayer, 2000b). Thus a worthwhile debate can be had regarding ethical assertions in competing conceptualisations of tenancy.

Two concrete comments can also be made about the impact of the moral stances on the research about tenancy. The first comment shows a limitation of some existing MPE studies, and the second shows a limitation of some existing NCE studies.

Firstly, most Marxist writers on Indian tenancy have assumed all tenants to be poor. Having done so they avoid dealing with reverse tenancy. Reverse tenants use their bargaining power to rent a desired amount of land from smallholders. The possibility that the smallholder would willingly and gainfully rent out their land to a more capital intensive, larger farmer was ignored by MPE researchers such as Bhaduri (for example Bhaduri, 1997). The a priori judgement that renters are exploited by landowners was questioned by Stiglitz (1986) because it regrettably closes down certain avenues of empirical investigation. The theoretical pluralist will need to have a balanced view of the possibilities rather than a predilection to find exploitation a priori.

Secondly, the NCE agenda of Pareto-optimal market exchange – usually also found in NIE – can cause analysts to avoid studying inequality per se. The discourse of Pareto optimality makes judgements about the distribution of land a matter of fact, not a question of values. Using bridging discourse it may be possible to broach questions of equality of access to land, but this is not normally done by NCE authors.

The discourse of Pareto optimality is persistent in part because of its tendency not to threaten vested interests. Poverty alleviation debates, by contrast, are at times full of controversy and do challenge existing distributions of assets. Pluralist approaches may raise thorny issues about the distribution of land, of which Agarwal's (1994,

2003) discussion is one illustration. Agarwal has engaged the Indian government with policy possibilities regarding changed individual access to land (ibid.) In discursive terms, intertextuality is the technical word for writings like hers that use mixtures of NCE and MPE arguments (or in other words those which mix discourses). Intertextuality occurs when two traditions are merged, or appear as contrasts side-by-side, in a single text (Fairclough, 1992: chapter 4). Fairclough argues that the study of inequality benefits from conscious meta-study of intertextuality (ibid: 200–07). The possibility that orthodox economic theory has been implicitly conservative has been suggested by a range of meta-analysts (for example Byres, 2003). The case for a more explicit discussion of values in poverty research links together the present collection of papers.

In this sub-section I have argued that pluralists explicitly do moral political economy, that in doing so the poverty of some ideal-typical agents (in this case tenants) should not be assumed a priori, and that bridging discourses might bring substantive moral issues into focus – notably the substantive moral issue of the distribution of assets. These arguments bring the economics of tenancy toward a heterodox paradigm within which ethics are not easily, or even desirably, separated from the description of a concrete situation. Such an ethically self-conscious moral political economy would cross the disciplines of politics and economics as well as sociology.

Relational Approaches to Poverty Studies are Preferred

The studies reviewed in Section II were of two broad types. One type uses an individualistic framework, often anthropomorphising households as if they were rational people, and examines the rationality of their decisions. An example is Agrawal (1999), who studied moral hazard in a model that was methodological individualist in its ontology. In this context poverty is seen as a characteristic of person/households, and poverty's causes are seen as being hidden, or as residing in the person's inadequate resources. The inadequate nature of such rational choice theories for the study of poverty is self-evident. It appears to blame the victim of poverty without recognising the background causes and history of poverty.

The other type of study sees households in dynamic relation to each other, socially grounded in groups like castes and classes (Bernstein and Byres, 2001). In these studies, the structures of society interact with the intentional agency of actors in society. These dynamic, relational models are difficult to put into mathematical format (Sayer, 1992: chapter 6). They offer explanations that are rich in historical and social background. They also help to place poverty in its social context. Relational studies of poverty examine the meanings of poverty to actors within social structures. By contrast, residual approaches to poverty often separate out the poor from the rest as if they were a separable, distinct group. The political economy models in this paper took a relational approach to poverty. The pluralist research by Lanjouw and Stern et al. (1998) also takes a relationship approach to poverty by repeatedly offering glimpses of the whole income- and wealth-distribution. Athreya et al. (1990) is more overtly relational in its approach to the class structures of south India.

The Danger of Undisciplined Research

However, pluralist research has one main disadvantage; it might be seen as having no boundaries. Empirical research might have to cut across several disciplines. Local studies would have to be integrated with larger-scale studies, and geography, biology and ecology would have to be linked to the social sciences. The wise research team will know that having a focused set of research questions is important. However, limiting one's theoretical basis to a single theory has been shown to be a weakness. This weakness brings to mind the image of the 'seven blind people feeling different parts of an elephant'. Each person, with their own standpoint, gets a different finding (it's hairy, it's smooth; it's flat, it's round). Talking to one another, they can reach a more rounded conclusion (it's an elephant). At the literature review stage a pluralist will be quite wide ranging, and may make use of teamwork to extend their knowledge. At the later empirical stages they must make some strategic decisions to narrow their focus.

Advantages of Having Competition Among Schools

Even for those who do econometric statistical work, pluralism may have its advantages. In this paper I advocated recognising that theories are constructed in specific social milieus. An economist might self-consciously choose a range of theories, not exclusively using those of the rational-choice kind. One example of such pluralist research is Sharma and Dreze (1998). They conduct a new institutionalist analysis whilst showing awareness of the land distribution and of the political economy debates about 'the social distance between tenants and landlords' (Sharma and Dreze, 1998: 499). Sharma and Dreze note that over the decades 1970-1993 there are both inegalitarian developments and increasing equality between landlords and tenants in Palanpur (north India) (ibid: 500). Their results thus refer to the political economy school's claims. In choosing to refer to both NIE and MPE theories, the rationale is not simply to make conclusions from empirical testing. Sharma and Dreze are aware that empirical tests tend not to falsify the underlying theories. Their pluralist theorization may respond to the needs of their audience and it need not be restricted to the models typical of a particular theory.

Lanjouw and Stern (1998) also illustrate pluralism by compiling chapters on inequality and poverty alongside new institutionalist chapters and historical background chapters. Their pluralism is both theoretical and methodological, as seen in Dreze et al's (1998) introductory chapter where social mobility is considered alongside economic change. They use methodological pluralism in the sense of mixing statistical methods with qualitative field data. Their qualitative research makes the introductory descriptions (ibid: 1–113) and concluding chapters particularly convincing, although they do not go so far as to use a hermeneutic method that investigates meanings.

IV. Summary and Conclusions

In this paper I have surveyed an area of research which illustrates the benefits of methodological and theoretical pluralism. In Section I some dangers of 'essentialism' were mentioned. In Section II I reviewed the choice *vs.* power debate in the theorization of tenancy. Several authors cut across borderlines, used bridging discourses, and tried to integrate or challenge competing theories. Power and poverty issues are taken up by all four schools of thought on tenancy. Choice and freedom, too, have been the subject of research in political economy as well as in neoclassical economics. Productivity and its measurement create an interesting area for further operationalisation work, since disaggregated measures of inputs and remuneration are needed if tenancy is to be linked empirically to poverty outcomes. In Section III, issues of commensurability were highlighted. I showed that both economic theories and political-economy theories of tenancy moved toward an analysis of beneficial collective action. The exemplar used here (Indian tenancy regulation) illustrated aspects of interdisciplinarity commonly found in poverty research. In Section IV I reviewed some strengths and limitations of theoretical pluralism.

For some, it is self-evident that crossing disciplines is enriching. Bridging the quantitative-qualitative divide leads to a challenging empirical agenda, which has not yet been fully explored. For instance, the subjective views of the agents involved can be explored (Olsen, 1998). Testing, using empirical data alone, is unlikely to resolve theoretical debates. Dow (2002) describes how an oversimplified Popperian testing was used in earlier (for example 1980s) neoclassical economic practice (Popper, 1963). Dow argues that

> The 'Duhemian problem' is particularly difficult in economics; the complexity of economic phenomena and questions about the empirical basis of the discipline make empirical testing an extremely complex affair. (Dow, 2002: 102–03)

Combining qualitative insights with primary survey data as seen in Banerjee et al. (2002: 255–65) in particular may be extremely useful in development economics. Such research is relevant for the reduction of adverse incorporation of peasants into market activity, and hence for reducing poverty. In conclusion, it is good to avoid a bifurcation in which development economists develop mathematical models which others do not understand or read (Layder, 1993: 202).

Acknowledgements

The support of the UK Economic and Social Research Council is gratefully acknowledged. The work was part of the programme of the ESRC Global Poverty Research Group (grant no. M571255001). I am grateful for comments received after presenting this paper at a GPRG workshop and at the conference of the Development Studies Association, Glasgow, September 11, 2003. The reviewer's and editors' comments were valuable in improving the paper.

Notes

1. Figure 1 defines the terms used in the paper. See also Smith (1998) for a full discussion of most of these terms.
2. Sayer suggests that comparing the results of extensive methods with the findings of intensive methods may be useful.

3. In the philosophy of science a technical term, idealism, is used to draw a contrast between purely idea-based and purely reality-based research. However this polarity can easily be exaggerated. Realist research requires conceptual frameworks, and therefore it is not completely divorced from the mental maps of those who make mathematical models.
4. According to atomism, structures, rather than being self-transforming and organic, are simply sets of related objects. In realist literature the most widely criticized form of atomism is methodological individualism. Toye (2003) offers a review of the role of atomism within development economics.
5. The literature on critical realism per se dates back to about 1979 whereas Berger and Luckmann's work dated 1966 would place itself under the different heading of a moderately realist social constructivism. The origins of critical realism however lie in marxism, critical social science, and the idea of progressive social science, which arose in earlier centuries (Archer et al., 1998).
6. This claim is often referred to as the Duhem–Quine thesis. An excellent summary is provided by Quine (1953).
7. The debate over how to interpret Kuhn has taken place in economics (for example Cook, 1999), and in the history of science (reviewed by Manicas, 1987). Two variants predominate in the interpretation of Kuhn's thesis. The weaker variant argues that scientific paradigms are socially grounded, but can nevertheless be compared and contrasted. According to this weak interpretation it is a worthwhile project to make rational judgements about the worth of competing theories. A stronger school of interpretation of Kuhn's work argues that paradigms are simply incommensurate and that there is no possibility of rationally comparing them. This latter interpretation (the 'strong' school in the sociology of science) argues that paradigms are primarily socially constructed. In this paper, the weaker interpretation of Kuhn is applied. For a general discussion of this debate, and a review of its implications for economics, see Dow (2002).
8. The 8 per cent figure for India is likely to be an underestimate because land reforms have created an atmosphere within which landowners avoid giving details of tenancy to outsiders. The 15 per cent figure is from Shankar (1999).
9. There is not enough space to cover all the schools in depth here. For instance, development research links tenancy to basic problems of poverty, food security, and the evolution of rights (see Ellis, 2000; Sawadogo and Stamm, 2000); sociologists studying tenancy include Grigsby (1996) and Gray and Kevane (2001); feminist studies include Agarwal (1984, 1994, 2003) and Jackson (2002). In the sociological and feminist literature, the meanings of tenancy are unpacked for differentiated actors.
10. The Washington consensus refers to a synthesis of neoliberal and neoclassical thought favouring free markets.

References

Agarwal, B. (1984) Women, poverty and agricultural growth in India, *Journal of Peasant Studies*, 13(4), pp. 165–220.

Agarwal, B. (1994) *A Field of One's Own: Gender and Land Rights in South Asia* (Cambridge: Cambridge University Press).

Agarwal, B. (2003) Gender and land rights revisited: exploring new prospects via the state, family and market, *Journal of Agrarian Change*, 3, pp. 184–224.

Agrawal, P. (1999) Contractual structure in agriculture, *Journal of Economic Behavior and Organization*, 39(3), pp. 293–325.

Allen, T. and Thomas, A. (2000) *Poverty and Development into the 21st Century* (Oxford: The Open University).

Archer, M., Bhaskar, R., Collier, A., Lawson, T. and Norrie, A. (1998) *Critical Realism: Essential Readings* (London: Routledge).

Athreya, B. V., Djurfeldt, G., and Lindberg, S. (1990) *Barriers Broken: Production Relations and Agrarian Change in Tamil Nadu* (New Delhi: Sage).

Banerjee, A. V., Gertler, P. J. and Ghatak, M. (2002) Empowerment and efficiency: tenancy reform in west Bengal, *Journal of Political Economy*, 110(2), pp. 239–80.

Bardhan, P. K. (1985) Agricultural development and land tenancy in a peasant economy – reply, *American Journal of Agricultural Economics*, 67(3), pp. 691–2.

Bardhan, P. K. and Rudra, A. (1984) Terms and conditions of sharecropping contracts: an analysis of village survey data in India, in P. K. Bardhan (ed.), *Land, Labour and Rural Poverty: Essays in Development Economics*, (New York: Columbia University Press).

Basu, K. (1984) Implicit interest rates, usury and isolation in backward agriculture, *Cambridge Journal of Economics*, 8, pp. 145–59.

Berger, P. and Luckmann, T. (1966) *The Social Construction of Reality: A Treatise in the Sociology of Knowledge* (London: Penguin).

Bernstein, H. and Byres, T. J. (2001) From peasant studies to agrarian change, *Journal of Agrarian Change*, 1(1), pp. 1–56.

Besley, T. (1995) Property rights and investment incentives – theory and evidence from Ghana, *Journal of Political Economy*, 103(5), pp. 903–37.

Bhaduri, A. (1977) On the formation of usurious interest rates in backward agriculture, *Cambridge Journal of Economics*, 1, pp. 341–52.

Bhaduri, A. (1983a) Cropsharing as a labour process, *Journal of Peasant Studies*, 10(2/3), pp. 88–93.

Bhaduri, A. (1983b) *The Economic Structure of Backward Agriculture*, (London: Academic Press).

Bhaduri, A. (1986) Forced commerce and agrarian growth, *World Development*, 14(2), pp. 267–72.

Bhaduri, A. (1997) Productivity, production relations, and class efficiency: illustrations from Indian agriculture, in A. Bhaduri and R. Skarstein (eds), *Economic Development and Agricultural Productivity* (Cheltenham: Edward Elgar).

Bhaskar, R. (1979) *The Possibility of Naturalism: A Philosophical Critique of the Contemporary Human Sciences* (London: Routledge).

Boylan, T. A. and O'Gorman, P. (1995) *Beyond Rhetoric and Realism in Economics: Towards A Reformulation of Economic Methodology* (London: Routledge).

Brass, T. (1986) Unfree labour and capitalist restructuring in the agrarian sector: Peru and India, *Journal of Peasant Studies*, 14(1), pp. 50–77.

Brass, T. (ed.) (1993) *Some Observations on Unfree Labour, Capitalist Restructuring, and Deproletarianization* (Netherlands: Int'l Inst. for Social History).

Brass, T. and Van der Linden, M. (1998) *Free and Unfree Labour: The Debate Continues* (Berlin: Peter Lang AB).

Braverman, A. and Stiglitz, J. E. (1989) Credit Rationing, tenancy, productivity and the dynamics of inequality, in P. K. Bardhan (ed.), *The Economic Theory of Agrarian Institutions*, pp. 185–201 (Oxford: Clarendon Press).

Braverman, A. and Kanbur, R. (1987) Urban bias and the political economy of agricultural reform, *World Development*, 15(9), pp. 1179–87.

Bryman, A. (1996) *Quantity and Quality in Social Research* (London: Routledge).

Bryman, A. (1998) Quantitative and qualitative research: strategies in knowing the social world, in T. May and M. Williams (eds), *Knowing the Social World* (Buckingham: Open University Press).

Byres, T. J. (1998) Economic development and agricultural productivity, *Journal of Peasant Studies*, 26(1), 159–69.

Byres, T. J. (2003) Agriculture and development: the dominant orthodoxy and an alternative view, in H.-J. Chang (ed.) *Rethinking Development Economics* (London: Anthem Press).

Chang, H.-J. (2003) The market, the state and institutions in economic development, in H.-J. Chang (ed.), *Rethinking Development Economics* (London: Anthem Press).

Chaudhuri, A. and P. Maitra (2002) On the choice of tenancy contracts in rural India, *Economica*, 69, pp. 445–59.

Cook, S. (1999) Methodological aspects of the encompassing principle, *Journal of Economic Methodology*, 6, pp. 61–78.

DaCorta, L. and Venkateswarlu, D. (1999) Unfree relations and the feminisation of agricultural labour in Andhra Pradesh, 1970–95, *Journal of Peasant Studies*, 26(2/3), pp. 73–139.

Danermark, B. (2001) *Explaining Society: An Introduction to Critical Realism in the Social Sciences* (London: Routledge).

Dow, S. (2002) *Economic Methodology: An Enquiry* (Oxford: Oxford University Press).

Dreze, J., Lanjouw, P. and Sharma, N. (1998) Economic development in Palanpur, 1957–93, in P. Lanjouw and N. H. Stern (eds), *Economic Development in Palanpur Over Five Decades*, pp. 114–238 (Oxford: Clarendon Press).

Ellis, F. (2000) The determinants of rural livelihood diversification in developing countries, *Journal of Agricultural Economics*, 51(2), pp. 289–302.

Fairclough, N. (1992) *Discourse and Social Change* (London: Polity Press).

Fleetwood, S. (2002) Boylan and O'Gorman's causal holism: a critical realist evaluation, *Cambridge Journal of Economics*, 26, pp. 27–45.

Genicot, G. (2002) Bonded Labor and serfdom: a paradox of voluntary choice, *Journal of Development Economics*, 67(1), pp. 101–27.

Gray, L. C. and Kevane, M. (2001) Evolving tenure rights and agricultural intensification in southwestern Burkina Faso, *World Development*, 29, pp. 573–87.

Grigsby, W. J. (1996) Women, descent, and tenure succession among the Bambara of West Africa: a changing landscape, *Human Organization*, 55, pp. 93–8.

Hacking, I. (2002) Inaugural lecture: Chair of Philosophy and History of Scientific Concepts at the Collège de France, 16 January 2001, *Economy and Society*, 31(1), pp. 1–14.

Harding, S. (1995) Can feminist thought make economics more objective, *Feminist Economics*, 1(1), pp. 7–32.

Harding, S. (1999) The case for strategic realism: a response to Lawson, *Feminist Economics*, 5(3), pp. 127–33.

Harre, R. (1998) When the knower is also the known, in T. May and M. Williams (eds), *Knowing the Social World*, pp. 37–49 (Buckingham: Open University Press).

Harriss, J. (2002) The case for cross-disciplinary approaches in international development, *World Development*, 30(3), pp. 487–96.

Harriss-White, B. (1999) *Agricultural Markets from Theory to Practice: Field Experience in Developing Countries* (Basingstoke: Macmillan).

Hoff, K. and Stiglitz, J. E. (1997) Moneylenders and bankers: price-increasing subsides in a monopolistically competitive market, *Journal of Development Economics*, 52(2), pp. 429–62.

Hoff, K. and Stiglitz, J. E. (1998) Moneylenders and bankers: price–increasing subsides in a monopolistically competitive market, *Journal of Development Economics*, 55(2), pp. 485–518.

Hulme, D. and Shepherd, A. (2003) Conceptualizing chronic poverty, *World Development*, 31(3), pp. 403–23.

Hulme, D. and Toye, J. (this volume) The case for multidisciplinary social science research on poverty, inequality and well-being, *Journal of Development Studies*.

Hussain, A. (1991) The underdevelopment of theory: some conceptual elements of mainstream economics, in P. Wignaraja, A. Hussain, H. Sethi & G. Wignaraja (eds), *Participatory Development: Learning from South Asia* (Tokyo: UN University Press).

Jackson, C. (2002) Disciplining gender? *World Development*, 30(3), pp. 497–509.

Jain, K. K. and Singh, P. (2000) Trends in tenancy and labour use pattern in Punjab agriculture, *Indian Journal of Agricultural Economics*, 55(3), p. 356.

Kanbur, R. (ed.) (2001) *Qual-Quant: Qualitative and Quantitative Poverty Appraisal: Complementarities, Tensions and the Way Forward*, contributions to a workshop held at Cornell University, March 15–16.

Kanbur, R. (2002) Economics, social science and development, *World Development*, 30(3), pp. 477–86.

Kaul, S. and Pandey, R. K. (2000) Economic study of tenancy structure in India, *Indian Journal of Agricultural Economics*, 55(3), pp. 346–7.

Kuhn, T. S. (1970) *The Structure of Scientific Revolutions* (Chicago: University of Chicago Press).

Kvale, S. (1996) *Interviews: an introduction to qualitative research interviewing* (London: Sage Publications).

Lanjouw, P. and Stern, N. H. (1998) *Economic Development in Palanpur Over Five Decades* (Oxford: Clarendon Press).

Lawson, T. (1997) *Economics and Reality* (New York: Routledge).

Layder, D. (1993) *New Strategies in Social Research* (Cambridge: Polity Press).

Layder, D. (1998) The reality of social domains: implications for theory, in T. May and M. Williamson (eds), *Knowing the Social World* (Buckingham: Open University Press).

Lee, F. (2002) Theory creation and the methodological foundation of post-Keynesian economics, *Cambridge Journal of Economics*, 26(6), pp. 789–804.

Lukes, S. (2005) *Power: A Radical View* (Hampshire: Palgrave Macmillan).

MacIntyre, A. (1985) *After Virtue: A Study in Moral Theory* (London: Duckworth).

MacIntyre, A. (1998) *A Short History of Ethics* (London: Routledge).

Majid, N. (1994) *Contractual Arrangements in Pakistani Agriculture: A study of Share Tenancy in Sindh*, D.Phil. thesis, Oxford: Oxford University.

Manicas, P. T. (1987) *A History and Philosophy of the Social Sciences* (Oxford: Basil Blackwell).

Olsen, W. K. (1993) Competition and power in rural markets: a case study from Andhra Pradesh, *IDS Bulletin*, 21(3), pp. 83–9.

Olsen, W. K. (1996) *Rural Indian Social Relations* (Delhi: Oxford University Press).

Olsen, W. K. (1998) Marxist and neo-classical approaches to unfree labour in India, in T. Brass and M. Van der Linden (eds), *Free and Unfree Labour: The Debate Continues*, pp. 379–404 (Berlin: Peter Lang).

Olsen, W. K. (2003a) Methodological triangulation and realist research: an Indian exemplar, in B. Carter and C. New (eds), *Making Realism Work: Realist Social Theory and Empirical Research* (London: Routledge).

Olsen, W. K. (2003b) Triangulation, time and the social objects of econometrics, in P. Downward (ed.), *Applied Economics and the Critical Realist Critique* (London: Routledge).

Outhwaite, W. and Bottomore, T. (1993) *The Blackwell Dictionary of Twentieth-Century Social Thought* (Oxford: Blackwell Reference).

Patomaki, H. and Wight, C. (2000) After postpositivism? The promises of critical realism, *International Studies Quarterly*, 44(2), pp. 213–37.

Popper, K. R. (1963) *Conjectures and Refutations: The Growth of Scientific Knowledge* (London: Routledge).

Quine, W. V. O. (1953) Two dogmas of empiricism, in W. V. O. Quine (ed.), *From a Logical Point of View* (Boston, MA: Harvard University Press).

Ramakumar, R. (2000) Magnitude and terms of agricultural tenancy in India: A statewise analysis of changes in 1980s, *Indian Journal of Agricultural Economics*, 55(3), p. 337.

Ray, L. J. and Sayer, R. A. (1999) *Culture and Economy After the Cultural Turn* (London: Sage).

Roth, P. A. (1987) *Meaning and Method in the Social Sciences: A Case for Methodological Pluralism* (Ithaca: Cornell University Press).

Sawadogo, J. P. and Stamm, V. (2000) Local perceptions of indigenous land tenure systems: views of peasants, women and dignitaries in a rural province of Burkina Faso, *Journal of Modern African Studies*, 38(2), pp. 279–94.

Sayer, A. (1992) *Method in Social Science* (London: Routledge).

Sayer, A. (1997) Essentialism, social constructionism and beyond, *The Sociological Review*, 24(3), pp. 453–87.

Sayer, A. (2000a) *Realism and Social Science* (London: Sage).

Sayer, A. (2000b) Moral economy and political economy, *Studies in Political Economy*, 61, pp. 79–104.

Sen, A. (1964) Size of holding and productivity, *Economic Weekly*, 16, pp. 323–6.

Sen, A. (1966) Peasants and dualism with and without surplus labour, *Journal of Political Economy*, 74, pp. 425–50.

Shankar, K. (1999) Tenancy reforms: rhetoric and reality, *Economic and Political Weekly*, 34(46/47), pp. 3264–5.

Sharma, H. R. (2000) Tenancy relations in rural India: a temporal and cross–sectional analysis, *Indian Journal of Agricultural Economics*, 55(3), pp. 295–307.

Sharma, N. and Dreze, J. (1998) Tenancy, in P. Lanjouw and N. H. Stern (eds), *Economic Development in Palanpur Over Five Decades* (Oxford: Clarendon Press).

Singh, M. (1995) *Uneven Development in Agriculture and Labour Migration: A Case of Bihar and Punjab* (Shimla: Indian Institute of Advanced Study).

Skoufias, E. (1995) Household resources, transaction costs, and adjustment through land tenancy, *Land Economics*, 71(1), pp. 42–56.

Smith, M. (1994) Realism, in P. Singer (ed.), *Ethics* (Oxford: Oxford University Press).

Smith, M. J. (1998) *Social Science in Question: Towards a Postdisciplinary Framework* (London: Sage Publications).

Srinivasan, T. N. (1989) On choice among creditors and bonded labour contracts, in P. K. Bardhan (ed.), *The Economic Theory of Agrarian Institutions*, pp. 203–20 (Oxford: Clarendon Press).

Stiglitz, J. (1986) The new development economics, *World Development*, 14(2), pp. 257–65.

Stiglitz, J. E. (2003) *Globalisation and its discontents* (London: Penguin).

Swain, M. (1999) Agricultural tenancy and interlinked transactions – I and II – neoclassical and Marxist approaches, *Economic and Political Weekly*, 34, pp. 2752–8.

Swaminathan, M. (1991) Segmentation, collateral valuation and the rate of interest in agrarian credit markets, *Cambridge Journal of Economics*, 15, pp. 151–78.

Toye, J. (2003) Changing perspectives in development economics, in H. J. Chang (ed.), *Rethinking Development Economics* (London: Anthem Press).

Walker, T. S. and Ryan, J. G. (1990) *Village and Household Economics in India's Semi–Arid Tropics* (London: Johns Hopkins University Press).

Williams, M. (2000) Science and Social Science: An Introduction (London: Routledge).

Capabilities, Reproductive Health and Well-Being

JOCELYN DEJONG

I. Introduction

Lack of reproductive health constitutes a significant deprivation of well-being in developing countries and yet the field is often marginalised within development studies. This paper seeks to examine the usefulness of the capabilities approach to an analysis of reproductive health in developing countries. It focuses its content on the development of three research questions, the first being primarily theoretical, the second more policy-orientated and the third centering on methodological approaches. With its direct focus on defining development as enhancing people's freedom to lead the life that they value and to access the social opportunities that make that possible, the capabilities framework has strong potential to reinforce efforts to advance reproductive health.

As elaborated initially by Amartya Sen (see Sen, 1992, 1993, 1999) the capability approach represents a powerful critique of two prevailing views within development studies. Firstly, it criticises the notion that access to resources, such as income or goods is an appropriate measure of well-being. Secondly, it questions whether happiness is an adequate basis or 'space' for evaluative judgement (as in utilitarianism) (for further discussion of 'happiness' see the paper by Kingdon and Knight in this volume). This approach draws on a liberal philosophical framework emphasising the importance of the individual in terms of what he or she is able to do and become and the kind of life he or she is able to lead. In this view, individual capabilities are buttressed by so-called 'social arrangements' (for example Sen, 1993) that either support or deny capabilities. Nussbaum (2000) has further developed the capabilities framework with a particular focus on women's capabilities in developing countries. She distinguishes between: (1) 'basic capabilities' generally innate from birth; (2) 'internal capabilities' which are developed states of the person; (3) 'combined capabilities' *which require an appropriate political, economic and social environment for their exercise* (italics my own) (Nussbaum, 2000, 84–85). Using case studies from the emerging field of reproductive health, then, the paper addresses the question: How can we address the social arrangements that are said to mediate individual capabilities? In particular, to what extent does the capabilities approach help us in analysing biases within society along political, cultural or other lines that lead to deprivation of capabilities?

Secondly, within the policy arena, does the capability approach help us in framing the concerns of reproductive health within the broader debates concerning development? The objective of such a dialogue would be, on the one hand, to accord greater prominence to the costs to development of deprivation in this field. On the other hand, one would hope it would illuminate the social bases of poor reproductive health and explore the relationships between poor outcomes in that sphere with other types of socio-economic disadvantage, a surprisingly under-researched area.

Thirdly, methodologically, what specific approaches to measuring reproductive health would address the above questions? The prevailing and highly influential approach to measuring the burden of disease in a population developed by the World Health Organization (WHO) and the World Bank uses so-called disability adjusted life years (or DALYs).

To approach these questions the paper will first briefly elaborate on the field of reproductive health as it has emerged over the last two decades. It will then introduce the concept of DALYs and how they have been used to measure the disease burden posed by poor reproductive health. The third section will provide some background on the concept of capabilities as developed by Sen and elaborated by Nussbaum (but very much influenced by the ideas of Rawls) before reviewing the usefulness of this approach for reproductive health and its distinctiveness from other approaches. The fourth section will be based on analyses of three sample reproductive health problems of particular relevance to the developing world, namely maternal mortality, obstetric fistulae and female genital mutilation (or cutting). It will examine the extent to which the capabilities framework is useful in analysing these, and if so what methodological approaches are most appropriate. The paper will conclude with some discussion of the policy implications of the capabilities approach as applied to reproductive health and questions for further research.

II. The Emergence of Reproductive Health

At the International Conference on Population and Development (ICPD) in 1994 in Cairo the governments of 180 nations endorsed a new approach to population policy centred on the concept of reproductive health. Conceptually, the term has come to describe an approach which sees women's health and well-being as important in their own right, not as a means towards the ends of fertility reduction or child health. In the interpretation of the ICPD, reproductive health addresses the broad determinants of women's and men's autonomy in making reproductive decisions and focuses on the legal–social and ethical contexts in which these decisions are made. As a panel of the American National Academy of Sciences concluded, robust reproductive health implies that: (1) every sex act should be free of coercion and infection; (2) every pregnancy should be intended; and (3) every birth should be healthy (Tsui et al., 1997: 13–14). The reality of human reproduction in developing countries is, of course, far from these goals, as is most visibly illustrated by the escalating HIV/AIDS epidemic.

Programmatically, the RH approach calls for an expansion of the scope (in terms of health problems addressed) of reproductive health services, including, but not limited to, family planning. It also entails broadening the constituencies to which reproductive health services are addressed to include not only women in the child-bearing age but also those from adolescence to post-menopause. Reproductive health services that have been long been restricted to women should, it argues, open their doors to men. But the approach also makes a claim for inter-sectoral action to address gender inequality in social development more broadly.

Sen himself was in the forefront of those arguing that the alarmist perspectives on population growth that had dominated debates on the relationship between population and development in the 1960s and 1970s are not justified on empirical grounds. He was rightly concerned that they pose serious ethical problems in their programmatic consequences, encouraging a tendency towards coercion (see for example Sen, 1994a, 1999). Moreover, Sen argued that the redirecting of resource flows towards family planning – the logical extension of this alarmism – detracts from encouraging broader social development that is the most effective and ethical way of reducing population growth.[1] He underscores the potential 'unintended social costs' of such coercion in terms of loss of freedom and practices such as sex-selective abortion in countries such as China, where a prevailing preference for sons means that female foetuses are more likely to be aborted than male (Sen, 1994a, 1999).

Sen's arguments, however, were joined by those of other academics as well as advocacy groups concerned about the abrogation of human rights witnessed in some population programmes, with the example of abusive programmes in India during the state of emergency in 1975 and China widely cited as examples. Most critically a growing international women's movement since the 1970s had been arguing that women in the developing world often do not have reproductive autonomy in that their male partners and other household and community members influence their decisions, particularly where cultural norms value women primarily for their childbearing role (Sen et al., 1994). Women's health advocates pointed out that women's lack of control over reproductive decisions limits their quality of life, poses a heavy health burden on them and ultimately constrains their participation in development processes (Sen et al., 1994). They pushed for policy changes to make health services more responsive to women's needs and to treat the health consequences of reproduction, rather than being exclusively focused on lowering fertility, and they criticised the nature of many family planning programmes.

Thus the ground was laid for the shift that was observed in Cairo from an emphasis in international population policy on aggregate population growth to individual welfare and rights. Yet since 1994 implementation of this approach has faltered for a number of reasons including lack of political commitment, seeming contradictions between the exigencies of implementing reproductive health and health sector reform simultaneously, as well as funding constraints (DeJong, 2000; Standing, 2002).

III. Disability Adjusted Life Years

International discussion of public health priorities from a quite different perspective than the ICPD coincidentally ended up lending weight to the importance of reproductive health in developing countries. The publication in 1993 of the World Bank's World Development Report entitled *Investing in Health* ushered in a new method of comparing the burden of disease associated with different conditions. Devised by economists and epidemiologists, DALYs rely heavily on the techniques and assumptions of those academic disciplines. According to that World Development Report, they are a unit used for measuring both the global burden of disease and the effectiveness of health interventions, as indicated by reductions in the disease burden. DALYs are calculated as the present value of the future years of disability-free life that are lost as the result of the premature deaths or cases of disability occurring in a particular year. The use of DALYs is an attempt to move away from measuring health solely by a focus on mortality and to incorporate in a single summary measure the collective experience of disability over life times by discounting life-years to the present. As such, DALYs are a 'bad' to be avoided (Anand and Hanson, 2004, p. 183). Because of the claim that DALYs embody objectivity, comparability and authority, they have become the basic currency of international health policy debates.

The application of DALYs has been in some ways a boon to reproductive health advocates, in that there is now recognition that reproductive ill-health contributes five to 15 per cent of the global burden of disease at a minimum. Use of DALYs has also underscored the gender bias within reproductive health; whereas this figure represents three per cent of the total disease burden for men, the equivalent figure for women is 22 per cent (Abou Zahr and Vaughan, 2000: 657). Nevertheless, in its explicit rejection of the importance of socio-economic context and social relations – on the argument that this would undermine objectivity – this measure has many weaknesses with regards to analysing reproductive health. For, as will be argued further below, many reproductive health problems are not only at least partially determined by social factors and norms, but their social consequences – such as stigma and shame – are heavily influenced by cultural context. Does the capabilities approach provide an alternative approach that overcomes some of these deficiencies?

IV. The Capabilities Approach and Its Usefulness for Reproductive Health

Sen presents his capabilities approach as the culmination of a critique elaborated over many years of prevailing utilitarian approaches to measuring welfare within development studies and economics. In developing these ideas, he was heavily influenced by the ideas of John Rawls as elaborated in his *A Theory of Justice* of 1971. Rawls was highly critical of utilitarian approaches to measuring welfare, and in particular did not agree with the idea that some members of society should have to give up advantages for the greater good of society. He argued that social and economic inequalities should be 'arranged' so that the greatest benefit accrues to the least advantaged. In an approach analogous to (although clearly developed independently of) that of basic needs as a development strategy mooted in the 1970s, Rawls argued that each citizen should have access to what he called 'primary social goods,' ones that any rational person would choose and that this list would include, but not be limited to, income.

Sen, however, takes issue with the articulation of 'primary goods' in his argument that the yardstick should not be access to material 'goods' or income, but rather the well-being of people themselves. He also criticises Rawls for his lack of sufficient consideration of inter-personal differences in need (for example some may be handicapped in some way) and in the ability to convert commodities into welfare (Sen, 1994b). These inter-personal differences, Sen (1994b) argues, are of critical importance for social policy.[2]

Thus according to Sen's capabilities approach, policies should be evaluated not on the basis of their ability to satisfy utility or increase income, but to the extent that they enhance the capabilities of individuals and their ability to perform socially accepted functionings. For our purposes, the distinction between functionings and capabilites is critical. Functionings are the 'beings and doings' of a person whereas capabilities are 'the various combinations of (valued) functionings that a person can achieve. Capability is thus a set of vectors of functionings, reflecting the person's freedom to lead one type of life or another' (Sen, 1992: 40). In terms of reproductive health, therefore, capabilities would embrace such concepts as the ability to live through pregnancy and to a mature age without suffering premature mortality, whereas the equivalent measure of lack of functioning would be rates of maternal mortality.[3]

The distinction between capabilities and functionings is particularly important in its consideration of the role of human agency. Two people could be equally deprived in terms of functioning (such as being well-nourished for example), while one is a victim of famine and the other fasts for religious reasons, yet they do not have the same capability because the famine victim suffers from lack of choice. Similarly, in terms of reproductive health, an upper-class woman with recourse to abortion has quite different capabilities than a poor woman, and someone with HIV/AIDS in England has quite different capabilities from someone with HIV/AIDS living in Bangladesh. In all of these cases, Sen would use the capability approach to analyse the ways in which such differences are accounted for not only by differences in income, but also in terms of social arrangements and norms.

V. Nussbaum's Approach to Capabilities

Martha Nussbaum's (2000) work builds on Sen's ideas and represents an ambitious attempt to apply universalist principles of justice to gender equality in non-western contexts in a manner which purports to be sensitive to local specificities. Nussbaum's main preoccupation is the pervasive discrimination against women in most of the developing world and the fact that 'considerations of justice for women have been disproportionately silenced in many debates about international development' (Nussbaum, 2000: 33). However, Nussbaum goes much further than Sen (who never makes a list of basic capabilities and uses them primarily for cross-country comparisons)[4] by developing a list of capabilities on which she argues there can be cross-cultural consensus. These include life, health, bodily integrity, political participation, equal employment and secure property rights among others.

In doing so, Nussbaum parts ways with many development practitioners in her critique both of cultural relativism in general and of the labelling of any effort to develop universalist notions of women's rights as cultural imperialism in particular. This tendency, she argues, ignores traditions of protest against gender injustice within cultural and religious traditions outside the west, and does not sufficiently account for dynamism within and interpenetration between cultures and societies in a globalised era. It is not, however, my purpose here to analyse the arguments for and against developing such a global list, but rather the usefulness of the general approach.

Nussbaum (2000) acknowledges that her notion of capabilities is very close to Rawls' listing of 'primary goods'. Nussbaum, however, follows Sen's advocacy of a shift from goods to people when measuring welfare, and thus refuses to acknowledge the importance of commodities in any form. Nevertheless, in recognition of feminist assertions that Rawls' conception of justice does not take sufficient account of people's needs for belonging and affection, Nussbaum (2000) addresses the 'family' to analyse what happens when principles of equality between the sexes may conflict with competing claims from relatives and in-laws. Nonetheless, she remains adamant that it is above all each individual's capabilities that need to be protected, as opposed to those of households or other social groups, as the communitarian critics of Rawls, such as Charles Taylor, would argue.

Nussbaum (2000) argues that there are advantages to applying capabilities over notions of rights to questions concerning women's status and well-being in developing countries. Before elaborating on these ideas, the following section outlines the basic features of the reproductive rights framework.

VI. Reproductive Rights

Based on a more generalised rights-based approaches to development, an alternative perspective that has been used by many reproductive health advocates – before and after the ICPD – is one applying the notion of 'reproductive rights.' Scholars of reproductive rights, such as Rebecca Cook (1995) and Lynn Freedman (1999a), argue that a broad interpretation of reproductive rights is based on the same principles of social justice and dignity that Nussbaum attaches to the capabilities approach. Narrowly defined, such rights are codified in international covenants and conventions, but also in international customary law. Thus applying their underlying principles provides a mechanism to hold not only states accountable to fulfilling obligations to reproductive health, but even non-state actors under their jurisdiction (Freedman, 1999a). Freedman defines reproductive rights as:

> ... the constellations of legal and ethical principles that relate to an individual woman's ability to control what happens to her body and her person by protecting and respecting her ability to make and implement decisions about her reproduction and sexuality. (Freedman, 1999b: 149)

She admits, however, that the language of rights has often been co-opted or manipulated to reinforce or to maintain the status quo and existing structures of power. Much of the resistance to internationally notions of reproductive rights has emerged because of their association with western political traditions and the focus on individual civil and political rights, as opposed to social and economic rights. Moreover, there has been criticism of the implicit assumption that western historical experience is somehow universally valid despite cultural differences. Yet reproductive health provides an example of a field where civil and political rights are inextricably linked to social and economic rights. For example, the right to have access to fertility regulation which was lacking, for example, in Ceaucescu's Romania, cannot be implemented without access to adequate health care including family planning. Petchesky and Judd's publication, which included in-depth case studies from seven different countries, illustrates the fact that common principles of dignity and social justice may be expressed in quite different forms across varied cultural contexts (Petchesky and Judd, 1998). In Egypt, for example, women expressed a clear sense of multiple violations of their reproductive rights, but did not use the language of rights (El Dawla, 2000).

Nussbaum argues that there is significant value-added to approaching questions of social justice within development from the vantage-point of capabilities as opposed to using the language of rights: 'Rights have been understood in many different ways, and difficult theoretical questions are frequently obscured by the use of rights language, which can give the illusion of agreement where there is deep philosophical disagreement' (Nussbaum, 2000: 97). Among areas of disagreement among advocates of rights are whether the relevant unit of analysis is individuals or groups, and on the relationship between rights and duties. Perhaps the strongest argument she makes, however, is that rights may be *understood* quite differently across cultures whereas capabilities fulfil more fundamental and less contentious needs.

Therefore, despite the enshrining of reproductive rights in the language of international conventions, such as the ICPD, and international institutions, the implementation of reproductive rights and their definition across diverse cultural contexts remains a fraught area. The heated debate at the ICPD itself between advocates of reproductive rights and the delegations of the Catholic and Muslim countries in particular concerning such contentious issues as abortion, sexual orientation and the reproductive health services for unmarried youth provides a clear example. While the reproductive rights and capabilities approaches share common basic principles – of social justice and dignity – arguably the capabilities approach shifts the emphasis to actual well-being, and may provide a less controversial approach to addressing sensitive questions relating to sexuality and reproduction – as is discussed in the following section.

VII. Capabilities and Gender Inequalities

The capabilities framework can be particularly useful for examining areas of gender inequity, although to the author's knowledge there has been no application to questions of reproductive health (with the exception of Harcourt, 2001). As Robeyns (2002: 5) has argued, while capabilities are ethically individualistic with their focus on individual well-being, they are not, contrary to the claims of many of their critics, ontologically so – that is, they allow for the importance of social relations, care and cultural norms. As Robeyns expresses:

> This is attractive for feminist research, because ethical individualism rejects the idea that women's well-being can be subsumed under wider entities such as the household or the community, while not denying the impact of care, social relations and interdependence. (Robeyns, 2002: 5)

In this sense this framework is likely to be particularly helpful in analysing reproductive health, which inherently addresses relational processes of sexuality and reproduction while valuing the well-being of individual women. Moreover, this approach is able to address doings and beings in market as well as non-market settings (Robeyns, 2002) – again a positive feature for analysing health outcomes which are not necessarily improved by addressing income, poverty or health care in isolation of broader contextual parameters.

Moving way from income and utility as the yardstick can allow us to both reject instrumental approaches which subordinate women's health to the goals of fertility reduction or human capital, but also to see how poor reproductive health can apply across social classes. An interesting example of the latter point comes from the historical experience of maternal mortality in the UK. In the early twentieth century, upper class women were more prone to dying in childbirth because they tended both to rely on doctors who often interfered unnecessarily in childbirth and to be hospitalised when hospitals did not have adequate infection control. In contrast, the poorer classes relied on traditional midwives who had vast experience in dealing with complications and delivered at home (Loudon, 2000).

Above all, however, using the capabilities approach to analyse reproductive health puts questions of social justice, ethics and distributional concerns at the centre of the debate and provides a normative framework explicitly based on a theory of justice rather than abstract exhortations. One would expect, therefore, that such an approach would provide the missing bridge between broader development debates and narrow health sector interventions based on biomedical models of health.

VIII. Sen and Nussbaum on Health

In both of their writings, Sen and Nussbaum allude to the fundamental nature of health as a capability of intrinsic importance in its own right and instrumental to other capabilities. In a piece entitled 'Why Health Equity?' Sen argues that: 'Health equity may well be embedded in a broader framework of overall equity, but there are some special considerations related to health that need to come forcefully into the assessment of overall justice' (Sen, 2002: 663). He goes on to argue that health equity depends not only on the distribution of health care, which is the central issue in much of the debate about inequality in health internationally, and that assessing questions of equity in health by nature requires a multidisciplinary approach.

Sen typically takes issue with the 'procedural' approaches to justice of the so-called 'libertarians' whereby just procedures are the focus regardless of the outcomes (Sen 1999: 19). However, in the case of health as in other matters of social justice, he recognises that processes are important and that it is not only outcomes (functionings) that are of relevance. Thus discrimination in health care is an important issue no matter what the outcome (Sen, 2002). To support this case, he argues that despite the fact that women in most populations tend to have a longer life expectancy than men,[5] this does not mean that we should favour men in terms of access to health services – that is, processes and not only outcomes are important.

As for Nussbaum, she includes two items of particular relevance to reproductive health on her list of critical capabilities. The first is *bodily health* – being able to have good health, including reproductive health, to be adequately nourished; to have adequate shelter. The second is *bodily integrity* – being able to move freely from place to place; having one's bodily boundaries treated as sovereign, i.e., being able to be secure against assault, including sexual assault, child sexual abuse, and domestic violence; having opportunities for sexual satisfaction and for choices in matters of reproduction' (Nussbaum, 2000: 78). Given the fundamental nature of health capabilities, Nussbaum questions whether in this particular case, states should push for functioning not capability and undermine choice in certain aspects (Nussbaum 2000: 91).

Beyond underscoring the intrinsic and instrumental contribution of health capabilities in terms of social justice, neither Sen nor Nussbaum present an extensive discussion of how such capabilities may be approached methodologically, or indeed of the complexities of policy within this area. There tends to be the implicit assumption that access to health care is inevitably a 'good' without delving into the malfunctioning or systematic biases against women within particular health care processes. As Unterhalter (2002) notes of their work on education, more theorising of this area of social relations can reveal how education, for example, can also be a site of deprivation of capabilities. She gives the example of the use of education to promote the aims of the apartheid government in South Africa, or the current widespread sexual abuse of schoolgirls taking place in the same country to illustrate the disempowering nature of education in some contexts. Likewise, within the health and family planning field, certainly there is ample literature to indicate that women seeking health care – and particularly poor women – are often treated with disrespect and their needs are not always fully taken into account. In the worst case they are the victims of lack of ethical practice such as informed consent and even victims of abuse (for example Sen et al., 1994; Kabakian-Khasholian et al., 2000; Cottingham and Myntti, 2002). Thus at issue is not only differential access to health care but the very nature and processes of health care itself.

IX. Methodological Questions Concerning the Application of Capabilities to Reproductive Health

The first methodological question one needs to confront in endeavouring to apply a capabilities framework to reproductive health is *whether to address functioning or capability*. Both Sen and Nussbaum argue convincingly that in terms of public policy and claims on the state, capability should be the starting point. A focus on capabilities as opposed to functionings protects sensitivities to cultural differences and both avoids paternalism and allows for pluralism. Thus an appropriate role for the state would not be forcing the person fasting for religious reasons to eat but in ensuring that everyone avoids starvation. As Nussbaum expresses: 'For political purposes, it is appropriate that we shoot for capabilities, and those alone. Citizens must be left free to determine their own course after that' (Nussbaum, 2000: 87).

Yet however superior the concept of capabilities may be on philosophical grounds, we are left with the methodological issue of how to disentangle the two. Sen does argue that since it is difficult to observe the capability set, 'in practice one might have to settle often enough for relating well-being to the achieved – and observed – functionings, rather than trying to bring in the capability set' (Sen, 1992: 52, quoted in Comim, 2001: 9). In the case of reproductive health, however, we want to know not only the biological risks but the extent that the 'social arrangements' let women down and constrain their choices.

An interesting methodological approach to this conundrum was adopted by Burchardt (2002) in her analysis of unemployment of women in the UK relying on empirical data. She argues: 'It would be wrong to assume that someone is worse off because she is not working, while it is correct to assume that she is worse off if she lacks the *capability* for paid employment' (Burchardt, 2002: 3). She took a two-prong approach whereby on the one hand, she assumed the capability exists but then tried to identify constraints. On the other hand, she assumed the capability for employment was not there and then analysed subjective preferences. As she notes, however, the first approach requires normative judgements about unobservable constraints, but the second is subject to the methodological constraints of 'adaptive preferences'[6] although it does address the unobservable constraints. The findings from this study are quite striking: nearly three-quarters of women who were not in paid work lacked employment capability, of whom only one-third would be picked up in official unemployment statistics. Such findings have immediate policy relevance, and Burchardt concludes that especially for women, employment capability is more relevant for policy than usual measures of unemployment (or functioning).

Burchardt justifies this approach by arguing that unlike being well-nourished, where if this is within the individual's capability set it is likely to be achieved, functioning and capability diverge in employment, and arguably particularly for women. That is, a woman may want to be employed but not achieve that state for a number of non-market reasons. I would argue, however, that even in health and nutrition the matter is not so straightforward, particularly in developing countries. Indeed one of the critiques of Sen's theory of entitlements and famines was prompted by empirical evidence that in famine situations certain people may 'choose to starve' in order to safeguard assets (de Waal, 1990). However, it is extremely difficult to measure capability in health, and health indicators typically only tell us about functioning. This is particularly the case in reproductive health, as will be argued below, given the stigma and sensitivity associated with many health problems of this nature about which it is difficult to establish even functioning, let alone capability.

The relationship between capabilities and functionings is further complicated by the fact that there is a strong role of chance in determining health outcomes. That is, of two women of equal capability for good-health and equal access to quality health care, one may die of pregnancy-related mortality while the other with the same condition – for (as yet?) medically unexplained reasons – does not. Interestingly it was the influence of chance that convinced Rawls that he should not include health (at least initially) in his list of so-called 'primary goods'. That is, to Rawls, the state could not be expected to guarantee the health of its citizens. Nussbaum (2000) counters this argument by saying that states can, however, guarantee the social bases of health. The challenge, then, is to specify how these 'social bases of health' are linked to health outcomes which by nature calls for employing the techniques and data of epidemiology as well as the social sciences.

The second methodological question which is critical to consider is *which functionings matter?* According to Robeyns (2002) the capabilities approach by design does not tell us this, and yet when applying the approach to the concrete field of reproductive health there may be grounds on which the question must be broached. Robeyns (2000) further warns that the subjective judgements as well as the background of the researcher inevitably enter into these choices. She is particularly concerned that gender considerations may easily be ignored. That is, a welfare economist may not be concerned about gender differences in care responsibilities within the household and therefore not select these functionings for analysis (Robeyns, 2000).

Prioritising capabilities would require applying some form of weighting which could also be used to address the third methodological question of *how to aggregate capabilities?* This is a general problem in the operationalisation of capabilities (Comim, 2001; Kingdon and Knight, this volume). The capabilities approach itself does not tell us how capabilities should be aggregated into an overall well-being indicator (Robeyns, 2002). But there is a specific problem which arguably applies particularly in health in that many capabilities are inter-dependent. Malnutrition insofar as it affects a young girl's development, for example, may be a risk factor for many subsequent reproductive health problems (for example obstetric fistulae described below) and this is where the epidemiological evidence as well as knowledge of social context must inform our choices of functionings. Can we then specify a hierarchy of capabilities?

Using the language of capabilities, DALY's represent an attempt to measure an actual burden or the extent of deprivation of 'functionings', and as such have been praised in many quarters for providing some level of aggregation. Yet the measure tells us little about capabilities which are the appropriate claim for social justice. How do we address reproductive health capabilities and not only functionings (or outcomes)? Ultimately understanding why individual and social differentials in capabilities produce varied outcomes is necessary if we are to judge the virtue of policies to improve reproductive health.

An alternative approach has been to analyse all well-being indicators to assess where gender differentials in functionings are most marked. Saith and Harris-White (1999) attempt to do so just this and conclude that the under-10 female/male ratio is a suitable indicator for assessing gender differences in well-being. Thus where one would expect equality, deviation from the norm would indicate inequality. In reproductive health, however, it is known that biologically women bear a greater burden of ill-health independent of social constraints by virtue of the fact that only women get pregnant and are biologically more at risk of sexually transmitted infections (for example HIV/AIDS). However, at issue is whether 'social arrangements' exacerbate this biological inequality and how constraints on women's choices represent therefore an infringement of social justice. Thus distinguishing functionings and capabilities remains critical, as can be illustrated by considering the case of the following health problems.

X. Reproductive Health Problems

The following four reproductive health problems have been chosen as illustrative examples of the challenges of applying the capabilities framework to reproductive health. As the foregoing has hinted, the diversity of problems encompassed within the broad field of reproductive health calls for some disaggregation in order to investigate the implications of applying the capabilities framework to them. These examples represent a range along a number of dimensions, including (a) the extent to which there has been policy attention to these concerns; (b) the extent to which socio-environmental factors play a role in their occurrence; and (c) the importance of 'agency' in explaining their prevalence. All could be both objectively and subjectively defined as 'severe' both in their biological and socio-economic consequences for the women concerned.

Maternal Mortality

More than 1600 women die daily in the developing world for reasons connected to pregnancy, childbirth or its aftermath and this number constitutes 99 per cent of all maternal deaths internationally. Indeed, maternal mortality is the indicator of well-being showing greatest discrepancy between the developed and developing world. Until 1987, the date of the first Safe Motherhood Conference, this fact was surprisingly not widely recognised within development policy. Since then the tragedy of avoidable maternal mortality has commanded increasing international attention, and the target of reducing maternal mortality by half now constitutes one of the Millennium Development Goals.

Maternal mortality is particularly apt for exploring the conceptual and methodological challenges of an application of the capabilities framework to reproductive health for a number of reasons. First of all, the role of chance (as discussed above in the context of Rawls) is critical. Maine (1999) argues that maternal health is quite unlike child health which could be said to operate under an additive model; that is a series of environmental deficiencies (poor water and sanitation, malnutrition, etc) add up to weaken resistance and produce high levels of infant and child mortality. With maternal mortality, however, more of a 'binomial model' (like flipping a coin) applies: a woman either does or does not develop a life-threatening complication during pregnancy and her survival depends on getting prompt, adequate emergency obstetric care. Exposure to the risk of maternal mortality occurs with every pregnancy, however, and therefore the risk is higher in countries with high fertility.

It is immediately clear, therefore, that maternal mortality is an event which can occur across social classes (as the example from the historical experience of the UK illustrates). However, once the chance, and relatively rare (even in developing countries with higher rates of maternal mortality) event occurs, the 'social arrangements' are critical which allow or impede a response to a potential crisis. These include the multiple social constraints on accessing available care, from the responses of partners, families and communities, to availing and being able to afford transportation even before the health care system is reached.

Within public health, prevailing interventions to address maternal mortality have focused to a large extent on providing essential obstetric care. Over time, however, there has been increasing recognition within public health that maternal mortality provides a test for the entire health care system in terms of how well it is able to discriminate and detect those women at high risk and act promptly to treat them. Thus issues of overall quality and management of health care play a central role. In a national study of maternal mortality in Egypt, for example, over 50 per cent of the 'avoidable factors' leading to maternal deaths were due to medical mismanagement (Egyptian Ministry of Health, 1993). These findings then prompt broader questions concerning the implications of overcrowding in medical schools, the poor quality of medical education and poor regulation by governmental powers – issues which, in Egypt, transcend the remit of the Ministry of Health.

The legal context provides another important parameter for maternal mortality particularly because of the contribution of unsafe abortion to maternal deaths. It is estimated that unsafe abortion accounts for 13 per cent of maternal deaths (but less than one per cent in developed countries) (Maine, 1999). The real legal context may be even more relevant, in terms of how social and religious norms influence behaviour. Thus religious norms are particularly influential in Catholic and Islamic countries where public policy has tended to make abortion illegal.[7]

Despite an appropriate focus on health care and the legal context, however, there has been surprisingly little research on the link between socio-economic disadvantage and maternal mortality.[8] That is, neither socio-economic risk factors nor the socio-economic consequences of maternal deaths have been well-documented. This is in contrast to, for example, the field of HIV/AIDS where there has been significant research on the implications for families and orphans of a parent or both parents dying of HIV/AIDS. Borghi et al. (2003) found that in Benin, for example, in the cases of severe obstetric complications of a mother within a household, costs incurred reached 34 per cent of annual household cash expenditure. Thus economic burden may be one of many reasons why women do not get access to health care when complications arise. The longer term consequences on children and households of maternal death, in terms of education, economic prospects and both physical and psychological well-being are virtually unknown, partly because they have not been prioritised within development policy. The prevailing DALY approach, for example, in its focus on the suffering of individuals, does not take into consideration this burden on households or communities of maternal mortality or indeed of any other health condition.

Conversely, there has been little research addressing the question of how poverty may exacerbate risk to critical reproductive health problems such as maternal mortality. Graham et al. (2004) in a study based on analysis of eleven nationally representative demographic and health surveys found that there are significant associations between women's poverty status and their survival. In Indonesia, for example, approximately a third of maternal deaths occurred among women from the poorest quintile. The mechanisms through which this association acts, however, needs much further research. It is not clear, for example, whether the actual risk of reproductive complication is higher among the poor, or whether the likelihood of treatment is lower. As Graham and colleagues argue, without taking into account such intra-national inequalities, development targets such as the Millennium Development Goals which focus on reducing national averages may miss the key point. Moreover, the DALY approach – in its focus on aggregating individual well-being – tells us little about such inequalities.

Thus, in this case, the research base to address the 'social bases of health' which Nussbaum advocates should be the claim on the state (in countering Rawls' assertion that states cannot guarantee the health of their citizens) is relatively weak; that is the level of knowledge about which 'social bases' are pre-eminent is lacking. While Sen (1989) himself has addressed the issue of women's 'survival as a development problem' this has been in the context of the so-called 'missing women' in India. This term has been used to describe the women not accounted for if one were to apply the expected sex ratio to the Indian population, and who Sen and others argue have been victims of systemic disadvantage in terms of nutrition and health care (see for example Sen, 1999).

Epidemiologically, determination of maternal mortality ratios (calculated as the ratio of maternal deaths to live births) in a population requires large-scale surveys since the event is relatively rare. A particular innovation was the introduction of the 'sisterhood method' (see for example Graham and Campbell, 1992) in which live sisters of women who had died are interviewed to investigate circumstances of death. Typically such data is then referred to medical researchers to ascertain the cause of death and whether it was indeed maternal or not. Generally such surveys have not been used to generate information about socio-economic circumstances or social relations relevant to the maternal death in order to make analyses of the role of social class, region of residence or other factors. Such large-scale approaches need to be combined with much more micro-level and qualitative social science research to explore the social context and characteristics of individuals who experience life-threatening complications or subsequently die of them. Qualitative local studies at the community and household levels could start to address the true social bases of health and health care processes which population-level statistics, although critical, do not capture.

A potentially useful approach for a case control study would be to compare the response to the case of a woman who dies a maternal death with what have been called 'near misses'[9] or women who suffer from life-threatening complications but do not subsequently die. Were such women 'saved by the system' in the sense that either the health care system or social circumstances and relations were such as to prevent the maternal death? That is, were there characteristics of the social response to their condition or of the quality of health care they received that increased their chances of survival? It is only when such types of research have been conducted that we can start to address capabilities to achieve a healthy pregnancy and delivery without suffering from premature mortality. Only then could we make inter-personal comparisons of capabilities and thus perhaps inform public policies in ways that might prevent this tragedy from occurring.

Obstetric Fistulae

Obstetric fistulae,[10] a health problem which leaves women permanently incontinent, has been even less researched than maternal mortality, although both share some common risk factors, particularly prolonged and obstructed labour and lack of access to adequate obstetric care. As such it is a classic example of the 'measurement trap' (Graham and Campbell, 1992) in that lack of political commitment to reproductive health in turn leads to lack of available data, leaving a vacuum in terms of trying to stimulate greater political commitment. Although long discussed among obstetricians and gynaecologists, fistulae occupy no significant place in development policy debates.

There is extremely limited research on the issue, despite its severity, and data on its incidence is almost non-existent (Bangser et al., 1999; Donnay and Weil, 2004). It has been reported, however, in Asia and throughout Sub-Saharan Africa (particularly Sudan, Nigeria, Tanzania and Ethiopia) as well as in Yemen. In 1989, WHO estimated that approximately two million girls and women worldwide suffered from the condition and that there were approximately 50,000 to 100,000 new cases globally each year (Donnay and Weil, 2004). The limited research and anecdotal evidence from health care professionals indicates that girls and women at risk of obstetric fistulae are often malnourished, short in stature with small pelvises, come from extremely poor families and have difficulty accessing transport and health care during an obstetric emergency. Typically the women experiencing this condition are young, having married early.

Once fistulae of either type occur, they are very difficult medically to repair. The operation requires highly skilled surgeons and thus being very expensive. In some contexts, the expense of this complex and time-consuming operation means that for most poor women it is not a possibility (Donnay and Weil, 2004). Research from India suggests that some women had been living with the condition for over 20 years before it was repaired (Bangser et al., 1999: 161). Thus, while the woman with obstetric fistulae escapes mortality she suffers from a severe, debilitating condition with severe socio-economic consequences often over a prolonged period, if not her whole life. Yet again, these severe socio-economic consequences are left out of DALY calculations which are restricted to the reduced physical functioning of individuals.

The severe stigma attached to this condition means invariably that such women face public shame, social exclusion and in many cases their marital and family relations break down and they lose their source of livelihoods. In almost every case the foetus dies as well, leaving the woman with the added stigma of childlessness if it is her first child. In Nigeria, studies have found that 'Women with VVF often work alone, eat alone, use their own plates and utensils to eat and are not allowed to cook for anyone else. In some cases they must live on the streets and beg' (Bangser et al., 1999: 158).

In terms of the capabilities, then, there is little data on the extent of the lack of functioning relating to obstetric fistulae. Virtually no social science research has been conducted on this condition and its consequences for the women, their relations or their communities. Like for maternal mortality as a functioning, the relevant capabilities in this case include being able to live safely through pregnancy and delivery but being well-nourished is critical. Autonomy to marry at an age when women are physically mature is clearly also a relevant capability. Yet once women are afflicted by this condition, access to appropriate and affordable care is central.

It is immediately clear, however, that trying to research capabilities relating to such stigmatised health conditions confronts enormous methodological challenges. It calls for local-level anthropological methods to reach those afflicted, who tend to be socially marginalised and whose conditions are often left out of official statistics. Such observational approaches would also elucidate the health care processes which facilitate or hamper these women's capabilities.

Female Genital Mutilation (or Cutting)

In contrast to the problem of obstetetric fistulae, female genital mutilation (or FGM)[11] as it has become known, is one of the central advocacy points of the growing reproductive health movement internationally. Indeed, FGM is perhaps the mostly frequently cited example used by universalists in their critiques of cultural relativism. Thus Nussbaum (2000) pays more attention to this particular reproductive health concern than any other.

Since FGM often occurs in unhygienic settings, the risk of infection and potential later complication is high. The practice has been reported in more than 30 countries in Africa, but it also occurs in the Middle East (in Egypt, Sudan and Yemen) as well as to a much more limited extent in Asia. It is estimated to affect some two million girls every year ranging in age from infancy to adolescence (Tsui et al., 1997).

Over the last 10 years, the research-base on this practice has increased considerably and there now exist large-scale nationally representative data on many countries through the demographic and health surveys. These have enabled analyses to be made regarding the potential role of education, changing patterns over time and differences in the practice according to such factors as region and social class. Qualitative research has also revealed complex motivations and attitudes (of parents) underlying the practice, although to the author's knowledge no research has been conducted on the attitudes of young girls to the practice. Large-scale data in Egypt, for example, has revealed the potential role of religion on the practice, in the context of a growing politicisation of religion in that country, with a growing number of respondents claiming that the motivation for the practice is religious.[12]

From a capabilities perspective this is a particularly complex problem particularly in relation to agency, not least because the decision to circumcise is taken by adults and perpetrated on children who do not have the opportunity of giving their informed consent. Recent qualitative research from Egypt has shown that in a context of economic deterioration, the marriageability of daughters is a prime consideration motivating mothers to have their daughters circumcised (El Dawla, 2000). This research has revealed the complex trade-offs women may be making in sacrificing reproductive autonomy and bodily integrity to what they hope will bring greater economic security and arguably long-term well-being. That is, achieving greater economic capabilities may be overriding the promotion of capabilities to achieve reproductive and sexual well-being. There are also signs that increasingly private medical doctors are the main health providers carrying out this practice, reminding us yet again that health care itself can be the site of deprivation of capabilities.

Nussbaum makes the assumption that all women who have been subject to female genital mutilation are deprived of the capability of sexual expression, an assertion that might be challenged by Egyptian women in a country where 95 per cent of women are circumcised. Much more research is needed on the socio-economic and psychological consequences of this practice, however. Qualitative methods which would explore the motivations of parents in circumcising their daughters, as well as their interpretations of religious and social norms that sanction the practice, are critical.

Ultimately then, this returns us to the more theoretical questions concerning the limits of universalism as opposed to the need to engage the communitarian debates on justice which both Nussbaum and Rawls reject. Authors such as Gore (1997) have argued that although the capabilities approach cannot be accused of being morally individualistic, it does not go far enough in incorporating the intrinsic importance of institutional contexts and social norms.

XI. Methodological Problems in Applying Capabilities to Reproductive Health

As is evident from the foregoing discussion, all of the above illustrative reproductive health problems need to be analysed using different methodologies, and require different policy approaches. There are, however, some underlying commonalities. For example, shared by all of them, with the possible exception of maternal mortality, is the stigma and cultural sensitivity often associated with these health problems, which renders them very private and therefore seemingly invisible. In this sense, even functioning, let alone capability, is difficult to measure, and lack of political commitment has reinforced this methodological challenge in a vicious cycle whereby lack of data feeds policy silence.

While the DALYs approach does represent one attempt to capture the burden of disease independent of advocacy and special interest pleading, in the case of each of the above problems it misses a great deal. Part of this deficiency is due to informational constraints. The accuracy of DALY calculations depends on available epidemiological data and across the spectrum of reproductive health conditions these have tended to be under-reported (Sadana, 2000). However, there may be more fundamental problems with the DALY approach as applied to reproductive health (Hanson, 2002; Allotey and Reidpath, 2002). Most importantly, in its intentional omission of context, it fails to consider the differential impact and socio-economic consequences of these conditions on women in different life-circumstances. A more or less stigmatising or negative social response in different settings for example – may meet the same condition – such as infertility. As Reidpath and colleagues argue, when blindness in the UK and blindness in Niger are given the same disability weight,[13] in spite of a context in the UK which makes disability less severe than in

Niger, the social determinants of the impact of disease are ignored; the effect is thus to underestimate the burden associated with morbidity in disadvantaged populations and overestimate that in advantaged populations (Reidpath et al., 2003). Moreover, as Abou Zahr and Vaughan (2000) note, in its focus on individual suffering, the socio-economic and psychological burden of these conditions falling on households and communities (as in the case of maternal mortality or HIV/AIDS) is excluded from analysis.

An example of an innovative multidisciplinary study in Egypt (Khattab et al., 1999) illustrates this methodological conundrum well. After two years of anthropological fieldwork in a low-income community of Giza governorate outside Cairo researchers interviewed women about their experience of reproductive illness. At the same time, doctors from the team trained the staff at the local government health services to improve their screening of reproductive tract infections and other reproductive health problems (when hitherto such clinics had mainly catered to providing family planning or pregnancy services). Members of the study team then asked if the women wanted clinical exams at the local clinic and in many cases where the women were reluctant, offered to accompany them to the health services. The results of the combined survey of women in their homes and clinical exams were striking: over 50 per cent of the women had reproductive tract infections (which can lead to infertility and enhance the spread of sexually transmitted disease) but none of these women had previously complained of these conditions to the local health services. Thus measuring functioning is difficult enough, before one begins to analyse capability in a context of a pervasive 'culture of silence' about women's health. The insights provided by this study were arguably only possible because anthropological or sociological methodologies to elicit subjective perceptions of well-being were complemented by the 'hard evidence' of clinical examination.

XII. Conclusion

This paper has argued that using the capabilities approach to analyse reproductive health can be extremely useful in its focus on individual well-being while also taking into consideration relational processes of sexuality and reproduction. It shares with reproductive rights an underlying concern with social justice and human dignity, but it may be less controversial as an approach and less associated with western political traditions and experience in the minds of many in the South, and arguably more directly linked to well-being. As we have also seen, locating reproductive health within a capabilities approach also has advantages over the prevailing use of DALYs, which has nevertheless accorded significant weight to the disease burden associated with reproductive health, particularly for women. It is arguably the combination of the use of DALYs and an increasingly vocal lobby of reproductive health advocates at the international level that contributed to making at least maternal mortality a subject of the Millennium Development Goals. Capabilities nevertheless provide distinct advantages over DALYs in that firstly, they provide more room for an explicit consideration of the social context and consequences of poor reproductive health. Secondly, the framework underscores the connection between the latter and social inequalities and deprivation, a subject that, as has been argued here, has not been adequately researched.

Above all, since reproductive health advocates typically share the focus on social justice – and in particular a concern with gender inequalities – embodied within the capabilities approach, their adoption of this framework would allow them to engage with mainstream development practitioners without having to succumb to the utilitarian perspectives that promote family planning in order to enhance development as defined by the satisfaction of preferences, or to human capital approaches which see investment in education and health as a means of accelerating economic growth. If development is defined as enhancing well-being then efforts to promote reproductive health are inherent to that objective.

Yet if we follow Sen and Nussbaum and argue that capabilities, not actual functionings, are the appropriate claim for social justice, then there remain many methodological challenges in addressing the cultural, religious and ultimately political biases in society contributing to the widespread lack of capabilities to achieve reproductive health in the South. While both Sen and Nussbaum acknowledge such biases, the ultimate focus of capabilities is on the individual; even if buttressed by a concern with 'social arrangements,' this does not provide a clear path for addressing the social context of reproductive health methodologically.

What is clear is that far from being a technical and narrow biomedical concern, reproductive health is a field influenced by a complexity of social factors and social relations that require cross-disciplinarity if they are to be adequately understood (see introduction by Hulme and Toye to this volume). In this case, the barriers to such cross-disciplinarity lie in the divide between epidemiologists allied with economists on one side, with other branches of the social science – particularly those using qualitative approaches – on the other. Aggregate population statistics are critical, but they must be complemented by more localised qualitative studies that illuminate motivations, behaviours and health care processes as well as the social norms that stigmatise and obscure some of the most important reproductive health problems that blight the lives of women in developing countries.

Acknowledgements

The support of the UK Economic and Social Research Council is gratefully acknowledged. The work was part of the programme of the ESRC Global Poverty Research Group (grant no. M571255001). I am particularly grateful to John Toye for very useful comments on earlier drafts of this paper, and to two anonymous reviewers. I am also grateful to GPRG colleagues at the Universities of Manchester and Oxford for helpful comments when this paper was presented at a GPRG workshop.

Notes

1. Amartya Sen's lecture during the Preparatory Committee for the ICPD at the UN in New York, April 28, 1994, was arranged by the 'Eminent Citizens' Committee for Cairo '94' and was later published as Sen (1994a).
2. In this context, Sen (1994b: 334) notes that 'The case of the pregnant woman is quite different – this is exercise of a special *ability* rather than the existence of a disability, but she too has extra needs related to the act of procreation'.
3. Maternal mortality is officially defined as deaths to women in pregnancy, during childbirth or during the 40 days following delivery.

4. Sen's refusal to espouse a list is primarily due to his respect for democratic process and the danger of paternalism. According to Robeyns, Sen 'advocates equality of capability, but does not defend one particular aggregative principle' (Robeyns, 2000: Note 4) and in this sense, his approach to capabilities is not a full theory of justice.

5. In separate work, Sen has singled out exceptions to this ratio such as China and India with their 'missing women' where the ratio of women to men is less than 1. He argues this is due to systematic biases against girls and women in terms of health care and nutrition.

6. Sen and Rawls among others have written about how chronic disadvantage shapes preferences as one of the main arguments against utilitarian approaches to measuring welfare. In the case of women's employment, for example, a woman interviewed in a government survey may claim she is not looking for work merely because she lacks confidence in her own employability.

7. Views concerning abortion with Islam are beyond the scope of this paper but several schools of thought within Islam condone abortion so long as it occurs before the foetus is 'ensoulled' – widely understood to occur at three months (see Musallam, 1983). Among Middle Eastern countries, however, only Turkey and Tunisia have legalised abortion on request.

8. Graham et al. (2004); Drs. Oona Campbell and Veronique Filippi, London School of Hygiene and Tropical Medicine, personal communication, February 2003.

9. For further detail on the public health use of near misses, see Filippi (1998).

10. Vesico-vaginal fistulae (VVF) represent a health problem which occurs when a hole develops between the vagina and bladder of a pregnant woman during prolonged and obstructed labour. In some cases the fistulae develop between the rectum and the vagina causing recto-vaginal fistulae.

11. Female genital mutilation has been classified by the World Health Organization into four types ranging in severity from excision of the clitoris to 'infibulation', whereby the labia majora are sewn together, leaving only a small hole.

12. Again, the Islamic position on the practice of female genital mutilation is beyond the scope of this paper. Certainly however there is nothing in the Qur'an to condone the practice and it is widely perceived to be against it. In Egypt, however, there have been conflicting statements on the part of the religious establishment in a context of a growing politicisation of religion in that country.

13. In the calculation of the DALY, each health condition is assigned a disability weight ranging from 0 (health condition is equivalent to full health) to 1 (equivalent to death).

References

Abou Zahr, C. and Vaughan, P. (2000) Assessing the burden of sexual and reproductive ill-heath: questions regarding the use of disability-adjusted life years, *Bulletin of the World Health Organization*, 78(5), pp. 655–66.

Allotey, P. and Reidpath, D. (2002) Objectivity in priority setting tools: context and the DALY, *Reproductive Health Matters*, 10(20), pp. 38–46.

Anand, S. and Hanson, K. (2004) Disability-adjusted life years: a critical review, in S. Anand, F. Peter, and A. K. Sen (eds), *Public Health, Ethics and Equity*, pp. 183–99 (Oxford: Oxford University Press).

Bangser, M., Gumodoka, B. and Berege, Z. (1999) A comprehensive approach to vesico–vaginal fistulae: a project in Mwanza, Tanzania, in M. Berer and T. K. S. Ravindran (eds), *Safe Motherhood Initiatives: Critical Issues*, pp. 157–65 (Oxford: Blackwell).

Borghi, J., Hanson, K., Acquah, C. A., Ekanmien, G., Filippi, V., Ronsmans, C., Brugha, R., Browne, E. and Alihonou, E. (2003) Costs of near-miss obstetric complications for women and their families in Benin and Ghana, *Health Policy and Planning*, 18(4), pp. 383–90.

Burchardt, T. (2002) Constraint and opportunity: women's employment in Britain, paper presented at the conference on Promoting Women's Capabilities: Examining Nussbaum's Capabilities Approach, Von Hügel Institute, St Edmund's College, Cambridge University, 9–10 September.

Comim, F. (2001) Operationalising Sen's capability approach, paper presented at the confernce on Justice and Poverty: Examining Sen's Capability Approach, Von Hügel Institute, St Edmund's College, Cambridge University, 5–7 June.

Cook, R. J. (1995) Women's international human rights law: the way forward, in R. J. Cook (ed.), *Human Rights of Women: National and International Perspectives*, pp. 3–36 (Philadelphia: University of Pennsylvania Press).

Cottingham, J. and Myntti, C. (2002) Reproductive health: conceptual mapping and evidence, in G. Sen, A. George and P. Ostlin (eds), *Engendering International Health: the Challenge of Equity*, pp. 83–109 (London: MIT Press).

DeJong, J. (2000) The role and limitations of the Cairo international conference on population and development, *Social Science and Medicine*, 51, pp. 941–53.

De Waal, A. (1990) A re-assessment of entitlement theory in the light of recent famines in Africa, *Development and Change*, 21(3), pp. 469–90.

Donnay, F. and Weil, L. (2004) Obstetric fistula: the international response, *Lancet*, 363(9402), pp. 71–2.

Egyptian Ministry of Health (1993) *National Maternal Mortality Study* (Cairo: Ministry of Health).

El Dawla, A. S. (2000) Reproductive rights of Egyptian women: issues for debate, *Reproductive Health Matters*, 8(16), pp. 45–54.

Filippi, V. (1998) Near misses: maternal morbidity and mortality, *Lancet*, 351, pp. 145–6.

Freedman, L. (1999a) Reflections on emerging frameworks of health and human rights, in J. M. Mann, S. Gruskin, M. A. Grodin and G. J. Annas (eds), *Health and Human Rights: A Reader*, pp. 227–52 (New York: Routledge).

Freedman, L. (1999b) Censorship and manipulation of family planning information: an issue of human rights and women's health, in J. M. Mann, S. Gruskin, M. A. Grodin and G. J. Annas (eds), *Health and Human Rights: A Reader*, pp. 147–78 (New York: Routledge).

Gore, C. (1997) Irreducibly social goods and the informational basis of Amartya Sen's capability approach, *Journal of International Development*, 9(2), pp. 235–50.

Graham, W. J. and Campbell, O. M. (1992) Maternal health and the measurement trap, *Social Science and Medicine*, 5(8), pp. 967–77.

Graham, W. J., Fitzmaurice, A. E., Bell, J. S. and Cairns, J. A. (2004) The familial technique for linking maternal death with poverty, *The Lancet*, 363, pp. 23–7.

Hanson, K. (2002) Measuring up: gender, burden of disease and priority setting, in G. Sen, A. George and P. Ostlin (eds), *Engendering International Health: the Challenge of Equity*, pp. 313–45 (London: MIT Press).

Harcourt, W. (2001) The capabilities approach for poor women: empowerment strategies towards gender equality, health and well-being, paper presented at the conference on Justice and Poverty: Examining Sen's Capability Approach, Von Hügel Institute, St Edmund's College, Cambridge University, 5–7 June.

Kabakian-Khasholian, T., Campbell, O., Shediac-Rizkallah, M. and Ghorayeb, F. (2000) Women's experiences of maternity care: satisfaction or passivity? *Social Science and Medicine*, 51, pp. 103–13.

Khattab, H., Younis, N. and Zurayk, H. (1999) *Women, Reproduction, and Health in Rural Egypt: The Giza Study* (Cairo: The American University of Cairo Press).

Loudon, I. (2000) Maternal mortality in the past and its relevance to developing countries today, *American Journal of Clinical Nutrition*, 72(1), pp. 241–6.

Maine, D. (1999) What is so special about maternal mortality? in M. Berer and T. K. S. Ravindran (eds), *Safe Motherhood Initiatives: Critical Issues*, pp. 175–82 (Oxford: Blackwell).

Musallam, B. F. (1983) *Sex and Society in Islam: Birth Control Before the Nineteenth Century* (Cambridge: Cambridge University Press).

Nussbaum, M. C. (2000) *Women and Human Development: the Capabilities Approach* (Cambridge: Cambridge University Press).

Petchesky, R. and Judd, K. (1998) *Negotiating Reproductive Rights: Women's Perspectives Across Countries and Cultures* (London: Zed Books).

Rawls, J. (1971) *A Theory of Justice* (London: Oxford University Press).

Reidpath, D., Allotey, P. A., Kouame, A. and Cummins, R. (2003) Measuring health in a vacuum: examining the disability weight of the DALY, *Health Policy and Planning*, 18(4), pp. 351–56.

Robeyns, I. (2000) An unworkable idea or a promising alternative? Sen's capability approach re-examined, *Discussion Paper Series 00.30*, Centre for Economic Studies, University of Leuven.

Robeyns, I. (2002) Sen's capability approach and gender inequality, paper presented at the conference on *Promoting Women's Capabilities: Examining Nussbaum's Capabilities Approach*, Von Hügel Institute, St. Edmund's College, Cambridge University, 9–10 September.

Sadana, R. (2000) Measuring reproductive health: review of community-based approaches to assessing morbidity, *Bulletin of the World Health Organization*, 78(5), pp. 640–54.

Saith, R. and Harriss-White, B. (1999) The gender sensitivity of well-being indicators, *Development and Change*, 30, pp. 465–97.

Sen, A. K. (1989) Women's survival as a development problem, *Bulletin of American Academy of Arts and Sciences*, 43, pp. 14–29.

Sen, A. K. (1992) *Inequality Reexamined* (Oxford: Oxford University Press).

Sen, A. K. (1993) Capability and well-being, in A. K. Sen and M. C. Nussbaum (eds), *The Quality of Life*, pp. 30–53 (Oxford: Clarendon Press).

Sen, A. K. (1994a) Population: delusion and reality, *New York Review of Books*, 41(15), pp. 62–71.

Sen, A. K. (1994b) Well-being, capability and public policy, *Giornale degli Economiste Annali de Econ*, 3(7/9), pp. 333–47.

Sen, A. K. (1999) *Development as Freedom* (Oxford: Oxford University Press).

Sen, A. K. (2002) Why health equity? *Health Economics*, 11(8), pp. 659–66.

Sen, G., Germain, A. and Chen, L. (1994) *Population Policies Reconsidered: Health, Empowerment and Rights* (Boston: Harvard University Press).

Standing, H. (2002) An overview of changing agendas in health sector reform, *Reproductive Health Matters*, 10(20), pp. 19–28.

Tsui, A., Waserheit, J. N. and Jaaga, J. G. (eds) (1997) *Reproductive Health in Developing Countries* (Washington, DC: National Academy Press).

Unterhalter, E. (2002) The capabilities approach and gendered education: an examination of South African contradictions, paper presented at the conference on Promoting Women's Capabilities: Examining Nussbaum's Capabilities Approach, Von Hügel Institute, St. Edmund's College, Cambridge University, 9–10 September.

World Bank (1993) *World Development Report: Investing in Health* (Oxford: Oxford University Press).

Development and Social Capital

MARCEL FAFCHAMPS

I. Introduction

The purpose of this paper is to reflect, from an economist's point of view, on the methodological issues raised by the study of social capital. This term has been used in many different ways to cover a broad range of phenomena (e.g., Dasgupta and Serageldin, 2000; Grootaert and van Bastelaer 2002a; Durlauf and Fafchamps, 2005). Perhaps it is best seen as a way of federating research programs in various social sciences (Woolcock and Narayan, 2000). If so, the quest for an all-encompassing definition may be futile or even counter-productive, because different disciplines need to appropriate the term differently depending on how it fits in their paradigm. What is important is that the phrase social capital facilitates the exchange of ideas across disciplines.

Human societies are complex combinations of individuals, institutions and networks of personal relationships. Up to now, economists have focused primarily on individuals and institutions (e.g., markets, firms, governments, households). For a long time they did well by ignoring the middle ground, the networks of personal relationships that oil the system and bring it to life. These personal relationships are important because they are the locale where human emotions are realized. While economists can deal with subjective beliefs and with a wide range individual preferences (including addiction, criminal tendencies, thirst for power, etc), their models are not equipped to accommodate human emotions such as trust, anger and spite – especially when these emotions are directed at specific individuals. It is not that these emotions have been entirely ignored by economists (e.g., Akerlof and Kranton, 2000; Becker, 1968; Barr, 2002b, c), but they often violate the assumption of rationality and thus do not fit into the paradigm. This remains largely true to this day.

In my view, economists' reluctance to delve into the world of emotions is because they intuitively realize the possible consequences. They understand the usefulness of understanding emotions for positive work – as illustrated for instance in experimental work on shame and guilt (e.g., Barr, 2002a, b). But they fear the repercussions on their normative work. Economics concerns itself with government policy and firm behavior. By assuming that people are rational and cold-headed, economists propose policies that are organized around financial incentives. Individuals then respond to these incentives of their own free will. Focusing on emotions for policy design would produce a very different kind of policy instruments such as propaganda (for governments) and advertising (for firms). As a rule, economists see these as ways of manipulating the public by deceiving them and playing with their emotions – even if it is for a 'good cause'. Anyone who worries about the use fascist and communist governments made of propaganda should perhaps be grateful that economics, as a science, has resisted focusing on emotions and human irrationality.

Leaving emotions aside, there remains the issue of networks. Up to recently, the economist's toolbox was not powerful enough to deal with the complexity brought by networks. This, however, is slowly changing, with much new theoretical work on networks (e.g., Bala and Goyal, 2000; Kranton and Minehart, 2001). It is likely that, over the next few years, economic theory will move further into the study of networks. This should lay the foundations for a detailed economic research agenda focusing on social capital.

Empirical work on social capital by economists has already begun, without necessarily waiting for a detailed theoretical framework (e.g., Keefer and Knack, 1997; Narayan and Pritchett, 1999; Fafchamps and Minten, 2002). The World Bank has been particularly active in encouraging multidisciplinary research on social capital (e.g., Grootaert and van Bastelaer, 2002b; Woolcock and Narayan, 2000; Bebbington et al., 2004). This effort is best illustrated by the two volumes on the subject edited by Dasgupta and Serageldin (2000) and by Grootaert and van Bastelaer (2002a). The purpose of this paper is less ambitious. Our aim is to raise a number of issues relative to empirical work on social capital, with a particular emphasis on equity and development. We first discuss a number of conceptual issues, seeking to clarify some of the confusion surrounding work on social capital. We then draw lessons for empirical work.

II. Conceptual Framework

To organize the discussion, we focus on the role that interpersonal relationships and social networks play in the efficiency of social exchange. By social exchange, we mean any form of human exchange, whether material or immaterial, economic or social. The exchange of goods for money – i.e., the market – falls under this definition. So does the provision of public goods, which can be seen as the outcome of a joint production process.

As Hayek (1945) was the first to point out, information asymmetries are an inescapable feature of human society. As a result, exchange is hindered either because agents who could benefit from trade cannot find each other, or because, having found each other, they do not trust each other enough to trade. In either case, mutually beneficial exchange does not take place. Similar principles apply to the provision of public goods. Search and trust are thus two fundamental determinants of the efficiency of social exchange. If we can finds ways of facilitating search and of fostering trust, we can improve social exchange.

There are basically two ways of achieving this dual objective: via formal institutions (e.g., stock exchange) or via interpersonal relationships (e.g., word-of-mouth). The literature on social capital focuses principally on the latter. In the following pages we illustrate how social capital can raise efficiency. We begin by examining the possible effects of social capital on search. We then turn to trust. Public goods are discussed in the following sub-section. The relationship between social capital and development is examined next. The last sub-section explores the relationship between social capital and equity.

Social Capital and Search

In order to illustrate the role of social capital in search, it is useful to compare US equity and labor markets. Thanks to the existence of a stock market, it is very easy for a seller of stock to find a buyer at the market clearing price. This is not the case in labor markets where there is no equivalent institution circulating accurate and up-to-date information about jobs and workers.

In his path-breaking study of the US labor market, Granovetter (1995) brought to light the role played by interpersonal relationships in channeling information about jobs and job applicants. A large proportion of jobs are allocated on the basis of personal recommendation and word-of-mouth. Fafchamps and Minten (1999) provide evidence that agricultural traders often rely on personal relationships to obtain information about market conditions and to identify trade opportunities. These phenomena can be understood as an endogenous, spontaneous adaptation to the absence of a formal clearing house equivalent to the stock market.

As this comparison demonstrates, observing that social capital plays a role in markets does not, by itself, constitute evidence that social capital is necessary and should be nurtured. In economies with sufficient organizational capacity, the development of formal institutions may be a superior alternative. This is not to say that formal institutions are always superior. Setting up a stock exchange or commodity exchange, for instance, facilitates trade. But it is an extremely costly endeavor and it restricts entry into brokerage since brokers have to put a very large bond and the space on the exchange floor is typically restricted. For many markets, investing in a formal exchange would not make economic sense. In these markets, reliance on informal networks is likely to be optimal. Intervention can then focus on fostering 'social capital', that is, on a smoother and more accurate dissemination of information through informal networks and business associations.

By changing the cost of setting up a formal institution, technological change can improve the cost-effectiveness of formal solutions to information sharing and coordination problems. A good illustration of this idea is the partial replacement of personal network-based exchange by anonymous Internet-based exchange (e.g., Ebay) for goods such as collectibles or secondhand durables. Whether informal institutions are more efficient than formal institutions thus depends on the relative costs and benefits of each. While informal institutions typically generate smaller benefits because their reach is limited, they also cost less because they free-ride on other social activities – e.g., people exchanging information about job prospects while attending a wedding. Other things being equal, we expect the cost of formal institutions to fall with the organizational capacity of an economy. Consequently, we anticipate that technologies that improve organization capacity – such as telecommunication and information technology – may enable an economy to switch from informal to formal institutions for the purpose of solving information sharing and coordination problems, such as matching in thin markets.

Social Capital, Trust and Efficient Exchange

As argued in Fafchamps (2002), trust can be understood as an optimistic expectation or belief regarding other agents' behavior. The origin of trust may vary. Sometimes, trust arises from repeated interpersonal interaction. Other times, it arises from general knowledge about the population of agents, the incentives they face, and the upbringing they have received (Platteau, 1994). The former can be called personalized trust and the latter generalized trust. The main difference between the two is that, for each pair of newly matched agents, the former takes time and effort to establish while the latter is instantaneous.

In most situations, trusting others enables economic agents to operate more efficiently – e.g., by invoicing for goods they have delivered or by agreeing to stop hostilities. Whenever this is the case, generalized trust yields more efficient outcomes than personalized trust. The reason is that, for any pair of agents, generalized trust is established faster and more cheaply than personal trust. This observation has long been made in the anthropological literature on generalized morality. Fostering generalized trust can thus potentially generate large efficiency gains. How this can be accomplished, however, is unclear.

Clubs and networks are different concepts having to do with the structure of links among economic agents. Clubs describe finite, closed groupings. Networks describe more complex situations in which individual agents are related only to some other agents, not all. The term 'network' is sometimes used to describe the entire set of links among a finite collection of agents. Other times, it is used to describe the set of links around a specific individual. To avoid confusion, we call the second concept subjective network.

Among other things, clubs and networks can be used to describe the extent to which personalized and generalized trust exist in a population. Perfect generalized trust corresponds to the case where all agents belong to a single club (or complete network) and trust all other members. Situations in which generalized trust exists only among sub-populations (say, Jewish diamond dealers in New York–Bernstein, 1992) could be described as small clubs. Situations in which individual agents only trust a limited number of agents they know individually can be described as a network.

From the above discussion, it is immediately clear that, since trust is beneficial for economic efficiency, the loss from imperfect trust can be visualized as the difference between the actual trust network and the minimum network that would support all mutually beneficial trades. Following this reasoning, inefficiency is expected to be highest in societies where the trust network is very sparse (Granovetter, 1995). Inefficiency will also be large when sub-groups who could trade with each other are unconnected, even if many links exist within each sub-group (e.g., Bloch et al., 2004; Goyal et al., 2004).

Based on empirical work in a dozen of African countries, Fafchamps (2004) studies in detail the relationship between market efficiency and level of institutional development. From this work it appears that legal institutions play a minor role in African markets, except in some countries and among larger firms. The reason is that in a poor economy most market transactions are too small to justify court action and most people have no assets to foreclose upon. As a result, relational contracting dominates markets, especially in manufacturing. Social networks play a paramount role in circulating information and facilitating the formation of new exchange relationships. Similar processes are also present in developed economies, as shown for instance by the work of Bernstein (1992, 1996), although they probably play a less prominent role.

In a market environment dominated by relational contracting, formal institutions can broaden the scope for exchange in many different ways. Business registration and ID card allow contractual parties to be identified unambiguously – and thus to be traced in case of breach of contract. Grading, standards, and ISO certification facilitate quality assessment. Credit reference agencies circulate market information beyond the range of social networks, thereby facilitating screening. A free press (with safeguards against slandering and defamation) publicizes the most outrageous cases of opportunistic behavior. Labor exchange, temp agencies and headhunting firms circulate information about job applicants. Organized exchanges (e.g., stock and commodity exchanges, foreign exchange auction) reduce the risk of contractual breach through various institutional mechanisms – e.g., externally audited accounts, posting of bond, internal scrutiny). As the above list illustrates, lawyers and courts are only part of the formal institutional infrastructure required for efficient market exchange. In practice, markets work best when formal institutions serve to expand the scope of social networks and to broaden the range of possible exchange. Although they may be impersonal, true markets are nearly never anonymous: the identity of the other party is nearly always essential, to the point that a brand or firm name has a value per se (Tadelis, 1999). The only truly anonymous markets are the least developed ones, e.g., roadside vendors on streets and markets in the developing world.

Social Capital and Public Goods

In the preceding sub-section we discussed the role of trust in fostering exchange. Trust is also an essential ingredient in the delivery of public goods. In many cases, the state can organize the provision of public goods by taxing individuals.

Whenever this is true, trust is not essential. But there are many forms of public goods that cannot be harnessed through state intervention.

In his work on PTA run schools, for instance, Coleman (1988) shows that parental involvement in school affairs has a beneficial external effect on student achievement, probably because it leads children to believe their parents care about their education. Parental involvement, in turn, requires trust to reduce and solve interpersonal conflicts and to minimize fears of free-riding. In this example, the externality is a public good that cannot be harnessed by state intervention. Voluntary participation by parents is essential.

In poor countries, there are many situations in which the state could, theoretically, intervene to provide a public good, but is unable to do so because its tax base and its capacity to organize are limited. Collective action can serve as substitute to the state. However, because it cannot rely on the coercive action of the state (e.g., the ability to tax and enforce contracts), collective action is much harder to set in motion. Two essential ingredients are then required: leadership and trust. A leader is required who is capable of convincing community members that they should voluntarily contribute to the public good. Trust is necessary to resolve conflicts among competing interests and to reduce fears of free-riding. Leaders can also help raise the level of trust in the community.

What the above discussion indicates is that delivering public goods via voluntary organizations depends critically on local trust and leadership. If these ingredients are absent, for instance after a civil war, outside intervention by the state or by development agencies may in some cases be faster than waiting for trust between communities to be rebuilt (e.g., Bigombe et al., 2000; Collier and Hoeffler, 2002). The success of this approach depends critically on the state of the infrastructure and means of communication needed for outside intervention. Furthermore, good local leaders are rare. Projects that work well in one place because of strong local involvement need not be replicable elsewhere if local leaders are weak. Pilot projects of public good delivery through local communities may provide wrong signals if their placement is correlated with the presence of good local leaders who managed to attract the pilot project to their community.

Social Capital and Development

In a well publicized book, Putnam et al. (1993) argue that northern Italy developed faster than southern Italy because the former was better endowed in social capital – measured as membership in groups and clubs. This book triggered a plethora of research purposing to show that social capital favors growth (Keefer and Knack, 1997).

In his latest book, however, Putnam himself undermines the very foundation of the new mantra he created. Focusing on the US experience since the 1950s, Putnam shows that social capital, defined as membership in formal and informal clubs, has declined monotonically since the 1950s. This is true for all states, all decades, and all measures of social capital. Moreover, he finds no relationship between the speed of the decline and economic performance across US states or across time periods. For instance, the 1990s were a period of rapid growth in the US but also of rapid decline in social capital.

Putnam worries about the demise of social capital in the US. An alternative interpretation of his findings is that, because generalized trust has improved over the period studied, club membership has become less necessary. In contrast, the Italian experience related to an earlier period in which generalized trust was insufficient or incomplete and small clubs helped broaden the range of personalized trust.

This raises the possibility that clubs and networks are important at intermediate levels of development. Their function is to broaden the range and speed of social exchange beyond the confines of personalized trust. But once a sufficiently high level of generalized trust has been achieved, clubs and networks are no longer necessary and wither away (North, 2001).

This is not the interpretation given by Putnam, who presents the rise in lawyers and lawsuits per capita as evidence that generalized trust has fallen. An increased reliance on lawyers and courts does not, by itself, constitute evidence against generalized trust, however. As Bigsten et al. (2001) and Fafchamps and Minten (2001) have shown, when legal institutions are weak and generalized trust absent, economic agents are extremely careful in their dealings with people they do not know. As a result, breach of contract is fairly rare and when it occurs it is resolved through face-to-face negotiations. An improvement in legal institutions may induce economic agents to deal with people they do not know. The willingness to deal with strangers is precisely what we have called generalized trust. Because dealing with strangers is more risky, however, this normally leads to a rise in the absolute number of cases of breach which in turn results in more lawsuits.

This can easily be illustrated with a simple example. Consider an economy with two types of borrowers: weak and bad, in proportions $1 - \beta$ and β. Bad agents never repay. Weak agents repay if deterrence is high, and do not repay if it is low. When deterrence is low, nobody repays. Consequently lenders do not lend; there is market failure. When deterrence is high, lenders get repaid with probability $1 - \beta$. They can also sue defaulting borrowers and recover a fraction $\varepsilon > 0$ of the principal. Let the cost of funds be r. Competition between lenders sets the interest rate on loans i such that

$$\beta\varepsilon + (1 - \beta)(1 + i) \geq 1 + r \qquad\qquad (2.1)$$

As long as i satisfies (2.1), it is in the interest of lenders to lend. It follows that in the low deterrence state, there is no trade and no lawsuit while in the high deterrence state, there is trade and lawsuits on a proportion β of all loans. Better contract enforcement institutions have raised generalized trust and trade while at the same time resulting in more default and lawsuits.

Using detailed survey data from the 1990s, Fafchamps (2004) compares contract enforcement among manufacturers in Ghana, Kenya and Zimbabwe. He finds that Zimbabwe has better courts than the other two countries and that Zimbabwean firms are more likely to deal with people they do not know. But Zimbabwe also has more breach. Because Zimbabwean firms know each other less well, they are also less likely to resolve contractual disputes through negotiations and more likely to go to court. This empirical evidence illustrates that an increase in generalized trust can go hand in hand with an absolute rise in the incidence of breach and lawsuits.

A similar kind of reasoning can be followed for public goods. In undeveloped economies, the state is weak and underfunded. Consequently it cannot organize the delivery of all needed public goods. This is particularly true for local public goods or for public goods that require a modicum of voluntary involvement to limit free-riding (of which corruption is but one manifestation).

Social capital provides an alternative. This idea was first put forth by de Soto (1989) and recently revisited by Rose (2000b, 2000a) in his work on Russia. Clubs formed for non-economic purposes (e.g., religious worship, political parties) have leaders. In the absence of public good provision by the state, these leaders may decide to mobilize club members (e.g., the religious congregation) to provide missing public goods. History is replete with examples of churches and Islamic fraternities intervening to build schools and clinics and to provide a variety of public services. Here, sharing a common religious fervor is the basis for trust and the religious hierarchy provides the necessary leaders. Some large secular organizations have adopted similar practices – e.g., Communist parties yesterday, international NGOs today.

These issues have an immediate bearing on empirical work on social capital. The difficulty comes from the fact that first best can in principle be achieved without paying attention to clubs and networks. Generalized trust in commercial contracts, for instance, can theoretically be achieved via laws and courts. Thanks to taxation, public goods can in principle be organized by the state at lower cost in terms of public mobilization and leadership skills. As North (1973) has argued, the rise of the western world is precisely due to the invention of institutions that protect property rights and make the state more effective at delivering public goods. Clubs, networks and community-based voluntary organizations can improve efficiency in economic exchange and public good delivery. But they are second-best solutions. The first best approach is to get legal institutions and state organization in order.

Whether or not social capital raises efficiency therefore depends on the level of institutional development. Suppose that laws and courts are insufficient to ensure the respect of commercial contracts. This situation can arise anywhere (Bernstein, 1996) but it is probably most severe in poor countries where many transactions are small and buyers and sellers are too poor for court action to yield reparation (e.g., Bigsten et al., 2000; Fafchamps and Minten, 2001). In such an environment, market exchange relies on a combination of personalized trust, legal institutions (e.g., to enforce large contracts and to punish thieves) and informal institutions (e.g., reputation sharing within business networks and communities). Whether or not social capital facilitates exchange can then be seen as a test of the strength and reach of formal institutions.

A similar reasoning holds for public goods. Public good delivery is best accomplished when the power of the state to tax and mobilize resources is combined with trust and community involvement. The reason is that, without voluntarily accepted discipline, government action is ineffective: taxes do not get paid, rules are not followed, civil servants become corrupt, and free-riding reigns. Discipline in turn depends on the perceived legitimacy of government action and the degree of public involvement in the decision-making process. It also depends on identification with the political elites, sense of national urgency, and many other factors which are still poorly understood. The bottom line, however, is clear: without some form of voluntary acceptance by the public, government efforts to provide public goods are likely to fail. Social capital is thus probably essential for public good delivery. But the form it may take are likely to vary a lot, i.e., from generalized trust in government and formal institutions to interpersonal trust mobilized via clubs and networks.

Social Capital and Equity

We have argued that trust is essential to both economic exchange and public good delivery. We have also argued that clubs and networks can facilitate search and provide an imperfect substitute to generalized trust. Unlike generalized trust, however, clubs and networks often have distributional consequences that may be quite inequitable. The reason is that, compared to generalized trust, clubs and networks only offer a partial or uneven coverage of society.

Reading some of the literature on social capital, one sometimes has the impression that social capital naturally goes hand in hand with equity (e.g., Uphoff and Wijayaratna, 2000; Robison et al., 2002). In practice, whether social capital improves or worsens the distribution of welfare depends on the distribution of social capital and the strength of positive and negative externalities.

Consider first the case in which the benefits of social capital principally accrue to those who 'have it', e.g., to members of a club or network.[1] They benefit from increased efficiency while non-members benefit less or not at all. As Taylor (2000) and Fafchamps (2002) have shown, the creation of clubs or networks can penalize non-members. This is because members of a club or network find it easier to deal with each other and, as a result, may stop dealing with non-members. If non-members are richer to start with, building social capital among the poor may improve equity. There is no reason, however, to expect that social capital is in general easier to build among the poor. Social capital takes time and resources. While the poor may have more time,[2] they have fewer resources. In many cases, richer members of society are richer precisely because they have more social capital. In my work on firms and traders, I have often found that entrepreneurs with better social capital indeed have higher incomes, so that social capital has a unequalizing effect.

In some special cases, it is possible for social capital to increase efficiency but reduce the welfare of members relative to non-members. This arises when externalities are very strong so that members and non-members benefit from the existence of social capital, but only members bear the cost of creating the externality. An example of such a situation is when only some village members voluntarily contribute to the provision of a non-rival public good (Baland and Platteau, 1995). In this case, social capital raises welfare for the village as a whole but the cost of generating the welfare gains is unequally distributed. Whether this improves or worsens equity in the village depends on whether non-contributors are richer or poorer than contributors. We discuss externalities more in details in the next section.

As the above discussion illustrates, the distributional effects of social capital depend critically on club or network membership. Consider again the case in which social capital benefits those who have it. In this case, clubs and networks are least conducive to equity when membership is restricted to a specific group (e.g., men or Whites) or when new members are not accepted (e.g., established firms only). Even when new members are accepted without restriction, historical events can shape the composition of clubs for decades whenever entry is slow. In this case, equal opportunity need not be realized because old members have enjoyed the benefits of membership for much longer. By extension, clubs are likely to have undesirable consequences on equity whenever (1) club membership is beneficial to members; and (2) entry into the club is not instantaneous. Put differently, clubs raise equity concerns whenever they have real economic benefits.

The creation of clubs may thus reinforce polarization in society between the 'in' group and the 'out' group. Investing in social capital by promoting clubs can thus have serious equity repercussions. This is true even if we ignore the fact that certain clubs may collude to explicitly dominate or exclude others (e.g., Ku-Klux-Klan, mafia) (Gambetta, 1993). A similar situation arises with networks because better connected individuals profit from their contacts (Fafchamps and Minten, 2002). Social capital can be used by certain groups to overtake others, generating between-group inequality and political tension. To the extent that between-group inequality itself favors crime and riots and deters investment, promoting social capital by promoting specific groups may, in the long-run, be counterproductive. Of course, at a given point in time, fostering social capital among a specific group may appear as the best way to counteract an existing disadvantage. But once the group is successfully created, the forces we have discussed here kick in and may have unwanted consequences in the long run.

III. Estimating Returns to Social Capital

Having clarified the relationship between social capital and the efficiency of social exchange, we now turn to the statistical analysis of social capital. Borrowing heavily from Durlauf and Fafchamps (2005), we first ask whether it is possible to uncover social capital effects from the sorts of data available to social scientists. In particular, we discuss the issue of identification, that is, of whether a role for social capital can be distinguished from other social effects that may be present. Then, we revisit the points raised earlier, such as the distinction between individual and aggregate efficiency effects.

The inference questions that we raise here are not specific to economics or to the study of social capital. They apply to inference in general. But the form these inference questions take is shared by many empirical studies of social capital, so that it is useful to discuss them in this context. A growing number of empirical papers on social capital seek to address the various inference issues discussed here. A detailed review of the empirical literature can be found in Durlauf and Fafchamps (2005). What this reviews shows is that, although progress has been made, much remains to be done. Here we limit ourselves to a brief overview of the main estimation issues.

Identification

The first problem that empirical work on social capital must solve is that of identification. In practice, much work on social capital takes the form of comparing groups or individuals with different levels of social capital. How social capital is measured varies from study to study. But it is common to use membership in a group or network as measure of social capital. For instance, Putnam (2000) uses membership in choirs and business association as well as indicators of socialization. Coleman (1988) compares school performance depending on whether parents participate to the management of the school through parent-teacher associations. Granovetter (1995) measures membership in networks. Fafchamps and Minten (2002) use the number of traders known.

In all these cases, a performance indicator – regional development, school performance, job market performance, or productivity – is compared across groups or individuals with different values of the social capital measure. Formally, let O_i be the performance indicator for individual or group i and let S_i be its social capital measure. Inference is then organized by testing whether:

$$E[O_i|S_i \text{ is high}] > E[O_i|S_i \text{ is low}]$$

In economics, this is typically achieved by regressing O_i on S_i and a series of controls Z_i. The same idea can be implemented via a simple t-test or, in a case study framework, by compiling evidence from multiple sources without necessarily imposing a formal statistical test.

In all these cases, correct inference requires that, conditional on Z_i, the two populations – those with low S_i and those with high S_i – be similar in other respects. If this condition is not satisfied, a difference in O_i levels between the two populations might be mistakenly interpreted as the result of social capital differences while it is due to other factors correlated with the social capital measure.

There are many possible sources of such omitted variable bias in the study of social capital. Here are a few:

- Leadership: In Section II we discussed the role of leadership in harnessing voluntary contributions to a public good. Suppose communities with good leaders have better outcomes. If leaders choose to set up associations to channel local efforts, then communities with an association will have a better outcome even though an association without a leader would not deliver equivalent performance. This problem is particularly severe when performance is measured in term of public good delivery. Community leaders often play a crucial role in fostering the creation of social capital – e.g., membership drive – that they can harness for a particular goal. Observing a relationship between social capital and the presence of a public good may be due to the presence of a third, unobserved factor: leadership. The distinction between the two effects is important for policy because good community leaders are rare and leadership is much harder to replicate than groups.

  One possible solution to this difficulty is to collect information about potential leaders in all populations, for instance by gathering information about the education level, entrepreneurial experience, and the like. This is difficult to do because the researcher does not know a priori who could be a leader. This means that, in practice, controlling for leadership is extremely cumbersome unless one is willing to assume that the identity of the leader is exogenous – e.g., the village chief.

Another possible solution is to opt for an experimental design and to exogenously change leadership, for instance by introducing an NGO into the community. For the experimental design to be convincing, the treatment effect must be randomly distributed; it cannot be correlated with the social capital measure. Experimental methods are gaining ground in development economics, and we can hope to soon have results of such experiments.

- Institutions: In Section II we discussed the role of trust in social exchange and argued that trust can be fostered either by formal institutions or by interpersonal relationships. We made the point that social capital can be a second-best response to the absence of formal institutions: in the absence of a labor exchange, interpersonal relationships facilitate job search. Should formal institutions be more effective, however, relying on interpersonal exchange may become unnecessary (Kranton, 1996). This reasoning can be used to explain Putnam's (2000) finding of a widespread decrease in measures of association at a time when the US economy was growing rapidly. Reliance on interpersonal relationships and networks may thus be seen as a symptom that formal institutions do not work well.

To illustrate how this might impact statistical analysis, suppose we have data on labor markets in different countries and we seek to estimate whether the density of social networks raises the average quality of the match between workers and employers. Suppose for the sake of argument that we have a convincing measure for the average quality of the match. Regressing this measure on the density of social networks is likely to yield incorrect results if the researcher does not control for differences in formal institutions across the countries. For instance, employment offices may play an active match-making role in some countries.[3] Failing to control for employment offices would underestimate the effect of social capital. In fact, if employment offices channel information more efficiently than interpersonal networks and if these networks arise in response to the absence of employment office, countries with more networks will have less efficient labor markets.[4]

This reasoning can be generalized as follows. Depending on the context, social capital can either be a complement or a substitute for formal institutions, a point that has been investigated empirically for instance by Grootaert and Narayan (2004). In the example above, social capital is a substitute for formal institutions. To the extent that formal institutions achieve more efficient social exchange than social capital, this may explain Putnam's reverse finding that:

$$E[O_i|S_i \text{ is high}] < E[O_i|S_i \text{ is low}]$$

If social capital is a complement, such as a formal business association (e.g., Hendley, 1999; Ayouz et al., 2002), we will observe a positive association between social capital and performance, without being able to disentangle the respective effects of institutions and social capital. To distinguish the two, one would need observations with and without institutions as well as with and without social capital. In general this is difficult to obtain while keeping the populations similar in other respects. Here too an experimental approach is possible, for instance by phasing in a new institutions over a period of years in a random fashion.

- Group effects: Leadership and institutions are examples of unobserved group effects, i.e., of a factor not observed by the researcher that favors both performance and social capital. There are potentially many other source of group effects, such as commonality of language and religion, co-residence, common interests, and the like. Depending on the context, these factors may have an effect on performance while at the same time be correlated with the social capital measure. In all these cases, inference can be distorted by omitted variable bias. The solution is to collect information about all these possible group effects. As the number of controls grows, so does the size of the sample required for inference purposes.

- Self-selection: This is a concept similar to group effects, but operating at the level of individuals. Say unobserved individual effects cause certain people to self-select into the association or group used as measure of social capital. Further suppose that these individual effects are correlated with individual performance, i.e., that people more likely to join the association are also more likely to be high performers. For instance, suppose that smooth-talking is important for business. Further suppose that smooth-talkers, because they enjoy talking, join more association and have more acquaintances. Comparing performance across members and non-members without controlling for self-selection would attribute to social capital – membership in the association – what might in fact be due to unobserved individual effects – smooth-talking.

- Endogeneity: In a world where formal institutions are insufficient and social capital is a substitute for good institutions, the need for social capital will be highest where the need for social exchange is highest. Consequently, individuals are likely to make more effort creating social capital when the potential returns are high. If one uses returns to social exchange as performance measure, one would obtain a positive association between O_i and S_i due to reverse causation: it is when O_i is high that S_i is created. A good example of this situation is agricultural trade: large traders may know more traders precisely because they trade with more people. The econometric solution to this problem is to 'instrument' S_i by regressing it on factors unaffected by O_i (such as parental background, education, and the like). Illustrations of this approach can now be found in numerous papers, notably in many of the papers on social capital produced by the World Bank as well as in Carter and Maluccio (2003), Maluccio et al., (2000), Haddad and Maluccio (2003), Fafchamps (2003) and Fafchamps and Minten (2002).

- Reflexivity: as first pointed out by Manski (1993), the empirical study of group externalities is subject to a special king of econometric problem which he called the reflection problem. The difficulty comes from the fact that, if my actions are influenced by the action of others, then my own action influences that of others as well. Consequently regressing my action (or the outcome of my action) on that of others is subject to endogeneity bias. Reflexivity bias is particularly a concern when seeking to document peer effects, for instance by regressing the school performance of a pupil on the test scores of other children in the class. Brock and Durlauf (2001) have discussed in detail the identification issues raised by reflexivity, with a special emphasis on applications to social capital analysis. More work is necessary in this area.

What the above discussion illustrates is that empirical work on social capital is fraught with danger. While the problems listed above are not specific to social capital, they have often been ignored in early empirical analysis. The purpose of our discussion is to convince the reader that one should be cautious not to make exorbitant claims about social capital without having sought to minimize the various sources of bias listed above.

Aggregate versus individual effects

Durlauf and Fafchamps (2005) discuss the difficulty of disentangling aggregate and individual effects of social capital. They begin by noting that identifying the effect of social capital from data on groups (e.g., associations, countries) is difficult. Estimating individual returns is easier because the number of observations is higher, therefore making it easier to control for the various effects discussed in the previous sub-section. Unfortunately, individual returns to social capital often are poor predictors of aggregate effects.

This is best illustrated by focusing attention on two specific processes: fallacy of composition and strong externalities. A fallacy of composition arises whenever social capital pegs individuals against each other. Relative to a situation without social capital, competition for a finite resource or market means that the gains made by those with more social capital lead to losses for those without. Strong externalities can lead to the opposite result in which social gains are larger than those appropriated by the owners of social capital. Once again these problems are not specific to social capital – they also arise in the study of human capital, for instance. But they are sufficiently pervasive in social capital analysis to deserve a detailed discussion.

We illustrate how fallacy of composition may affect the estimation of social capital effects with the help of a simple job search example. Suppose there are M job openings and N job seekers, all identical, with $N > M$. Suppose that employer and workers do not know each other and are matched at random. Since $N > M$, all positions are filled and each worker has an equal probability of getting a job M/N. Total surplus is the sum of employer and worker surplus. Since all workers are equivalent, total surplus is the same irrespective of which workers get the available jobs.

Next suppose that, thanks to interpersonal connections, a group of workers C hears about the open positions before other workers. Further suppose that $C < M$. Consequently C workers get a job with probability 1. Other workers get the remaining jobs with probability $\frac{M-C}{N-C}$ which is smaller than $\frac{M}{N}$. Total surplus is unchanged since workers are equivalent. Social capital – in this case the existence of a better connected group of workers – thus has no effect on the efficiency of social exchange. But it has important distributional consequences, which can be measured by regressing the probability of obtaining a job on group membership. Doing so in our example would yield a coefficient of $1 - \frac{M-C}{N-C}$ on membership in the group even though the net effect of social capital on aggregate welfare is zero. What this example illustrates is that social capital can have private returns even when it has no effect other than distributional on the efficiency of social exchange. Observing private returns to social capital should therefore not be construed as evidence that social capital is socially beneficial. In our example, it is actually discriminatory. The above reasoning can be extended to situations where groups, not individuals, compete with each other (Durlauf and Fafchamps, 2005).

It is also possible that social capital has beneficial effects on social welfare but yields no individual returns. This may arise when social capital only has 'external' effects, such as the provision of a non-rival public good. To illustrate this possibility, consider N groups of fisherman tapping the same fishing ground.[5] Without collective action, there is over-fishing. Suppose that fishing groups with better social capital enforce self-restraint while others do not. Gains from self-restraint are shared among all fishermen, irrespective of whether they have social capital or not. Social capital increases social welfare but fishermen with less social capital have higher profit because they benefit from the self-restraint of others without having to incur the cost. Regressing fish catch on social capital would result in a zero or negative coefficient on social capital even though it has a positive social return for fishermen.

The externality can also be pecuniary, as for instance would obtain if the fishing groups does not share a common fishing ground but sell their fish on the same market: social capital makes collusion to restrict supply possible but all fishermen benefit from higher fish prices. In this case, the effect of social capital can only be ascertained by comparing fishing groups who do not compete with each other, either by accessing the same fishing ground or by selling fish on the same market.

What these examples demonstrate is that individual returns from social capital can be poor indicators of aggregate returns. If social capital enables certain individuals or groups to capture rents at the expense of others, then individual returns to social capital are likely to exceed social returns, and social capital results in unequal outcomes. In contrast, if social capital generates positive externalities not fully appropriated by owners of social capital, individual returns will underestimate social returns. While these considerations complicate empirical analysis, they do not make it impossible, as evidenced by much recent work on social capital.

IV. Conclusions and Lessons for Policy

In this paper we have discussed various issues surrounding empirical work on social capital and drawn a number of lessons for empirical work. Starting from a simple conceptual framework, we clarified a number of methodological problems that have plagued the literature. Much work remains to be done and, as the literature begins to mature, the prospects for valuable scientific contributions remain very high.

A proper understanding of the relationship between social capital, efficiency, development and equity also has important implications for policy. In the remaining part of this paper, we illustrate these implications by drawing a number of simple lessons from the conceptual framework presented in Section II. These tentative lessons are only meant to be indicative since the conceptual framework I have proposed has not been formally tested, at least not in its entirety.

Lesson 1: Focusing only on legal institutions and government may not be sufficient to achieve efficiency in exchange and public good provision. This is particularly true in underdeveloped economies where the state is weak and the majority of the population is beyond the reach of courts. Good development policy must pay attention to legal institutions and government as well as trust and leadership.

Lesson 2: Abstracting from cost considerations, promoting generalized trust is in general better than expanding the reach of personalized trust via the promotion of associations (clubs) and networks. This is because generalized trust is more efficient and more equitable (in the Jeffersonian sense of equal opportunity).

Lesson 3: While it is relatively easy to foster the creation of associations and networks, there is no easy way to promote generalized trust in societies where laws have little bite on the majority of firms and economic agents. For this reason, expanding personalized trust is often a more cost-effective way of improving efficiency in developing countries with limited administrative capacity to develop formal institutions.

In some cases, it is possible to move towards generalized trust by expanding the reach and inclusiveness of existing associations and networks. One example, discussed in Fafchamps (2002), is the switch from informal to formal information-sharing, such as a credit reference bureau, quality certification agency, or grading system.

Lesson 4: If generalized trust cannot be fostered directly because setting up formal institutions is too costly given the resources of the economy, promoting associations and interpersonal networks may be envisaged provided special care is given to equity issues. Pending further research on these issues, I speculate that equity is best protected if: (1) entry in associations and networks is free and unrestricted; (2) association and network composition are representative of the general population in terms of gender, ethnicity, regional origin, etc; (3) associations and networks do not create entrenched interests that will subsequently slow the replacement of personalized trust with generalized trust.

Lesson 5: Government intervention and community participation are complimentary in the provision of public goods and services. Government can reduce free-riding via taxes and compulsory contributions. Community involvement is required to ensure that the public participates in a disciplined and trustworthy manner to government programs.

Lesson 6: If governments are too weak or disorganized to provide public goods directly, provision can be organized via community-based organizations. In the absence of the state, participation in community-based projects is purely on a voluntary basis. This opens room for adverse selection and free-riding. Effective delivery of public goods on a voluntary basis requires trust and strong leadership. For this reason, successful community-based programs need not be replicable everywhere because of a dearth of strong local leaders.

Lesson 7: Large hierarchical organizations such as Churches, Islamic fraternities and other faith-based organizations can substitute themselves to the state for the provision of public goods. The same is true of international NGOs. Although these organizations do not have the right to raise taxes, they share some of the attributes of the state (large organization with institutional memory, selection of trained leaders, pooling of resources across space). Consequently they are better equipped than small community-based organizations to provide public goods. For this reason, donors dissatisfied with states may choose to work with faith-based organizations and international NGOs for the provision of public goods.

Lesson 8: Working with faith-based organizations and NGOs, however, is fraught with danger because these organizations often have their own social and political agenda (e.g., Hamas). To the extent that faith-based organizations are like clubs with exclusive membership and fairly restrictive entry requirements, they may ultimately get in the way of generalized trust. This was the view of Smith, Jefferson and Voltaire and the reason why they favored a secular state and sought to weaken the power of the Church.

Lesson 9: Social capital must not become a new mantra. It must not be used to justify pouring resources into community development efforts that have a low chance of success and low replicability (because of the dependence on unpredictable local leadership). Social capital is not an easy or cheap replacement for an effective state. If the state is broken, why not fix it. Investing in social capital should be seen as a complement to investing in government capacity. The two cannot and should not be separated.

Acknowledgements

The support of the Economic and Social Research Council (UK) is gratefully acknowledged. The work is part of the programme of the ESRC Global Poverty Research Group.

Notes

1. This case does not rule out the presence of positive externalities on non-members, as long as social capital effects are stronger for members.
2. This may be true of the rural poor, who find little to do. But it need not be true of the urban poor.
3. In practice, employment offices often play a minor role in matching employers with workers. Perhaps a better comparison is between the US and European markets for academic economists or medical interns: in the US, these markets benefit from a strong coordinating device; in Europe, job matching is uncoordinated and probably less efficient.
4. The presence of credit reference firms such as Dun and Bradstreet is another example of formal information sharing device that can be partially substituted by informal networks.
5. This example is inspired of the work of Platteau and Seki (2002) on Japanese fishermen.

References

Akerlof, G. A. and Kranton, R. E. (2000) Economics and identity, *Quarterly Journal of Economics*, 115(3), 715–53.
Ayouz, M. K., Fares, M. and Tassou, Z. (2002) Association des commerçants, capital social et compétitivité: Tests économétriques sur les données des commerçants des produits vivriers du Bénin (mimeograph).
Bala, V. and Goyal, S. (2000) A non-cooperative model of network formation, *Econometrica*, 68(5), 1181–229.
Baland, J. M. and Platteau, J. P. (1995) *Halting Degradation of Natural Resources: Is There a Role for Rural Communities?* (Oxford: Food and Agriculture Organization; Clarendon Press).
Barr, A. (2002a) *Familiarity and Trust: An Experimental Investigation* (Oxford: CSAE, Oxford University).

Barr, A. (2002b) Risk pooling and limited commitment: an experimental approach (mimeograph).

Barr, A. (2002c) Cooperation and shame (mimeograph).

Bebbington, A., Guggenheim, S., Olson, E. and Woolcock, W. (2004) Exploring social capital debates at the World Bank, *Journal of Development Studies*, 40(5), 33–64.

Becker, G. S. (1968) Crime and punishment: an economic approach, *Journal of Political Economy*, 76, 169–217.

Bernstein, L. (1992) Opting out of the legal system: extralegal contractual relations in the diamond industry, *Journal of Legal Studies*, XXI, 115–57.

Bernstein, L. (1996) Merchant law in a merchant court: rethinking the code's search for immanent business norms, *University of Pennsylvania Law Review*, 144(5), 1765–821.

Bigombe, B., Collier, P. and Sambanis, N. (2000) Policies for building post-conflict peace, *Journal of African Economies*, 9(3), 323–48.

Bigsten, A., Collier, P., Dercon, S., Fafchamps, F., Gauthier, B., Gunning, J. M., Isaksson, A., Oduro, A., Oostendorp, R., Patillo, C., Soderbom, M., Teal, F. and Zeufack, A. (2000) Contract flexibility and dispute resolution in African manufacturing, *Journal of Development Studies*, 36(4), 1–37.

Bloch, F., Gerciot, G. and Ray, D. (2004) Social networks and informal insurance (mimeograph).

Brock, W. A. and Durlauf, S. N. (2001) Interactions-based models, in J. Heckman and E. Leamer (eds), *Handbook of Econometrics*, Vol. 5, pp. 3297–380 (Amsterdam: North Holland).

Carter, M. R. and Maluccio, J. (2003) Social capital and coping with economic shocks: an analysis of stunting of South African children, *World Development*, 31(7), 1147–63.

Coleman, J. S. (1988) Social capital in the creation of human capital, *American Journal of Sociology*, 94(Supplement), S95–S120.

Collier, P. and Hoeffler, A. (2002) *Greed and Grievances in Civil War* (Oxford: Center for the Study of African Economies, Oxford University).

Dasgupta, P. and Serageldin, I. (2000) *Social Capital: A Multifaceted Perspective* (Washington DC: The World Bank).

de Soto, H. (1989) *The Other Path: The Invisible Revolution in the Third World* (New York: Harper and Row).

Durlauf, S. and Fafchamps, M. (2005) Social capital, in P. Aghion and S. Durlauf (eds), *Handbook of Economic Growth* (New York: Wiley).

Fafchamps, M. (2002) Spontaneous market emergence, *Topics in Theoretical Economics*, 2(1), accessed at www.bepress.com

Fafchamps, M. and Minten, B. (1999) Relationships and traders in Madagascar, *Journal of Development Studies*, 35(6), 1–35.

Fafchamps, M. and Minten, B. (2002) Returns to social network capital among traders, *Oxford Economic Papers*, 54, 173–206.

Fafchamps, M. (2003) Ethnicity and networks in African trade, *Contributions to Economic Analysis and Policy*, 2(1), accessed at www.bepress.com

Fafchamps, M. (2004) *Market Institutions in Sub-Saharan Africa* (Cambridge, MA: MIT Press).

Fafchamps, M. and Minten, B. (2001) Property rights in a flea market economy, *Economic Development and Cultural Change*, 49(2), 229–68.

Gambetta, D. (1993) *The Sicilian Mafia: The Business of Private Protection* (Cambridge, MA: Harvard University Press).

Goyal, S. van der Leij, M. and Moraga-Gonzalez, J. S. (2004) Economics: an emerging small world? (mimeograph).

Granovetter, M. S. (1995) *Getting a Job: A Study of Contacts and Carreers* (Chicago: University of Chicago Press).

Grootaert, C. and Narayan, D. (2004) Local institutions, poverty and household welfare in Bolivia, *World Development*, 32(7), 1179–798.

Grootaert, C. and van Bastelaer, T. (2002a) *The Role of Social Capital in Development: An Empirical Assessment* (Cambridge: Cambridge University Press).

Grootaert, C. and van Bastelaer, T. (2002b) *Understanding and Measuring Social Capital: A Multidisciplinary Tool for Practitioners* (Washington DC: World Bank).

Haddad, L. and Maluccio, J. (2003) Trust, membership in groups, and household welfare: evidence from KwaZulu-Natal, South Africa, *Economic Development and Cultural Change*, 51(3), 573–601.

Hayek, F. A. (1945) The use of knowledge in society, *American Economic Review*, 35(4), 519–30.

Hendley, K. (1999) Beyond the tip of the iceberg: business disputes in Russia (mimeograph).

Keefer, P. and Knack, S. (1997) Why don't poor countries catch up? A cross-national test of institutional explanation, *Economic Enquiry*, 35(3), 590–602.

Kranton, R. and Minehart, D. (2001) A theory of buyer–seller networks, *American Economic Review*, 91(3), 485–508.

Kranton, R. E. (1996) Reciprocal exchange: a self-sustaining system, *American Economic Review*, 86(4), 830–51.

Maluccio, J., Haddad, L. and May, J. (2000) Social capital and household welfare in South Africa, 1993–98, *Journal of Development Studies*, 36(6), 54–81.

Manski, C. F. (1993) Identification of endogenous social effects: the reflection problem, *Review of Economic Studies*, 60, 531–42.

Narayan, D. and Pritchett, L. (1999) Cents and sociability: household income and social capital in rural Tanzania, *Economic Development and Cultural Change*, 47(4), 871–97.

North, D. (2001) Comments, in M. Aoki and Y. Hayami (eds), *Communities and Markets in Economic Development*, pp. 403–8 (Oxford: Oxford University Press).

North, D. C. (1973) *The Rise of the Western World* (Cambridge: Cambridge UP).

Platteau, J. P. (1994) Behind the market stage where real societies exist: Part II – the role of moral norms, *J. Development Studies*, 30(4), 753–815.

Platteau, J. P. and Seki, E. (2002) Community arrangements to overcome market failure: pooling groups in Japanese fisheries, in M. Aoki and Y. Hayami (eds), *Communities and Markets in Economic Development* (Oxford: Oxford University Press).

Putnam, R. D. (2000) *Bowling Alone* (New York: Simon and Schuster).

Putnam, R. D., Leonardi, R. and Nanetti, R. Y. (1993) *Making Democracy Work: Civic Institutions in Modern Italy* (Princeton: Princeton University Press).

Robison, L. J., Schmid, A. A. and Siles, M. E. (2002) Is social capital really capital? *Review of Social Economy*, 60(1), 1–21.

Rose, R. (2000a) Getting things done in an antimodern society: social capital networks in Russia, in P. Dasgupta and I. Serageldin (eds), *Social Capital: A Multifaceted Perspective*, pp. 147–71 (Washinston DC: The World Bank).

Rose, R. (2000b) Uses of social capital in Russia: modern, pre-modern, and anti-modern, *Post-Soviet Affairs*, 16(1), 33–57.

Tadelis, S. (1999) What's in a name? Reputation as a tradable asset, *American Economic Review*, 89(3), 548–63.

Taylor, C. R. (2000) The old-boy network and the young-gun effect, *International Economic Review*, 41(4), 871–91.

Uphoff, N. and Wijayaratna, C. M. (2000) Demonstrated benefits from social capital: the productivity of farmers organizations in Gal Oya, Sri Lanka, *World Development*, 28(11), 1875–90.

Woolcock, M. and Narayan, D. (2000) Social capital: implications for development theory, research, and policy, *World Bank Research Observer*, 15(2), 225–49.

Subjective Well-Being Poverty *vs.* Income Poverty and Capabilities Poverty?

GEETA GANDHI KINGDON & JOHN KNIGHT

I. Introduction

Empirical research by economists on poverty in developing countries has generally been concerned with its measurement in terms of income and consumption. Behind this metric lies the concept of utility, or welfare, which people are assumed to derive from income and consumption. Yet there has been little attempt to measure poverty in terms of reported utility, that is subjectively perceived welfare. In this paper we shall explore the latter approach, attempting to gain insights from new research on the economics of happiness for understanding poverty in developing countries.

Economic research on reported happiness (or subjective well-being – we use the terms interchangeably) is sparse and recent but growing rapidly. It is apparent from this literature that there are two important gaps to be filled. First, reflecting the availability of data, there is little research on subjective well-being on poor countries (Diener and Biswas-Diener, 2000).[1] Second, within any country, there is little research on the relationship between subjective well-being and conventional measures of poverty. The purpose of this paper is to help bridge these two gaps.

Some theoretical research on poverty in developing countries has eschewed income or consumption as the evaluative criterion. Alternative criteria have been put forward, some in a form which eschews utility as the evaluative criterion, for example the fulfilment of basic needs and the extent of peoples' capabilities to be and to do things of intrinsic worth. Such approaches suggest a broader set of measures for assessing poverty than just income and consumption, including public provision of non-marketed services, such as sanitation, health care and education (inputs) or healthiness, life expectancy and literacy (outputs). While retaining utility as our evaluative criterion, and using subjectively perceived well-being, that is reported satisfaction, as our measure of utility, we shall propose a method of incorporating not only income or consumption but also other determinants of the quality of life (such as these) into the analysis of poverty.

In this paper we shall consider the relationship between what we shall call 'subjective well-being poverty' and poverty as it is otherwise measured in poor countries. The paper is methodological in emphasis, setting out the issues, the appropriate methods and the data requirements for a programme of research.

Section II will provide a review of the literature on happiness, explaining the solid results so far and the hypotheses that they suggest for the study of poor people in poor countries. Section III provides the methodology, explaining the estimation of subjective well-being functions, their relationship to income functions, and their relationship to various other concepts of poverty. The argument is illustrated in Section IV with an available data set, the SALDRU national household survey for South Africa, 1993. Section V draws conclusions from the analysis.

II. Literature Survey

This section contains four parts. We start with relevant aspects of the literature on subjective well-being, and then turn to relevant aspects of the literature on poverty. We examine the research on the interface between these two topics and, finding little, we put the case for exploring the subjective well-being approach to poverty.

There is a good survey of the literature on economic aspects of happiness – some of it interdisciplinary and some by non-economists – by Frey and Stutzer (2002). Their evaluation of this growing field is upbeat and their prognosis is promising. Layard (2003), in surveying the field, takes an even more sanguine view: 'The scientific study of happiness is only just beginning. It should become a central topic in social science'. Much of the research has involved the estimation of happiness functions, in which happiness (subjectively rated on an ordinal or cardinal scale) is the dependent variable and various socio-economic characteristics of the individual, household or community are used as explanatory variables. Some of the research relates to particular countries (generally advanced economies), using either cross-section or panel data sets; and some covers many countries, normally using comparable data sets derived from the *World Values Survey*.

The main findings from the general literature are the following. First, happiness increases with absolute income, ceteris paribus, but not proportionately and at a diminishing rate (Frey and Stutzer, 2002). Moreover, differences in income explain only a small proportion of the variation in happiness among people. The importance of income appears to vary among countries: happiness levels are lowest in the poorest countries but the relationship between income and happiness is weak beyond a fairly low international level of income per capita. This is consistent with the argument that happiness depends in part on the gratification of certain absolute biological and psychological needs (Veenhoven, 1991).

The limited role of absolute income is further suggested by the fact that income and happiness are positively related in cross-section but not in time-series studies. For instance, in the United States and in Japan, real income per capita increased over time but the mean happiness score remained constant. It is possible that mean happiness did not rise over time because aspiration levels adjusted to, and so rose along with, mean incomes in the society, and happiness varied positively with income but negatively with aspirations (Easterlin, 2001). The second main finding, therefore, is that happiness depends on relative income, defined by the reference group or the reference time that people have in mind.

This finding is consistent with the long-established literature on relative deprivation (Duesenberry, 1949; Runciman, 1966). Perceptions of subjective well-being depend on the context: people compare themselves with others in society or with themselves in the past, and they feel deprived if they are doing less well than the comparator. This raises the questions: what comparisons do people make; how wide are the orbits of comparison? Duesenberry (1949) stressed previous income or consumption, and better-off people, as the frames of reference. Runciman (1966) suggested informational and social reasons why the frame of reference can be narrow. Perceptions of relative deprivation are expected to reduce happiness. It is also possible that perceptions of relative advantage will raise happiness. Thus, a person's position in the income distribution of the relevant reference group may govern happiness. Happiness might be responsive to income ranking over the range (say, below the median) in which people feel relatively deprived, or it might increase monotonically throughout the income distribution.

Absolute and relative incomes are not the only economic determinants of happiness. Being unemployed is found to reduce happiness independently of its effect on income (Clark and Oswald, 1994; Winkelmann and Winkelmann, 1998). The general unemployment rate also has a depressing effect, suggesting that having a higher risk of becoming unemployed reduces happiness. Another indication of economic insecurity is inflation: countries and periods with higher inflation display lower happiness, ceteris paribus (Di Tella et al., 2001). Subjective well-being is influenced by several factors that are non-economic or potentially so, such as age, sex, marital status, health status, education, social capital, religion, and social and political institutions (Helliwell, 2002).

We turn to the literature on poverty. Sen (1983) introduced the concept of a person's 'capabilities' to be and to do things of intrinsic worth, that is resources adequate to achieve a specified set of 'functionings'. He argued that absolute deprivation in terms of a person's capabilities can imply relative deprivation in terms of income, resources or commodities, for example for taking part in the life of the community, for the avoidance of shame, or for the maintenance of self-respect. He favoured the capability to function as the criterion for assessing the standard of living, and by implication poverty, rather than the utility that might be derived from using that capability. Thus, Sen eschewed the 'welfarist' approach to poverty with its underlying assumption that the evaluative criterion is the utility that people derive from goods and services. However, he neither offered a practical criterion for evaluating the various capabilities to function nor sought any aggregation of the social values of the separate capabilities.

Atkinson and Bourguignon (1999) use the same framework but from a welfarist perspective. They regard poverty as 'inadequate command over economic resources' but view this as an intermediate concern, the ultimate concern being in terms of 'capabilities' in the sense of Sen. The absolute set of capabilities translates into a set of goods requirements which is relative to a particular society and its standard of living. This leads them to formulate a concept in line with the World Bank's *World Development Report* (1990), that a:

> ... poverty line can be thought of as comprising two elements: the expenditure necessary to buy a minimum level of nutrition and other basic necessities and a further amount that varies from country to country, reflecting the cost of participating in the everyday life of the society. (World Bank, 1990: 26)

There is a hierarchy of capabilities. The first concerns physical functioning and requires a set of goods fixed in absolute terms; this capability has priority. The second capability concerns social functioning and requires a set of goods that depends on the mean level of income. These authors see capabilities and functionings as contributing to welfare, but they do not consider subjective well-being as the measure of welfare nor do they explicitly adopt an encompassing approach.

Attempts have been made to compare and combine different measures of poverty. For instance, Laderchi et al. (2003) examine and contrast four different approaches to the definition of poverty (not including the subjective well-being approach). They show empirically that there is little overlap in individuals falling into the different types of poverty, for instance (their definitions of) income poverty and capabilities poverty. They favour aggregation of the various dimensions of poverty but conclude that 'in general there is no right way of aggregating' (246). Clark (2005) espouses the capabilities approach to poverty but, on the basis of a South African case study of poor peoples' perceptions of a good life, reaches the qualitative conclusion that both income and utility are important components of functioning.

Little has yet been written on the interface between subjective well-being and poverty. Ravallion and colleagues have pioneered the use of subjective perceptions in the analysis of poverty in developing countries. Pradhan and Ravallion (2000) use household surveys for Jamaica and Nepal which ask whether total consumption (or consumption of food, or housing, etc.) is adequate for household minimum needs. This enables them to estimate 'subjective poverty lines'. They compare these with objective poverty lines and note interesting differences, for example a greater subjective than objective urban–rural difference in poverty, and greater perceived than actual household scale economies in consumption.

Ravallion and Lokshin (2001, 2002) use a household panel data set for Russia which asked people to classify themselves on a nine-step ladder along a dimension from 'poorest' to 'rich'. Households are ranked both according to their subjective poverty/wealth status and according to their income (normalised by the relevant objective poverty line). The two rankings are significantly positively correlated but the matching is nevertheless weak: many who classify themselves as subjectively poor are not objectively so, and vice versa. The reason for the discrepancy is explored by incorporating into the subjective ranking equation such factors as education, employment status, health status and permanent income. The subjective classification takes these factors into account as well as current income. Although rank changes are treated as representing changes in utility (Ravallion and Lokshin, 2001), the ranking is not necessarily an indication of subjective well-being. Rather, it appears to ask people to gauge their relative position in the hierarchy of poverty and wealth, and is partly a test of how well informed they are about this.

The underlying criticism of happiness as a measure of poverty is that it represents a particular mental reaction to the use of a capability rather than the capability itself (Sen, 1983, 1984), that it need not be closely related to subjectively perceived poverty (Ravallion and Lokshin, 2002), that it is too broad (Sen, 1983; Ravallion and Lokshin, 2002), and that it is a necessary but not a sufficient condition for assessing quality of life (Diener and Biswas-Diener, 2000, 2003). In our view the most serious criticism is the first of these. In the words of Sen:

> The most blatant forms of inequalities and exploitations survive in the world through making allies out of the deprived and exploited. The underdog learns to bear the burden so well that he or she overlooks the burden itself. Discontent is replaced by acceptance... suffering and anger by cheerful endurance. As people learn to adjust... the horrors look less terrible in the metric of utilities. (Sen, 1984: 308–9)

We intend nevertheless to explore the happiness approach, for the following reasons. First, we place value on individual freedom, and thus on the individual's clearly expressed views about her own well-being, and we are loath to have these over-ruled by values emerging unclearly from elsewhere. However, if another value judgement is sought, the objective of alleviating subjectively felt misery and raising peoples' sense of well-being is a commonly held value judgement, which underlies much of the concern that is voiced about poverty in developing countries. Second, the use of a multivariate analysis makes it possible to isolate the average effects of selected particular determinants of happiness without having to worry about the many unobservables that contribute to human happiness and which make some people naturally happier than others (unless these are correlated with the observed determinants). Third, provided that utility is accepted as the evaluative criterion, it is possible to treat subjective well-being as an encompassing concept, which enables us to quantify the relevance and importance of the other approaches to poverty and of their components. It will be necessary, however, to consider how human ability to adapt and to take a rosy view of a bad situation can affect our estimates of the relationship between subjective well-being and its determinants.

III. Methodology and Hypotheses

Our objective is to discover whether and how happiness can be explained by economic and non-economic variables, and what light this can throw on the concept of poverty. We therefore begin with the subjective well-being function

$$W_i = a_i + b_n \cdot X_{ni} + u_i \qquad (1)$$

where W_i represents subjective well-being and X_n is a vector of n socio-economic variables. W_i is normally available as a multiple choice variable (of the sort 'are you 1. very happy; 2. happy; 3. so-so; 4. unhappy; 5. very unhappy?'). The appropriate estimation procedure is therefore by means of a polychotomous probit or logit equation. The selection of X_n depends on the research hypotheses but also on what variables the data set has to offer. In the absence of a well-articulated model carrying theoretical predictions, our approach is exploratory and is influenced by the criteria that have been proposed in the literature for defining and assessing poverty.

The vector of estimated coefficients b_n provides the weights that indicate the relative importance of different contributors to subjective well-being. The potential value of this exercise can be illustrated by the deficiencies of the UNDP's Human Development Index. This is calculated by according equal weights to its three components – income per capita, educational attainment, and life expectancy (UNDP, 2000). The value judgement implicit in this weighting need not correspond at all well to the valuations of these capabilities made by individuals in society. Subjective well-being may be a narrow metric but at least it corresponds to individual valuations and it is a metric that can be measured.

The estimated subjective well-being function can be harnessed to examine the relationships between the subjective well-being criterion for poverty and other criteria. These include the conventional income criterion and, within the capabilities approach, the physical functioning criterion and the social functioning criterion. Consider first the relationship between subjective well-being poverty and income poverty. An obvious question concerns the extent of overlap between the two. This can be examined by dividing the sample into m quantiles according to the values of W and then into m quantiles of corresponding sizes according to income ranking. A second exercise is to include income (X_y) among the explanatory variables in the subjective well-being equation and to examine its importance in determining W relative to other determinants (the importance of income is indicated by the coefficient b_y and the contribution of X_y to explaining the variation in W).[2]

Although they are conceptually distinct, there is potentially a good deal of overlap between the capabilities and the subjective well-being approaches to poverty. Both capabilities and subjective well-being are likely to be positive functions of income. The various other characteristics that are normally hypothesised to give people the capability to function well are also prime suspects for raising happiness. The subjective well-being function should thus include variables $(X_1, \ldots, X_e)$ that correspond to physical functioning. These might comprise components of 'basic needs' such as nutrition, clothing, shelter, sanitation, health and literacy. The function should also include variables $(X_{e+1}, \ldots, X_h)$ that correspond to social functioning. These might take the form of proxies for the capability to meet the norms of society and to interact well with society. Relative concepts are likely to figure: the relevant reference groups need to be investigated. The group might be defined in terms of income, ethnicity, residence or even time. It is thus possible to attach weights to physical and to social functioning, and to their components. It is also possible to measure the relative importance of the variables hypothesised to denote capabilities in the determination of subjective well-being.

By introducing a time dimension and using panel data, the literature on poverty often distinguishes between chronic and transient poverty. Underlying this distinction is the notion that the ill-effects are best measured by aggregating the indicator of poverty over time. Expectations do not necessarily enter the story. However, by introducing proxies for insecurity into the subjective well-being function, the subjective well-being approach can be used to incorporate expectations. It is possible to examine the effect of prospective future poverty on current happiness.

Finally, it is appropriate to include certain variables which do not fit into any of the approaches to poverty outlined above, some of which fall outside the normal purview of economists or policy-makers. These might include such demographic, geographic and social variables as age, gender, family composition, marital status, residential location, religion, social network, trust, and social participation. In part they serve as control variables; in part they serve to emphasise that subjective well-being can depend on a broad range of factors, many of which are non-economic.

The notion that both absolute and relative poverty measures are relevant has implications for the use of happiness measures in poverty analysis. We expect inadequate physical functioning (such as hunger, lack of shelter and lack of warmth) to cause unhappiness. It is also plausible that inadequate social functioning (such as alienation, shame and lack of self-respect) causes unhappiness. Insofar as inadequate functioning reduces happiness, ceteris paribus, the relationship between income and functioning determines the relationship between income and happiness. When an individual's income rises from a low level, happiness rises as the extent of both absolute and relative poverty is reduced; when physical functioning is achieved, a further rise in income can still raise happiness if social functioning is improved. Ceteris paribus, a negative relationship between inadequacy of functioning and happiness might therefore produce diminishing gains in individual happiness as income rises beyond first the absolute and then the relative poverty level.

The coefficients estimated in the subjective well-being function isolate the average effects of each explanatory variable for the sample as a whole, whereas we are interested primarily in the poor. Consider the relationship between subjective well-being (W) and the vector of 'resources' (X) that produce subjective well-being. For simplicity, assume that resources can be aggregated and measured cardinally (X). Figure 1 illustrates. If the poor (those with low X) are subject to the same 'happiness production function' as the non-poor (the continuous curve $W = W_1(X)$), we might expect the function to exhibit diminishing returns to resources, that is to be concave (to the X axis). Apart from their corresponding to the normal assumption of diminishing marginal utility, diminishing returns might reflect the fulfilment first of physical functionings (basic needs) and then of social functionings (position in society). By contrast, we have noted Sen's argument (*Sen*, 1984) that the poor manage to adjust to hardship, that is of necessity they become more efficient

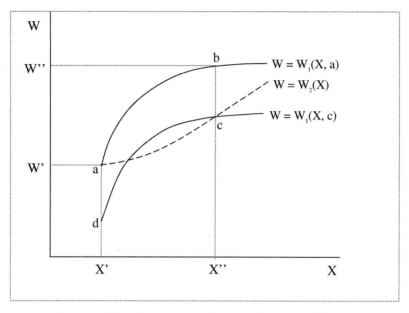

Figure 1. The effect of adaptation on subjective well-being

'pleasure machines', so increasing their happiness relative to their resources. In that case the subjective well-being function can be linear instead of concave, or even convex (the continuous curve $W = W_2(X)$).

It is possible that both functions are relevant: the effect of additional resources on the subjective well-being of the poor might depend on whether there is an accompanying change in attitudes or aspirations. The current poor (at point a, corresponding to (X', W')) may experience the steeper, continuous curve, $W = W_1(X, a)$ in the short run, given an expectation of remaining poor. Thus they move to point b if their resources increase to X''. Gradually over time, however, they adjust to the higher level of resources, so moving to point c. Thus the long run subjective well-being function is depicted by the flatter, dashed curve $W = W_2(X)$, reflecting full adjustment to each level of resources. Similarly, a fall in resources from point c corresponding to (X'', W'') involves a short term move along $W = W_1(X, c)$ to point d at X'. Given time to adjust to their new situation, however, the newly poor become reconciled to their lot, their aspirations are lowered and point a is restored. We need to discover whether and how the poor and the non-poor differ in the way that their happiness responds to additional resources.

The subjective well-being concept of poverty might be treated as competing with income, capabilities and other concepts of poverty. We prefer to view it as an encompassing concept, which permits us to quantify the relevance and importance of the other approaches and of their components. Ultimately, the concept of poverty requires a value judgement as to what constitutes a good life or a bad one. Our starting point is that an approach that examines the individual's own perception of well-being is less imperfect, or more quantifiable, or both, as a guide to forming that value judgement than are the other possible approaches.

IV. An Illustration From South Africa

The SALDRU national household survey of 1993 in South Africa was carried out by the South African Labour and Development Research Unit (SALDRU) of the University of Cape Town. The dataset contains information on about 8,800 households and is patterned on the World Bank's Living Standards Measurement Studies, with modules on household demographics, employment, health, income and expenditure, etc. as well as community information. Section 9 of this survey is on perceived quality of life and it contains, *inter alia*, the question: 'Taking everything into account, how satisfied is this household with the way it lives these days?' The five options available in the pre-coded response were 'very satisfied', 'satisfied', 'neither satisfied nor dissatisfied', 'dissatisfied' and 'very dissatisfied' (SALDRU, 1994, Annex: 52).

While the individual respondent to the survey answered the question, the question itself related to the satisfaction of the household as a whole rather than to that individual's personal subjective well-being only. This raises the possibility that the individual was giving the answer mostly with his own personal satisfaction level in mind rather than that of the household as a whole. In order to address this concern, we check the robustness of the findings to inclusion of the individual respondent's own personal characteristics in the analysis. Appendix Table 2 shows that, controlling for household characteristics, individual characteristics are generally unimportant in our subjective well-being equations. This is not surprising if, as is likely, there are interdependencies in perceived well-being among members of the household.[3]

The discussion comes in two parts. First, we ask to what extent our measure of subjective well-being corresponds with the income measure that is most commonly used as a proxy for well-being. We also examine whether the determinants of these two measures affect them in the same direction and with similar intensity. Second, we examine the impact on subjective well-being of factors that meet basic needs (physical functioning), social needs (social functioning), and security needs of households.

Subjective Well-being Poverty Versus Income Poverty?

The survey yields data on about 8,300 households after removing observations with missing values for key variables. Table 1 presents a cross-tabulation of subjective well-being category and income category. The former takes five values, from 'very dissatisfied' (coded as 1) to 'very satisfied' (coded as 5). The distribution of households across happiness categories is uneven: 23 per cent of all households reported being 'very dissatisfied'; 33 per cent as being 'dissatisfied'; only 10 per cent as 'neither satisfied nor dissatisfied'; 26 per cent as 'satisfied' and a mere 8 per cent as being 'very satisfied'. Instead of using household per capita income quintiles, therefore, we have divided the data into income categories as follows: the poorest 23 per cent of the households (in terms of per capita income) are in Income Category 1

Table 1. Cross-tabulation of subjective well-being category and income category

	Subjective well-being category					
Income category	1	2	3	4	5	Total
1	568	880	156	296	44	1,944
	29.2	45.3	8.0	15.2	2.3	100
	29.2	31.7	19.8	13.5	7.1	23.3
2	781	1,078	257	568	96	2,780
	28.1	38.8	9.2	20.4	3.5	100
	40.2	38.8	32.7	25.9	15.4	33.4
3	167	265	81	214	60	787
	21.2	33.7	10.3	27.2	7.6	100
	8.6	9.5	10.3	9.8	9.7	9.5
4	406	498	248	793	250	2,195
	18.5	22.7	11.3	36.1	11.4	100
	20.9	17.9	31.5	36.1	40.2	26.4
5	22	59	45	324	172	622
	3.5	9.5	7.2	52.1	27.7	100
	1.1	2.1	5.7	14.7	27.7	7.5
Total	1,944	2,780	787	2,195	622	8,328
	23.3	33.4	9.5	26.4	7.5	100
	100	100	100	100	100	100

Note: The numbers in each cell present the frequency, row percentage, and column percentage respectively.

(to correspond with the 23 per cent of households in the lowest subjective well-being category); the next 33 per cent of households – in the ordering of households by per capita income – are in Income Category 2, to correspond with the 33 per cent that are in the second happiness category, and so on.

The table shows that there is a poor degree of coincidence between these two measures. Only in the second and fourth cells on the leading diagonal is the cell percentage frequency highest among all cells in that row. For instance, of all the households in the poorest income category, only 29 per cent are in the lowest happiness category, although 75 per cent are in the lowest two happiness categories. Similarly, of those in the richest income category, only 28 per cent are in the highest happiness category. The best fit comes when we consider the two lowest categories together: 70 per cent of households defined as income-poor in this way were also subjective well-being poor (and, by construction, vice versa). The overall correlation coefficient between income category and subjective well-being category is +0.358. Thus, while income is positively correlated with happiness, it is an imperfect predictor of happiness.

Table 2 examines whether various factors affect income and happiness in the same way. Since our subjective well-being variable, and thus by design our income variable, is discrete and takes values from 1 to 5 that are inherently ordered, the ordered probit is used to model both income category and happiness category.[4] The pseudo R-square in an ordered probit can be expected to take a low value. However, it has a higher value in the income than in the happiness equation. All variables are defined in the notes to the table. The gender and education level of individual members of the household are averaged across all household members aged 16 and above. Thus the variable *male* represents the proportion of male members and the education dummy variables *primary*, *junior*, *secondary* and *higher* represent the proportion of household members with these levels of education. The age variables represent the proportion of adult household members (16-years and older) within the specified age ranges. Persons aged 0–15 are included by way of the variable 'number of children in the household' (*hhnchild*). Other variables are household-level variables or community-level variables.

In Table 2, household per capita income category is significantly determined by productive characteristics such as age and education, but also by the household unemployment rate (*hhurate*), race (*African, Coloured, Indian*), and location (*urban, metropol, province*), etc. Several variables have quite different, or even opposing, effects on income and life-satisfaction levels. For instance, comparing Columns A and B, youth (*age 16–25*) is associated with low income but high subjective

Table 2. Comparison of ordered probit of income and of subjective well–being

	Income category (A)		Subjective well-being category (B)		Subjective well-being category (C)	
	Coefficient	Robust t	Coefficient	Robust t	Coefficient	Robust t
Age 16–25	−0.421	−4.6***	0.216	2.5***	0.258	3.0***
Age 26–35	0.443	6.5***	0.056	0.9	0.012	0.2
Age 46–55	0.368	5.2***	0.078	1.0	0.037	0.5
Age 56–65	0.732	7.5***	0.206	2.1***	0.132	1.3
Age ≥ 66	1.197	10.3***	0.379	3.6***	0.231	2.1***
Hhsizem	−0.063	−5.0***	−0.009	−0.7	−0.004	−0.4
Hhnchild	−0.196	−9.5***	0.017	1.0	0.035***	2.0***
Hhurate1	−1.487	−23.1***	−0.400	−8.3***	−0.238	−4.8***
Nolfpb	−1.133	−19.8***	−0.183	−3.8***	−0.063	−1.2
Primary	0.143	2.0***	−0.015	−0.2	−0.028	−0.4
Junior	0.468	6.2***	0.039	0.6	−0.005	−0.1
Secondary	1.158	13.1***	0.215	2.8***	0.100	1.4
Higher	1.937	15.0***	0.523	5.4***	0.347	3.8***
Migrate	0.170	2.6***	0.229	2.0***	0.221	1.9
Ownship_	0.121	2.5***	0.104	2.4***	0.099	2.3**
Hhdaysic	0.001	0.2	−0.006	−2.3**	−0.006	−2.3**
N_victim	0.102	2.3**	−0.074	−1.9*	−0.085	−2.2**
Male	0.680	7.6***	0.060	0.7	−0.012	−0.1
African	−1.500	−15.2***	−1.042	−10.4***	−0.908	−8.9***
Colored	−0.948	−8.8***	−0.458	−4.1***	−0.374	−3.4***
Indian	−0.728	−4.8***	−0.343	−3.3***	−0.280	−2.8***
Metropol	0.340	3.5***	−0.171	−1.5	−0.208	−1.8*
Urban1	0.091	1.0	−0.197	−2.1**	−0.211	−2.2**
Homeland	0.029	0.3	0.014	0.1	0.012	0.1
Wcape	−0.293	−3.1***	0.163	1.6	0.192	1.8*
Ncape	−0.351	−1.5	0.344	1.8*	0.379	1.9*

(continued)

Table 2. (*Continued*)

	Income category (A)		Subjective well-being category (B)		Subjective well-being category (C)	
	Coefficient	Robust t	Coefficient	Robust t	Coefficient	Robust t
Ecape	−0.345	−3.7***	0.107	0.8	0.156	1.2
Natal	−0.230	−2.5**	0.361	2.8**	0.385	2.9***
Ofs	−0.123	−0.8	0.311	1.9*	0.319	2.0**
Etvl	0.029	0.2	0.523	2.6**	0.523	2.5***
Ntvl	−0.394	−4.2***	0.247	1.7*	0.295	2.0**
Nw	0.113	1.0	0.307	1.6	0.299	1.5
Impass	−0.186	−3.4***	−0.177	−3.0***	−0.156	−2.6***
Pubtran	0.106	2.0**	0.045	0.7	0.037	0.6
Lnhhpci	–	–	–	–	0.146	6.7***
N	8279		8279		8279	
LogL	−7555.56		−11251.83		−11205.38	
Restr LogL	−12203.979		−12199.69		−12199.69	
Pseudo R^2	0.3809		0.0777		0.0815	

Note: The age variables = proportion of persons in each age range within the household. Hhsizem = household size; hhnchild = number of children below age 16 within the household; hhurate1 = household unemployment rate, that is proportion of household labour force participant members that are unemployed. Hhurate is undefined (missing) for households with no labour force participants, so for these households, the included variable hhurate1 takes value 0 and the indicator variable nolfpb takes the value 1; nolfpb = 0 for households with ≥1 labour force participant; Primary, junior, secondary and higher = proportion of household members with these different levels of education; migrate = whether household migrated to its current area within the past 5 years; ownship_ = whether household lives in owned home; hhdaysic = total number of person days that household members were sick in the past 14 days; n_victim = number of times in the past 12 months that household members have been victims of crime (robbery, assault, rape, murder, and abduction and 'other'); male = proportion of males in household; African, coloured, Indian = race dummies (base category is 'white'); metropol = household lives in metropolitan city; urban1 = household in urban non–metropolitan area (base category is rural); homeland = household lives in a former 'homeland'/Bantustan. Wcape – nw = province dummies; impass = whether community roads become impassable at certain times of the year; pubtran = whether community has public transport; lnhhpci = natural log of household per capita income. *, ** and *** denote statistical significance at the 10%, 5% and 1% levels respectively.

well-being. Living in a metropolitan city (*metropol*) raises income but lowers happiness. Poor health, as measured by number of days household members have been sick in the past 14 days (*hhdaysic*), has no significant impact on income but lowers perceived well-being significantly. The percentage of male members in the household (*male*) significantly raises income but has no impact on happiness. Six of the eight coefficients on the province dummy variables have opposing signs in the income and happiness equations. Thus, not all factors or conditions that raise income also raise happiness, and some even lower happiness.

Even when the signs are the same, the extent of association of several variables with income differs substantially from that with happiness. For instance, while being African depresses both income and happiness, the negative coefficient on *African* is very significantly greater in the income equation than in the happiness equation.

Similarly the association of age with income rank is much greater than its association with happiness rank. The same remarks apply to the coefficients on household size (*hhsize*), number of children aged 15 or below (*hhnchild*), household unemployment rate *(hhurate)* and the education variables (*primary, junior, secondary, higher*). We cannot assume that if a characteristic is good for generating income, it is commensurately good, or even good at all, for generating happiness.

Several of the variables included in the subjective well-being equation in Column B have a direct impact on perceived well-being and also an indirect impact via their effect on household income. Column C adds the natural log of household per capita income (*lnhhpci*) to the happiness equation. Happiness increases powerfully with income, but the inclusion of income does not affect the coefficients of other variables. The marginal effect of *lnhhpci* on the probability of being in subjective well-being poverty (that is being in the lowest two life-satisfaction categories) is 0.0572. Given a standard deviation of 1.4121, an increase in *lnhhpci* from one standard deviation below to one standard deviation above the mean would reduce the risk of subjective well-being poverty by 16.2 percentage points, which is not a particularly large effect, given that 55 per cent of all households are in the bottom two satisfaction categories. When income is not constrained to enter linearly, there appear to be increasing returns to income: if *lnhhpci* and its square are included, only the squared term is positive and significant; when no quadratic form is imposed and log of household per capita income quintiles are included instead (quintile one being the base or reference quintile), the coefficients on quintiles two, three, four and five are 0.073, 0.166, 0.377, and 0.505 respectively, and all four are statistically significant.[5] These cross-section results suggest that the relationship between subjective well-being and income corresponds to the dashed, convex curve in Figure 1, that is people do to some extent adjust and accommodate their perceptions of well-being to their economic circumstances.

A comparison of Columns B and C shows that the effect of education on happiness falls (but the effect of higher education does not disappear) when income is included, suggesting that much of the effect of education on happiness comes via its effect on income. Similarly, just under half of the negative association between unemployment and happiness is due to the impact of unemployment on income. In common with other studies (Clark and Oswald, 1994), unemployment has a powerful negative relationship with life-satisfaction even after controlling for income, perhaps because it imposes a psychological cost. The lack of panel data means that we are unable convincingly to test the direction of causality. However, Winkelmann and Winkelmann (1998), who control for individual fixed effects, find that causality runs from unemployment to unhappiness.

Table 3 re-estimates the income and subjective well-being equations with cluster fixed effects, that is a set of cluster dummy variables. Variables that do not vary within clusters, such as location (*urban, metropol, homeland* and *province*) and cluster characteristics such as whether community roads become impassable at certain times of the year (*impass*) and whether community is served by public transport (*pubtran*), are excluded from the estimation. Including cluster fixed effects increases the explained variation in income from 38 to 43 per cent and in happiness from 8 to 15 per cent. Table 3 shows that apart from the effect of race – which changes dramatically – the coefficients on unemployment, education, home ownership,

Table 3. Comparison of ordered probit of income and of subjective well-being, with cluster fixed effects

	Income category		Subjective well-being category		Subjective well-being category	
	Coefficient	Robust t	Coefficient	Robust t	Coefficient	Robust t
Age 16–25	−0.319	−4.3***	0.183	2.7***	0.208	3.0
Age 26–35	0.428	6.5***	0.017	0.3	−0.023	−0.4
Age 46–55	0.398	4.8***	−0.003	0.0	−0.041	−0.6
Age 56–65	0.788	8.4***	0.129	1.5	0.057	0.7
Age ≥ 66	1.214	11.6***	0.263	2.8***	0.127	1.3
Hhsizem	−0.061	−5.7***	−0.004	−0.4	0.000	0.0
Hhnchild	−0.198	−11.3***	0.004	0.3	0.020	1.3
Hhurate1	−1.528	−30.9***	−0.334	−7.8***	−0.186	−4.0***
Nolfpb	−1.138	−22.4***	−0.094	−2.1**	0.012	0.3
Primary	0.006	0.1	0.040	0.7	0.041	0.7
Junior	0.303	4.8***	0.095	1.6	0.072	1.3
Secondary	0.929	12.5***	0.237	3.5***	0.156	2.3**
Higher	1.691	17.4***	0.431	5.2***	0.298	3.5***
Migrate	0.063	1.2	0.040	0.9	0.036	0.8
Ownship_	0.184	4.6***	0.104	2.8***	0.089	2.4***
Hhdaysic	−0.001	−0.5	−0.006	−3.0***	−0.006	−3.0***
N_victim	0.056	1.4	−0.127	−3.5***	−0.134	−3.7***
Male	0.523	9.2***	0.115	2.2**	0.070	1.3
African	−1.622	−15.5***	−0.194	−2.1**	−0.055	−0.6
Colored	−1.356	−7.0***	−0.208	−1.2	−0.107	−0.6
Indian	−0.452	−1.8*	0.090	0.4	0.145	0.7
Lnhhpci	–	–	–	–	0.141	8.4***
Cluster dummies	Yes		Yes		Yes	
N	8279		8279		8279	
LogL	−7004.32		−10365.02		−10329.37	
Restr LogL	−12203.98		−12199.69		−12199.69	
Pseudo R^2	0.4261		0.1504		0.1533	

Note: Variable definitions in Table 2. *, ** and *** denote statistical significance at the 10%, 5% and 1% levels respectively.

health, crime and income remain more or less unchanged with cluster fixed effects. The fact that race coefficients collapse in size and significance suggests that race per se is not associated with happiness (members of certain races are not intrinsically happier than those of others) but rather that unobserved circumstances that matter to happiness differ across the races. For instance, the huge negative coefficient on the *African* (and to a lesser extent on *Coloured* and *Indian*) race dummies in Table 2 may be due to the fact that Africans are concentrated in locations where public services and amenities – what might be termed 'social wages' – are very poor. While we do include certain measures of community characteristics, such as whether community roads become impassable at certain times of the year (*impass*) and whether public transport passes by the community (*pubtran*) – and also experimented with others[6] – these arguably do not capture all the relevant amenities and services that matter to perceived well-being.

To summarise, income is the most commonly used proxy for well-being – being apparently objective, accurately measurable and readily available – and the most commonly used measure of poverty. However, although household per capita income is indeed positively correlated with household subjectively evaluated well-being, the correlation is not strong. Subjective well-being is also related to a range of non-monetary factors, including education, employment, health and safety from crime. The ways in which these factors affect income differ substantially from the ways in which they affect happiness. Researchers who adhere to the income approach to poverty do so at peril of oversimplifying.

Subjective Well-being Poverty Versus Capabilities Poverty?

This section examines the relationships between the subjective well-being criterion for poverty and, within the capabilities approach, the physical functioning (or basic needs) criterion and the social functioning (or social needs) criterion. The methodology based on Equation 1 in Section III allows us to attach weights to different measurable components of physical and social functioning to estimate their contribution to subjective well-being.

Table 4 presents ordered probits of subjective well-being. Province dummies are included in all specifications but not reported. The first column (Column A) starts with the inclusion only of control variables, namely age, household demographics, gender and whether the household migrated to its current location in the previous five years. Column B includes basic needs variables such as education, health, employment and living conditions that can affect physical functioning. The last set includes household variables such as distance to water (*dwater*), type of house roof – *ironroof* (a corrugated iron roof would mean that the home is too hot in the summer and too cold in the winter), electricity connection (*connecte*), and persons per room (*personpr*), as well as cluster variables such as the condition of roads (*impass*) and whether public transport is available in community (*pubtran*). The inclusion of these variables causes the pseudo R-square to rise dramatically. Almost all the basic needs variables are statistically significant determinants of happiness.

Column C adds to A only the monetary poverty variables, that is income (log of household per capita income) and wealth (value of assets owned). Both *lnhhpci* and *assetval* are important determinants: the inclusion of these two variables raises the pseudo R-square by more than does the set of 14 basic needs variables (Column B).

Column D includes control variables together with both basic needs and income/asset variables. The coefficient on income falls significantly compared with Column C, but remains large and statistically highly significant. Controlling for income and assets reduces the coefficients of the basic needs variables and renders most of them insignificant. The physical functioning variables that have a statistically significant relationship with subjective well-being even after controlling for monetary poverty are health, employment and condition of community roads (which probably proxies for other community factors as well). Higher education is the only level of education that remains significant, but that is hardly a *basic* need.

Column E of Table 4 adds three types of social functioning variables: race dummies (*African, Coloured, Indian* – the base category being *White*), location dummies (*urban, metropol,* and *homeland*) and whether the household is a racial

Table 4. Determinants of subjective well-being

	With only control variables (A)		Control plus basic needs (B)		Control plus income/assets (C)		Control plus basic needs and income/assets (D)	
	Coefficient	Robust t	Coefficient	Robust t	Coefficient	Robust t	Coefficient	Robust t
Control variables								
Age 16–25	0.118	1.1	0.247	2.5***	0.388	3.9***	0.390	4.0***
Age 26–35	0.026	0.3	0.006	0.1	0.076	1.2	0.075	1.2
Age 46–55	0.191	2.2**	0.150	1.9*	0.059	0.8	0.071	0.9
Age 56–65	0.223	2.0**	0.292	2.7***	0.177	1.7*	0.201	1.9*
Age ≥ 66	0.306	2.9***	0.505	4.8***	0.306	3.2***	0.359	3.3***
Hhsizem	−0.028	−2.2**	−0.005	−0.4	−0.049	−4.2***	−0.028	−2.2**
Hhnchild	−0.005	−0.3	0.042	2.2**	0.083	4.7***	0.070	3.7***
Male	0.008	0.1	0.005	0.1	−0.017	−0.2	−0.022	−0.2
Migrate	0.370	3.5***	0.244	2.4***	0.259	2.2**	0.233	2.2**
Basic needs variables								
Primary			−0.047	−0.6			−0.036	−0.5
Junior			0.013	0.2			−0.072	−1.1
Secondry			0.300	3.7***			0.010	0.1
Higher			0.838	7.5***			0.256	2.8***
Hhdaysic			−0.004	−1.8*			−0.005	−1.9*
Ironroof			−0.094	−1.4			−0.087	−1.3
Pipeint			0.310	2.8***			0.080	0.7
Wdist			0.000	1.6			0.000	1.6
Personpr			−0.078	−3.6***			−0.031	−1.5

(*continued*)

Table 4. (*Continued*)

	With only control variables (A)		Control plus basic needs (B)		Control plus income/assets (C)		Control plus basic needs and income/assets (D)	
	Coefficient	Robust t	Coefficient	Robust t	Coefficient	Robust t	Coefficient	Robust t
Connecte			0.143	1.9*			0.037	0.5
Hhurate1			−0.373	−7.7***			−0.193	−3.8***
Nolfpb			−0.121	−2.5***			−0.018	−0.3
Impass			−0.164	−2.8***			−0.144	−2.5***
Pubtran			−0.029	−0.5			0.000	0.0
Income/assets variables								
Lnhhcpi					0.174	8.2***	0.117	5.9***
Assetval					0.027	12.7***	0.022	8.7***
Province	Yes		Yes		Yes		Yes	
LogL	−12000.89		−11405.41		−11291.39		−11228.89	
Psuedo R^2	0.0163		0.0651		0.0745		0.0796	

Notes: $N = 8279$, restricted LogL = −12199.69. Variable definitions as in Table 2 and as follows: Racialm = household is a racial minority in its cluster; assetval = value of assets owned by the household, calculated as follows: assetval = (ncar * 8) + (nphone * 3) + (nkettle * 0.5) + (nradio * 0.2) + (nfridge * 5) + (nbike * 1) + (nestove * 0.5) + (ngstove * 0.5) + (ntv * 3) + (ngeyser * 2), where the preface 'n' before each variable means 'number of'. Thus, ncar is number of cars, nbike means number of bikes, ntv means number of TVs, nestove is number of electric stoves and ngstove is number of gas stoves, etc.; debt = whether household owes any debt; urateb = cluster unemployment rate. *, ** and *** denote statistical significance at the 10%, 5% and 1% levels respectively.

(*continued*)

Table 4. (*Continued*)

	Control, basic needs, income, social needs (E)		Control, basic needs, social needs, security and income (F)		Parsimonious version of (F) (G)		
	Coefficient	Robust t	Coefficient	Robust t	Coefficient	Robust t	Marginal effect on probability of being dissatisfied or very dissatisfied
Control variables							
Age 16–25	0.318	3.6***	0.322	3.7***	0.339	3.9***	−0.133
Age 26–35	0.062	1.1	0.060	1.1	0.067	1.1	−0.026
Age 46–55	0.043	0.6	0.031	0.4	0.036	0.5	−0.014
Age 56–65	0.148	1.5	0.117	1.2	0.128	1.2	−0.050
Age ≥ 66	0.295	2.7***	0.253	2.3**	0.266	2.4***	−0.104
Hhsizem	−0.015	1.3	−0.014	1.2	−0.018	−1.6	0.007
Hhmchild	0.047	2.7***	0.051	2.9***	0.052	3.1***	−0.020
Male	0.005	0.1	0.000	0.0			
Migrate	0.217	2.1**	0.213	2.1**	0.213	1.9*	−0.084
Basic needs variables							
Primary	−0.017	0.2	−0.031	0.4			
Junior	−0.032	0.5	−0.036	0.6			
Secondary	0.033	0.5	0.018	0.3			
Higher	0.205	2.3**	0.199	2.2**	0.218	2.8***	−0.086
Hhdaysic	−0.006	2.4***	−0.005	2.3**	−0.005	2.2**	0.002
Ironroof	−0.127	2.0**	−0.123	2.0**	−0.120	1.9*	0.047
Pipeint	−0.012	0.1	−0.047	0.4			
Wdist	0.000	0.7	0.000	0.8			
Personpr	−0.025	1.2	−0.023	1.1			
Connecte	0.061	0.8	0.041	0.6			
Hhurate1	−0.218	4.4***	−0.152	3.2***	−0.145	3.0***	0.057

(continued)

Table 4. (*Continued*)

	Control, basic needs, income, social needs (E)		Control, basic needs, social needs, security and income (F)		Parsimonious version of (F) (G)		
	Coefficient	Robust t	Coefficient	Robust t	Coefficient	Robust t	Marginal effect
Nolfpb	−0.053	−1.0	−0.010	−0.2	0.001	0.0	−0.001
Impass	−0.086	−1.4	−0.072	−1.2	−0.057	−0.9	0.023
Pubtran	0.088	1.4	0.103	1.7*	0.107	1.7*	−0.042
Income/assets variables							
Lnhhcpi	0.104	5.2***	0.105	5.2***	0.110	5.0***	−0.043
Assetval	0.014	5.7***	0.014	5.4***	0.014	5.9***	−0.006
Social functioning variables							
African	−0.664	−6.0***	−0.597	−5.3***	−0.576	−5.0***	0.227
Colored	−0.287	−2.4***	−0.225	−2.0**	−0.228	−1.9*	0.087
Indian	−0.224	−2.1**	−0.193	−1.8*	−0.209	−2.0**	0.080
Racialm	0.233	2.5***	0.246	2.7***	0.249	2.6***	−0.099
Metropol	−0.276	−2.2**	−0.244	−1.9*	−0.291	−2.8***	0.112
Urbanl	−0.238	−2.4***	−0.212	−2.2**	−0.251	−3.0***	0.097
Homeland	0.041	0.4	0.103	1.0			
Security variables							
N_victim			−0.091	−2.3**	−0.089	−2.3**	0.035
Ownship_			0.079	1.8*	0.097	2.2**	−0.038
Debt			−0.065	−1.6*	−0.062	−1.5	0.024
Urateb			−0.581	−3.2***	−0.529	−2.7***	0.208
Province	Yes		Yes		Yes		
LogL	−11140.15		−11111.19		−11117.50		
Psuedo R^2	0.0869		0.0892		0.0887		

$N = 8279$; Restricted LogL = −12199.69.

minority in the cluster in which it lives (*racialm*). In order to function socially, people must be able to relate well to others in society. Each of these variables can affect the ability to function within the society: race can reflect discrimination and prejudice, location can identify the type of community or lifestyle to which one relates, and being a racial minority in a cluster can reflect social disadvantage. The inclusion of the race and location variables raises the explanatory power of the model but makes little difference to the original variables. Race is important even after controlling for income and physical functionings. As discussed in Section IV, when cluster fixed effects are used, race becomes insignificant, suggesting that here it is picking up the effect of unobserved cluster conditions that matter to life-satisfaction. People in urban areas and metropolitan cities are significantly less happy than those in rural areas. Households that are racial minorities in their cluster are happier than others. This is contrary to our expectation, but it is possible that *racialm* proxies for the high achievement among non-White households which enables them to live in predominantly White areas.

Column F adds what we have termed 'security/insecurity' variables. These capture how insecure the household is physically (in terms of exposure to crime, *n_victim*) and economically, in terms of *debt*, risk of unemployment (as captured by the cluster unemployment rate, *urateb*) and lack of assets that could be liquidated in time of need (home ownership, *ownship*).[7] Inclusion of these variables does not alter the existing coefficients, and it raises explanatory power only modestly. The variables themselves are mostly statistically significant, and have the expected signs: insecurity reduces subjective well-being.

A comparison of Columns C and F shows that the introduction of all the other poverty variables reduces the coefficient on log of household per capita income (*lnhhpci*) substantially from 0.174 to 0.105. It suggests that the direct influence of income is 60 per cent, and the indirect influence is 40 per cent, of its total effect. However, this may exaggerate the indirect influence of income if their association does not reflect the causal effect of income on the other variables.

Column G provides our preferred, parsimonious version of Column F, together with the marginal effects of the variables on the probability of being subjective well-being poor, that is of being dissatisfied or very dissatisfied with life. The means, standard deviations and the full set of marginal effects of the variables are shown in Appendix Table 1. If the proportion of household members aged 16–25 increases from one standard deviation below to one standard deviation above the mean, the probability of being in the bottom two life-satisfaction categories falls by 7 percentage points. A rise in log of per capita household income from one standard deviation below to one standard deviation above the mean reduces the probability of subjective well-being poverty (that is of being dissatisfied or very dissatisfied with life) by 12 percentage points. Considering that overall probability of being dissatisfied/very dissatisfied is 55 per cent, this is not a large reduction. The African probability of being subjective well-being poor is 23 percentage points higher than that of Whites, even after controlling for observed income, education and employment, etc. Those who live in metropolitan cities are 11 percentage points more likely to be in subjective well-being poverty than are rural-dwellers. The household's own unemployment rate has a smaller effect on the probability of being in the bottom two happiness categories than does the cluster unemployment rate.

Going from one standard deviation below to one standard deviation above the household unemployment rate increases that probability by 4 percentage points but doing the same for the cluster unemployment rate reduces it by 10 percentage points. The effects of higher education, health, crime and debt are also small, compared with the effect of household income, household assets, and race.

What do these results enable us to say about the relationships among the various criteria for poverty? Subjective well-being poverty is related to both income poverty and capabilities poverty. The comparison of the R-squares in Columns B and C of Table 4 suggests that it is somewhat better related to income poverty than it is to capabilities poverty but this may be because our measures of capabilities poverty are imperfect. Certainly the results do not support the notion that income poverty is an adequate measure of capabilities poverty since variables that measure physical and social capabilities to function – such as health, employment, mobility, and freedom from forms of insecurity – matter to happiness even after controlling for economic factors such as income and assets. The parsimonious version of the all-inclusive equation (Column G) indicates that, in addition to the control variables, the economic variables (income and assets), some physical functioning variables, some social functioning variables and some security variables have a statistically significant influence on subjective well-being. The subjective well-being approach to poverty is not necessarily in competition with the other approaches. Rather, it can be viewed as an encompassing approach which incorporates, evaluates and weights the others.

We experimented with the inclusion of both the income (*lnhhpci*) and also the race-specific income quintile of the household (r_pciqj, $j = 1, \ldots, 5$); r_pciq1, the lowest quintile being the omitted category). Table 5 shows the results for these variables; a full set of conditioning variables were included but are not reported. The equation was estimated for two groups: the income-poor and the income-non-poor. There is an interesting difference between the income-poor (who represent roughly half of the households) and the non-poor. The coefficient on *lnhhpci* is significantly positive for

Table 5. The effect of absolute and relative income variables on subjective well-being, by poverty status

	Below poverty line		Above poverty line	
	Coefficient	Robust t	Coefficient	Robust t
	Absolute income variable			
Lnhhpci	0.071	2.2**	−0.087	−1.0
	Relative income variables			
R_pciq2	0.072	1.3	0.071	0.8
R_pciq3	0.038	0.6	0.149	1.3
R_pciq4	0.103	1.0	0.449	3.3***
R_pciq5	–	–	0.536	2.7***

Notes: A full set of conditioning variables is included but not reported. Income poverty is defined by the 'Household supplementary level' poverty line for South Africa of Rand 251 per month in 1993 (Julian May, 1998). The omitted quintile dummy variable is the lowest income quintile r_pciq1. ** and *** denote statistical significance at the 5% and 1% level respectively. *Source*: Kingdon and Knight (2007, forthcoming).

the poor but not for the others. However, the coefficients on the race-specific income quintiles rise monotonically, and the highest two are highly significant, in the non-poor group, whereas there is no such relationship in the poor group. For those in income poverty, it is absolute income that matters, whereas for others it is relative income – in particular relative income within their race-group – that affects their subjective well-being. It suggests that the need to function physically predominates when income is low but that social functioning takes over as income rises.[8]

V. Conclusions

We have developed a methodology for using a measure of subjective well-being as the criterion for poverty, and have illustrated its use by reference to a South African data set. We conclude generally that the new research on the economics of happiness, although still in its infancy, does indeed offer promise of successful adaptation for the analysis of poverty in poor countries.

Our main conceptual and empirical conclusions are the following. Survey-based indicators of subjective well-being are amenable to quantitative analysis, and can be explained in terms of numerous socio-economic variables. There are powerful regularities to be found, both generally and in our own illustrative analysis. This raises the possibility of using explanations of subjective well-being to examine poverty. Any attempt to define and describe poverty involves a value judgement as to what constitutes a good quality of life or a bad one. We argued that an approach which examines the individual's own reported perception of well-being is less imperfect, or more quantifiable, or both, as a guide to forming that value judgement than are the other potential approaches. Thus, we combined positive and normative analysis. We used the positive results on the determinants of subjective well-being to infer value judgements about the nature and components of poverty that were based on the aggregation of individual perceptions.

In our illustrative case study we found that income and happiness are positively correlated but that the association is not exclusive. Income enters positively and significantly into the subjective well-being function but so also do several other variables. These include proxies for the fulfilment of various needs which cannot normally be met by spending income. Many of the variables that determine income also determine subjective well-being, but their effects can differ in relative importance and even in direction.

Provided that the metric of utility is accepted as the evaluative criterion, the subjective well-being approach to poverty does not compete with the income, capabilities and security approaches, but rather encompasses them. Our main contribution is to view subjective well-being as an encompassing concept, permitting us to quantify the relevance and importance of the other approaches to poverty and of their component variables. In estimating subjective well-being functions for South Africa we found that our preferred equation contained some variables corresponding to the income approach, some to the basic needs (or physical functioning) approach, some to the relative (or social functioning) approach, and some to the security approach. Our methodology effectively provided weights of the relative importance of these various components of subjective well-being poverty. We regard this approach as superior to one that arbitrarily attaches weights – quite likely equal weights, for lack of a reasoned alternative – to certain pre-selected components. Although those who regard functionings as having value irrespective of people's feelings about them may reject our approach, they in turn face the problem of finding operational measures of poverty.

Two caveats are in order. First, the possibility that some of the explanatory variables are endogenous or causally interrelated, and our inability to correct for these problems in this data set, means that the estimated weights on the explanatory variables might be a somewhat misleading guide to their causal effects on subjective well-being. Second, we would not wish to generalise from the South African case: the possibility that different preferences across countries will generate different sets of weights opens a new avenue of research.

Acknowledgements

We would like to thank John Helliwell for stimulating discussions about the ideas in this paper. In addition to workshop participants at the GPRG workshop, Oxford, and seminar participants at the Wellbeing in Developing Countries (WeD) Research Group at Bath University, we would like to thank Alan Krueger, Allister McGregor, Wendy Olsen, John Toye and an anonymous referee for helpful comments on the paper. Any errors are ours. The support of the UK Economic and Social Research Council is gratefully acknowledged. The work was part of the programme of the ESRC Global Poverty Research Group (grant M571255001).

Notes

1. Ravallion and Lokshin (2001) and Graham and Pettinato (2002) are exceptions.
2. There are obvious issues of endogeneity and causality which will be discussed below.
3. Powdthavee (2005) and Moller (1998) have also written on perceived quality of life in South Africa.
4. In Table 2 (and throughout the paper) standard errors have been corrected for clustering.
5. An instrumentation procedure can in principle be used to address the likely endogeneity of income in a happiness equation. Empirically justifiable instruments available are the variables proportion of males in the household and household size, both of which are statistically significant in the income equation and insignificant in the happiness equation. However, there is no strong a priori theoretical justification for them. Studies using panel data and exogenous variation in income (for example a lottery win) have found that causality runs from income to happiness (for example see Gardner and Oswald, 2001).
6. We experimented with variables from the cluster questionnaire including distance from the cluster to various facilities (such as health clinic, school, shops, bank, post office, market, etc), number of such facilities within the cluster, and distance to nearest source of transport, as well as with cluster averages of household variables such as distance to nearest source of water for the household, etc.
7. The *ownship*, *debt* and *urateb* variables could be included under the monetary variables category, together with income and assets, and the crime variable included under the physical functionings (basic needs) category.
8. Kingdon and Knight (2007, forthcoming) explore the influence of relative income on subjective well-being in greater detail.

References

Atkinson, A. B. and Bourguignon, F. (1999) Poverty and inclusion from a world perspective. Typescript, July. Also published as (2000) Pauvrete et inclusion dans une perspective mondiale, *Revue d'Economie du Developpement*, June, pp. 13–32.
Clark, A. and Oswald, A. (1994) Unhappiness and unemployment, *Economic Journal*, 104, pp. 648–59.

Clark, D. A. (2005) Sen's capability approach and the many spaces of human well-being, *Journal of Development Studies*, 42(8), pp. 1339–68.

Diener, E. and Biswas-Diener, R. (2000) New directions in subjective well-being research: The cutting edge, mimeo, University of Illinois.

Diener, E. and Biswas-Diener, R. (2003) Findings on subjective well-being and their implications for empowerment, Workshop on Measuring Empowerment: Cross-Disciplinary Perspectives, Washington DC: World Bank, February 2003.

Di Tella, R., MacCulloch, R. and Oswald, A. (2001) Preferences over inflation and unemployment: evidence from surveys of happiness, *American Economic Review*, 91, pp. 335–41.

Duesenberry, J. S. (1949) *Income, Savings and the Theory of Consumer Behavior* (Cambridge: University of Harvard Press).

Easterlin, R. A. (2001) Income and happiness: towards a unified theory, *Economic Journal*, 111, pp. 465–84.

Frey, B. and Stutzer, A. (2002) Can economists learn from happiness research? *Journal of Economic Literature*, 40, 402–35.

Gardner, J. and Oswald, A. (2001) Does money buy happiness? A longitudinal study using data on windfalls, mimeo, University of Warwick.

Graham, C. and Pettinato, S. (2002) Frustrated achievers: Winners, losers and subjective well-being in new market economies, *Journal of Development Studies*, 38, 100–40.

Helliwell, J. F. (2002) How's life? Combining individual and national variables to explain subjective well-being, *Economic Modelling*, 20, pp. 331–60.

Kingdon, G. G. and Knight, J. (2007) Community, comparisons and subjective well-being in a divided society, *Journal of Economic Behaviour and Organization*, forthcoming.

Laderchi, C. R., Saith, R. and Stewart, F. (2003) Does it matter that we do not agree on the definition of poverty? A comparison of four approaches, *Oxford Development Studies*, 31, pp. 243–74.

Layard, R. (2003) Happiness, *LSE Alumnus Magazine*, Summer, p. 10.

Moller, V. (1998) Quality of life in South Africa: post apartheid trends, *Social Indicators Research*, 43, pp. 27–68.

Powdthavee, N. (2005) *Essays on the use of subjective well-being data in economic analysis: An empirical study using developed and developing countries data.* Doctoral dissertation, Economics Department, Warwick University.

Pradhan, M. and Ravallion, M. (2000) Measuring poverty using qualitative perceptions of consumption adequacy, *Review of Economics and Statistics*, 82, pp. 462–71.

Ravallion, M. and Lokshin, M. (2001) Identifying welfare effects using subjective questions, *Economica*, 68, pp. 335–57.

Ravallion, M. and Lokshin, M. (2002) Self-rated economic welfare in Russia, *European Economic Review*, 46, pp. 1453–73.

Runciman, W. G. (1966) *Relative Deprivation and Social Justice* (Berkeley: University of California Press).

SALDRU (1994) *South Africans Rich and Poor: Baseline Household Statistics, Project for Statistics on Living Standards and Development* (Cape Town: South African Labour and Development Research Unit, University of Cape Town).

Sen, A. K. (1983) Poor, relatively speaking, *Oxford Economic Papers*, 35, pp. 153–69.

Sen, A. K. (1984) Rights and capabilities, in *Resources, Values and Development*, pp. 307–24 (Oxford: Basil Blackwell).

UNDP (2000) *Human Development Report 2000* (New York: Oxford University Press).

Veenhoven, R. (1991) Is happiness relative? *Social Indicators Research*, 24, pp. 1–34.

Winkelmann, L. and Winkelmann, R. (1998) Why are the unemployed so unhappy? Evidence from panel data, *Economica*, 65, pp. 1–15.

World Bank (1990) *World Development Report 1990* (Oxford: Oxford University Press for the World Bank).

Appendix

Table A1. Means, standard deviations, and detailed marginal effects of variables, using parsimonious specification of Table 4

	Descriptive		Marginal effects on probability of being			
	Mean	S.D.	Very dissatisfied	Dissatisfied	Satisfied	Very satisfied
Control variables						
Age 16–25	0.198	0.244	−0.094	−0.039	0.089	0.032
Age 26–35	0.186	0.282	−0.018	−0.008	0.017	0.006
Age 46–55	0.083	0.194	−0.010	−0.004	0.009	0.003
Age 56–65	0.059	0.166	−0.035	−0.015	0.034	0.012
Age ≥ 66	0.051	0.158	−0.073	−0.031	0.069	0.025
Hhsizem	4.562	2.984	0.005	0.002	−0.005	−0.002
Hhnchild	1.849	1.963	−0.014	−0.006	0.014	0.005
Migrate	0.117	0.310	−0.059	−0.025	0.056	0.020
Basic needs variables						
Higher	0.075	0.218	−0.060	−0.025	0.057	0.021
Hhdaysic	3.002	6.378	0.001	0.001	−0.001	0.000
Ironroof	0.561	0.496	0.033	0.014	−0.031	−0.011
Hhurate1	0.218	0.357	0.040	0.017	−0.038	−0.014
Nolfpb	0.156	0.363	0.000	0.000	0.000	0.000
Impass	0.387	0.487	0.016	0.007	−0.015	−0.005
Pubtran	0.731	0.443	−0.030	−0.012	0.028	0.010
Income/assets variables						
Lnhhcpi	5.578	1.412	−0.030	−0.013	0.029	0.010
Assetval	9.558	13.216	−0.004	−0.002	0.004	0.001
Social functioning variables						
African	0.746	0.435	0.140	0.087	−0.145	−0.070
Colored	0.076	0.266	0.068	0.019	−0.059	−0.018
Indian	0.029	0.169	0.063	0.018	−0.054	−0.017
Racialm	0.103	0.304	−0.063	−0.036	0.064	0.028
Metropol	0.283	0.450	0.085	0.028	−0.075	−0.025
Urban1	0.220	0.414	0.074	0.023	−0.065	−0.021
Security variables						
N_victim	0.115	0.356	0.025	0.010	−0.023	−0.008
Ownship_	0.650	0.477	−0.027	−0.011	0.025	0.009
Debt	0.447	0.497	0.017	0.007	−0.016	−0.006
Urateb	0.324	0.237	0.146	0.061	−0.138	−0.050

Table A2. Subjective well-being equation with individual respondent's personal characteristic

	Parsimonious equation from Table 4 (A)		(A) with personal characteristics of the household respondent (B)	
	Coefficient	Robust t	Coefficient	Robust t
Control variables				
Age 16–25	0.339	3.9***	0.267	2.9***
Age 26–35	0.067	1.1	0.020	0.3
Age 46–55	0.036	0.5	0.084	1.1
Age 56–65	0.128	1.2	0.200	1.8*
Age ≥ 66	0.266	2.4***	0.331	2.7***
Hhsizem	−0.018	−1.6	−0.012	−1.0
Hhnchild	0.052	3.1***	0.044	2.5***
Migrate	0.213	1.9*	0.218	2.0**
Basic needs variables				
Higher	0.218	2.8***	0.250	2.8***
Hhdaysic	−0.005	−2.2**	−0.005	−2.2**
Ironroof	−0.120	−1.9*	−0.114	−1.8*
Hhurate1	−0.145	−3.0***	−0.140	−2.7***
Nolfpb	0.001	0.0	0.013	0.2
Impass	−0.057	−0.9	−0.062	−1.0
Pubtran	0.107	1.7*	0.111	1.8*
Income/assets variables				
Lnhhcpi	0.110	5.0***	0.115	5.1***
Assetval	0.014	5.9***	0.015	6.2***
Social functioning variables				
African	−0.576	−5.0***	−0.566	−5.0***
Colored	−0.228	−1.9*	−0.210	−1.8*
Indian	−0.209	−2.0**	−0.197	−1.9*
Racialm	0.249	2.6***	0.247	2.6***
Metropol	−0.291	−2.8***	−0.300	−2.8***
Urban1	−0.251	−3.0***	−0.255	−3.2***
Security variables				
N_victim	−0.089	−2.3**	−0.092	−2.3**
Ownship_	0.097	2.2**	0.099	2.3**
Debt	−0.062	−1.5	−0.061	−1.5
Urateb	−0.529	−2.7***	−0.542	−2.8***
R_age			−0.010	−1.9*
R_agesq			0.000	1.3
R_edyrs			−0.006	−0.5
R_edyrsq			0.000	0.1
R_male			−0.021	−0.6
R_empld			0.003	0.1
Province	yes		Yes	
LogL	−11117.50		−10984.71	
Restr LogL	−12199.69		−12063.84	
Psuedo R^2	0.0887		0.0895	
N	8,279		8,190	

Note: r_age and r_agesq are respondent's age and its square; r_edyrs and r_edyrsq are respondent's years of education and its square; r_male is gender and r_empld whether the respondent is employed or not.

Poverty Persistence and Transitions in Uganda: A Combined Qualitative and Quantitative Analysis

DAVID LAWSON, ANDY MCKAY, & JOHN OKIDI

I. Introduction

Uganda's excellent record in reducing the national incidence of monetary poverty over the 1990s is widely known. However, longitudinal household survey data reveal that this net aggregate reduction was accompanied by substantial mobility into as well as out of poverty (Okidi and McKay, 2003). A majority of those that were poor in 1992 had escaped by 1999, but a substantial minority were left behind and many others fell into poverty. Against a background of strong macroeconomic performance in Uganda over this decade, there was a significant variation in individual experiences of poverty movements, and it is important to understand the factors, many of which are individual or local, that contributed to this.

We develop the understanding of these movements by combining qualitative and quantitative insights at the individual, household and community level.

The qualitative component draws on the results of the two assessments conducted as part of the Uganda Participatory Poverty Assessment Process (UPPAP), and this provides important insights about the processes and factors associated with poverty transitions and persistence. The quantitative analysis is based on longitudinal (or panel) household survey data sets where the same household is surveyed at more than one point in time. This component builds strongly on earlier work by Okidi, with different authors, exploiting these panel data sets (Deininger and Okidi, 2003; Okidi and McKay, 2003, among others). The qualitative sources add substantially to the information available from the panel survey data alone, by helping to identify key issues to investigate using the survey data and by providing important additional insights not available from the survey data, including about processes and contextual factors.

This paper is structured as follows. In Section II we briefly review general approaches to developing a dynamic understanding of poverty, including persistent or chronic poverty. Building on this, in Section III we outline the available qualitative evidence on the key factors and processes identified by communities and their members as lying behind their experiences of poverty transitions or non-transitions. In particular, we identify some clear individual, household, community and local policy factors contributing to impoverishment. Sections IV and V then builds on the qualitative evidence by presenting descriptive and econometric analysis drawing on household panel survey data. In this way we are able to consider the importance of different factors behind movements in monetary poverty. In Section VI we conclude by synthesising the qualitative and quantitative insights, and then comment on the methodological scope for combining qualitative and quantitative approaches to enhance the understanding of poverty dynamics.

II. Understanding Factors Underlying Poverty Persistence and Transitions

The key focus of this paper is to identify factors that are important drivers, interrupters and maintainers of poverty (Hulme et al., 2001: 33) in Uganda – that is, factors influencing respectively movements into poverty, escapes from poverty and the inability to escape from poverty. An important starting point for this paper is to review existing approaches to identifying determinants of poverty, seen in a dynamic perspective. Existing literature on factors underlying chronic, or persistent, poverty is particularly relevant, by helping identify the factors that prevent individuals and households from making poverty transitions. This can be viewed at different levels from the individual to national level and above, although the focus here will mostly be on the household and community level, reflecting available information for Uganda.

Chronic poverty is often seen as reflecting a lack of basic security, which is pervasive both over time and across different aspects of living conditions making it very difficult to escape poverty (Wresinski, 1987; Wood, 2003). A standard, and basic, economic approach views household income as reflecting the assets a household has command over and the returns it can earn on these. Income poverty therefore reflects inadequate levels of one or both of these.

Asset ownership and returns are therefore of key importance, but a livelihoods approach (Ellis, 2000) is one important way of generalising this approach to a broader understanding of poverty. In particular this represents a more dynamic approach, which is of particular relevance here. According to the livelihoods framework a household's livelihood strategy, and so its level of well-being, depends on the assets it has access to (classically financial, human, natural, physical and social capital); the factors that mediate their access (for instance, gender relations or how markets operate); and contextual factors (such as macro policies or shocks). Both local factors and wider regional, national and global factors can be important influences of living conditions.

Building on the livelihoods framework and drawing on Sen's freedoms approach (Sen, 1999), Hulme et al. (2001) develop an extended view of chronic poverty based on a wider range of 'assets', including political and security assets. Some of these factors may be what economists typically think of as factors influencing returns to assets. Whichever framework is used, this approach is useful in thinking about the wide range of factors influencing dynamic poverty status in Uganda.

Identifying the range of factors (or assets) referred to above of relevant to poverty dynamics calls for both qualitative and quantitative approaches, and so this paper combines insights from both sources. This combined approach (much of which has been based on participatory poverty assessment and household survey data) is increasingly applied in poverty research. Examples of this include the studies by Parker and Kozel (2004) for India, and Barahona and Levy (2003) for Malawi.

However, in many instances these studies are applied at local levels because of the absence of national participatory and qualitative information. For Uganda, and as noted above, we are particularly fortunate in that qualitative assessment can draw on two rounds of the Uganda Participatory Poverty Assessment Process (UPPAP), whose primary aim was to allow different communities across Uganda to express their local understanding of poverty and their perceptions about policy priorities. These intuitive understandings of poverty are often highly dynamic in nature, and the participatory poverty assessments (PPAs) also help identify commonly perceived causes of poverty transitions.

The PPAs do not though allow for an understanding of the relative importance of different factors, nor do they enable generalisation to a wider level. For these reasons understandings of the factors influencing poverty dynamics are frequently drawn from nationwide panel surveys. These are most commonly analysed in consumption/income terms but which can be related to a wide range of correlates also available from the survey data. In this case, we analyse the results of the 1992–1999 household panel formed by the 1992–1993 Integrated Household Survey (IHS) and the 1999–2000 Uganda National Household Survey (UNHS) for information on poverty correlates. Such analysis is theoretically based on a Ramsey consumption growth model (Jalan and Ravallion, 2000), which relates changes in household living conditions (or discrete representations of this capturing movements across poverty lines) to initial period levels of key household assets and other characteristics which are likely to influence their subsequent fortunes.

In this paper we seek to synthesise qualitative and quantitative insights on chronic poverty. We do this by first reviewing key insights about poverty transitions from the qualitative sources, and then see to what extent these are found to be a more widespread phenomenon in Uganda based on the quantitative data. The nature of the available information though is such that some factors can only be clearly identified from one approach or the other.

III. Qualitative Evidence on Factors Affecting Poverty Transition in Uganda

There is now a significant amount of qualitative information about poverty in Uganda, with the main source being the two large-scale participatory poverty assessments carried out as part of UPPAP in 1998–1999 and 2002. Drawing on detailed fieldwork in nine districts in 1998–1999 and 12 in 2002, the results provide a rich source of information on local understandings of poverty and of policy priorities (Republic of Uganda, 2000, 2002). Of specific relevance to this paper, they also provide valuable insights about factors contributing to poverty persistence and transitions, which we focus on in the following discussion.

Communities covered in both rounds typically express clear ideas of what poverty means to them, and these understandings have a clear and important dimension of persistence. Thus in the first PPA, poverty is described as a perpetual need for daily necessities of life and a feeling of powerlessness (Republic of Uganda, 2000: 11), and the difficulty of overcoming poverty is stressed. In both rounds a household's lack of assets, such as land or financial capital, is seen as a major factor contributing to the perpetuation of poverty (Republic of Uganda, 2002). But having adequate land is insufficient by itself if there is no effective access to markets, or excessive local taxes (a problem widely stressed). In addition, a lack local community leadership and the presence of corruption and insecurity are also seen as important factors behind poverty and its perpetuation.

However, the two factors most strongly identified in both PPAs were poor gender relations and alcohol abuse. Poor gender relations were regarded as 'causing and perpetuating poverty' (Republic of Uganda, 2000: 13). Key factors behind the perpetuation of unequal gender relations (identified very strongly as a central maintainer of poverty in the second PPA in particular) included the practice of paying a bride price; domestic violence (often linked to alcohol abuse); and conservative attitudes among both men and women. Excessive consumption of alcoholic drinks was widely regarded as a major and widespread problem by both women and men, in terms of the amount of money spent on it as well as its effects. At the same time, it was also recognised that the production and sale of alcoholic drinks was an important source of income, including for many women.

The participatory assessments also investigated the factors associated with movements into and out of poverty. Alcoholism was identified as one key factor underlying descents into poverty. Other important factors included being in a large (or polygamous) family; insecurity (especially in the north); loss of assets, a job, or remittances; loss of a spouse or marital breakup; and unfair taxation or lack of government support. The PPA results provided less information on how households were able to move out of poverty, but key factors identified were working hard and having access to assets.

Other qualitative evidence by Bird and Shinyekwa (2003) broadly supports such findings. They look at the factors behind downward mobility in poor rural communities in three Ugandan districts. Multiple shocks at the household and community level were found to be particularly important for leading to descents into poverty, with socio-cultural factors playing an important role in this. This leads to the likelihood that the individuals and households facing these multiple shocks and deprivations will be trapped in chronic poverty. Family defragmentation (following death of a key family member or marital breakdown) was a key shock, particularly impacting on women. Marginalised groups (such as the elderly, the disabled or internally displaced people), who typically have lower levels of assets, face the further disadvantage of commonly being excluded from the household and community support mechanisms that exist.

As in UPPAP, Bird and Shinyekwka found poor gender relations and excessive alcohol consumption to be key factors. Excessive drinking, reported by Bird and Shinyekwa to be widespread in rural areas, is identified as a major shock and contributor to further and persistent impoverishment in its own right, and prevents an escape from poverty.

In summary, available qualitative evidence identifies some clear messages about perceived causes of persistent poverty and descents into poverty (although less on causes of escaping from poverty) in the communities it relates to. The main results are clearly intuitive. But the extent to which these can be generalised across Uganda is unknown, and it is also difficult to identify the relative importance of different factors. In addition, little is known about escapes from poverty (which conceivably may be difficult for communities to recognise unless the changes are dramatic; those that are doing well have an obvious interest not to advertise it too widely).

For the aforementioned reasons, as well as to confirm results from the qualitative analysis where possible, there is a major benefit to complementing messages from qualitative sources with quantitative insights. This is especially the case when we can base such insights on a relatively large scale, nationwide panel survey over a period where the aggregate figures for monetary poverty show that quite a large number of households appear to have bettered their position and escaped poverty. This is the focus of the following section.

IV. The Nature of Poverty Transitions: Insights Based on Panel Data

The Uganda National Household Survey (UNHS) conducted in 1999–2000 was designed to include 1,398 households that had previously been surveyed in the Integrated Household Survey (IHS) of 1992–1993. The quantitative analysis in this paper is based on a subset of these intended panel households that can be matched with confidence.

Both the IHS and UNHS surveys were large multi-purpose household surveys, each based on stratified random cluster samples of around 10,000 households. The panel subcomponent of this was also designed to be nationally representative. The surveys collected information at household and community level on a wide range of characteristics, including demographic composition; education, health and housing; economic activities; household expenditures; and community infrastructure and characteristics. The analysis of monetary poverty here is based on the same approach used for the national level poverty studies (Appleton, 2001). The monetary measure of wellbeing is calculated as total household consumption expenditure per adult equivalent, adjusted for variations in prices between regions and the time period between the surveys, and the poverty line is defined with reference to minimum calorie requirements.

Data Matching and Attrition

To ensure that the panel households were the same in both periods, a two part matching process was undertaken. The first stage matched the sex and age of the household head, allowing for an acceptable error range given uncertainty about precise ages, etc.[1] A second stage focused on those households whose head had changed over the period, for example where a household head had died and another member of the family had become the new head. Therefore, in this phase, we checked to see if the current household head, referencing by sex and age, was in the household in the previous period.

Combining both stages of this matching process, results in 1103 households being matched for the 1992–1999 two wave panel. Thus 295 of the intended panel households could not be matched, in many cases perhaps because they were not interviewed in the second survey (due to factors such as mobility, household break-up, refusal to be interviewed etc.) survey, implying an attrition rate of 21 per cent. Although this may seem to be quite a high attrition rate, potentially raising sampling concerns, such levels of attrition are perhaps not surprising when considering that we are following households whose head in the second round is present in the household in the first round, over an eight year period. Furthermore, when we compare attrition levels, with similar empirical work (Alderman et al., 2000; Davis and Stampini, 2002), such levels are not unusual. Despite this however, we still consider it pertinent to test whether there are systematic patterns of attrition.

In order to assess the relevance of attrition in for selectivity we perform two kinds of analysis. Firstly, we compare the initial characteristics of both the reduced and full panel with the 1992 IHS, to see if the families which dropped out are different from those which stayed in. Secondly, we use statistical methods (estimation of probit models) in order to identify which variables predict attrition.

Appendix Table A2 outlines the means of the main household characteristics for those of the 1,398 households that were re-interviewed and could be matched across the two surveys (panel households) and those that dropped out (attrited households). Overall, we notice that the full sample of the 1,398 intended panel households are characterised by lower incomes than the full IHS sample. Reassuringly however, such differences and the mean incomes of the attrited and matched panel households, are not statistically significantly different from zero,[2] and this is the distinction that matters for current purposes.

In terms of other characteristics, statistically significant differences between the attrited and matched panel households are only observed in terms of the gender of the household head and level of spouse primary education. However, a further analysis using a probit model (a multivariate approach which seeks to identify significant correlates of whether an intended panel household was included in the panel) shows that such characteristics are statistically insignificant (Appendix Table A3).[3]

Overall therefore, the results indicate that attrition is not a major problem for this sample, with both the simple descriptive data and multivariate probit model showing that the household characteristics collectively are significant but explain only a small proportion of the probability of attrition. Given these results, we proceed by using standard data analysis and regression techniques.

Patterns of Poverty Dynamics in Uganda

Adopting the accepted poverty lines for Uganda calculated by Appleton (2001), which show the population identified as poor to have fallen from 55.7 per cent in 1992 to 35.2 per cent in 1999, we now focus on the dynamics of poverty change using the panels.

Although the panels represent small subsamples of the national surveys, as we can see from Table 1 the poverty incidence figures based on the panel households are broadly similar to the national level figures. Within the 1992–1999 panel, the poverty incidence fell from 48.6 per cent of households in 1992 to 29.3 per cent by 1999. 18.9 per cent of these panel households were chronically poor (poor in both periods), while nearly 40 per cent experienced transitory poverty over this period, 29.6 per cent of households moving out of poverty and 10.3 per cent slipping in.[4]

There are also important geographic differences in the distribution of chronic and transitory poverty (Table 1). Most striking are results relating to rural areas and particularly to the northern region. Almost one third of chronically poor households in Uganda reside in the Northern region, compared to just over one seventh of the population. Within this region almost two in every five households are chronically

Table 1. Poverty incidence (by region) – 1992/99 panel

Geographic location	Poverty status (per cent)				
	Chronic poverty	Moving out of poverty	Moving into poverty	Never in poverty	All
National	18.9	29.6	10.3	40.9	100
Urban/rural and region					
Column percentages					
Urban	8.1	12.2	8.8	21.9	15.0
Rural	91.9	87.8	91.2	78.1	85.0
Central region	23.4	32.0	26.3	37.2	31.9
East region	19.6	28.0	21.9	19.9	22.5
North region	30.1	11.3	25.4	6.8	14.5
West region	26.8	28.7	26.3	36.1	31.1
Row percentages					
Urban	10.6	23.9	6.0	59.1	100
Rural	20.5	30.7	11.1	37.6	100
Central region	13.8	29.7	8.5	47.8	100
East region	16.4	36.8	10.4	36.2	100
North region	38.9	22.8	18.1	20.1	100
West region	16.2	27.2	8.7	47.6	100

poor. They are also less likely to have escaped poverty and more likely to have fallen into poverty over this period compared to the other regions.

This evidence is corroborated by findings in the second UPPAP report, where the majority of the communities identified insecurity and displacement (key characteristic features of the northern region over this period) as a priority factor moving people into poverty. To the extent that insecurity had paralysed mainstream economic activities in the affected areas, some communities even viewed lawlessness such as corruption, theft and trafficking of illicit goods as a means of escaping poverty. Econometric results obtained by Deininger and Okidi (2003) also emphasise avoidance of civil strife as a critical determinant of households' ability to increase welfare and reduce the risk of falling into poverty.

In terms of other characteristics, in both years of the panel chronically poor households are larger on average, and have higher dependency rates than the corresponding national averages (Table 2). Further, they have lower levels of human capital with both the household head and (especially) the spouse having attended fewer years of school. They are less obviously disadvantaged in terms of physical assets, in that they cultivate similar land areas to the national (or rural) average. However, it is important to recognise that information on land quality is not available and these households are disproportionately in the northern region where land quality is poorer on average. Chronically poor households are, however, less likely to own cattle, and to own smaller quantities when they do. Also important are the economic activities in which they are engaged: the chronic poor are more likely to be reliant on own account agriculture and less likely to be engaged in non-farm wage work compared to the national average and especially compared to the never poor group. Again this latter fact may partly reflect their disproportionate numbers in the northern region.

Those that were transitorily poor over the period share many of the same initial characteristics as the chronically poor, if not always to the same extent: they tend to be larger households than the national average, with higher dependency rates and lower levels of human capital. However, as might be anticipated there are some important differences between escaping and descending households in how these characteristics change over the 1992 to 1999 period. In particular for those falling into poverty there is a large increase in average household size and in the proportion of dependents over the period, suggesting that in many cases this descent into poverty may reflect life cycle factors.

There are also other important distinctions. For example, there is an increase in the average area of land cultivated by those escaping poverty, but a modest decline for those falling in. The average number of cattle owned by those falling into poverty declines over this period. These are important examples of asset depletion, consistent with evidence from the second round of UPPAP, indicating that farming households that suffered severe drought problems had to sell off their assets, especially land, in order to pay taxes, medical bills and school fees. This is obviously self-defeating behaviour in the longer term and seems to have led some households into poverty, and trapped others in it. In addition, households falling into poverty are less likely to have had non-agricultural wage work initially, and are more likely to have a household head that has ceased to work or moved from own account agricultural work

Table 2. Key household characteristics by poverty status

| | Poverty status 1992/99 | | | | |
	Chronic poor (1)	Moving out of poverty (2)	Moving into poverty (3)	Never in poverty (4)	All (5)
Average household size					
1992	6.24	5.91	5.06	4.95	5.48
1999	6.7	5.74	6.79	5.84	6.07
Average ratio of dependents to non-dependents					
1992	1.52	1.41	1.40	1.29	1.38
1999	1.67	1.47	1.77	1.52	1.55
Percentage of female headed households	19.1	21.0	23.7	20.4	20.7
Percentage of households with polygamous head	5.3	7.3	6.1	3.9	5.4
Education: average number of primary years completed					
Head	3.47	3.54	3.92	4.51	3.96
Spouse	1.87	2.65	2.85	3.65	2.90
Asset ownership					
Average land area cultivated 1992	2.71	2.75	2.47	2.76	2.72
Average land area cultivated 1999	3.27	4.90	2.41	5.56	4.60
Average number of cattle owned 1992	0.85	0.98	1.02	1.01	0.98
Average number of cattle owned 1999	0.72	0.96	0.82	1.56	1.14
Economic activity category in 1992 (per cent)					
Agricultural wage labour	1.9	2.7	0.1	2.2	2.2
Agriculture: own account	76.6	69.5	77.1	54.9	65.5
Non-agricultural wage work	11.0	17.1	14.9	21.5	17.5
Non-agriculture: own account	4.8	5.2	3.5	16.4	9.5
Other	5.7	5.5	4.4	5.1	5.3
Changes in economic activity category 1992 to 1999 (per cent)					
No change	72.2	74.5	65.4	68.9	71.4
Agriculture own account to agricultural wage labour	0.5	0.6	4.4	0.6	0.9
Other to agricultural wage labour	0.5	1.5	0.9	1.5	1.3
Agricultural wage labour to agriculture own account	0.5	2.4	0.0	1.3	1.4
Other to agriculture own account:	10.5	9.1	14.0	15.3	12.5
to non-agricultural wage work	4.8	1.8	2.6	3.5	3.2
to non-agriculture own account	3.3	5.4	2.6	6.3	4.6
to Other (unemployed, disabled, etc.)	7.7	4.6	10.1	2.6	4.7

into agricultural wage employment compared to the national average. This strongly suggests that it is not just life cycle effects that lie behind descents into poverty.

Polygamy and excessive alcohol consumption are two drivers of poverty identified in the UPPAP assessments on which information is available in the panel data set. Households whose head is in a polygamous relationship, are more likely to be poor than average (Table 2), though not necessarily more likely to be chronically poor.

But data on the share of household budgets spent on purchases of alcoholic drinks show an emphatic relationship with poverty status (Table 3).[5] This is true even though such purchases are widely under-reported in surveys of this type (and the respondent is often not the best informed about these specific purchases). In 1992, chronically poor households and households that were not poor then but later fell into poverty were more likely to purchase alcoholic drinks, and devoted higher proportions of their budgets to them. Large numbers in these two groups devoted more than one quarter of their budget for the purchases of all food and drinks for the households to the purchase of alcoholic drinks. This reinforces very strongly the message from qualitative work.

Finally, it is important to consider the key characteristics of those that were not poor in either period. In many cases this is simply the absence of some of the impoverishing factors noted above; but a factor strongly associated with this is working in non-farm activities, whether for wages or on own account.

V. Factors Influencing Poverty Transitions: Econometric Analysis

Estimation Methods and Approaches

In practice, a number of different approaches have been adopted to understanding the factors associated with chronic and transitory poverty, or with poverty transitions. Some are based on careful descriptive analysis, for instance Sen (2003), who

Table 3. Alcohol consumption as a proportion of household food and beverage budgets

Consumption/purchases of alcoholic drinks	Poverty status				
	Chronic poor (1)	Moving out of poverty (2)	Moving into poverty (3)	Never in poverty (4)	All (5)
Average consumption as proportion of all food and beverages	4.5	3.7	4.5	3.3	3.8
Average purchases as proportion of all food and beverages	9.9	7.7	10.2	6.8	8.0
Percentage of hhs with any alcohol consumption expenditure	42.6	39.3	48.2	36.7	39.8
Percentage of hhs with any purchases of alcoholic drinks	40.6	33.9	41.6	34.2	36.1
Hhs for whom alcohol exceeds 25% of F&B consumption (%)	4.3	2.1	2.6	2.7	2.8
Hhs for whom alcohol exceeds 25% of total F&B purchases (%)	12.6	10.7	13.3	9.6	10.9

Note: F&B denotes food and beverage.

considers these factors within a livelihoods framework. Most studies complement descriptive analysis with an explicitly multivariate approach, generally based on econometric analysis. These generally take two forms, those modelling a discrete dependent variable measuring dynamic poverty status (such as a zero one indicator of whether a household is poor or not) and those modelling the (generally continuous) underlying variable measuring the standard of living. The former approach has been strongly criticised by Ravallion (1996) for the loss of information it implies among other factors; but if the poverty line is set at a meaningful absolute level, it is still valuable to consider modelling transitions across the poverty line.

Focusing first on the discrete dependent variable approach, McCulloch and Baulch (1999) distinguish chronically, transitorily and never poor households for Pakistan. They then use econometric modelling techniques to identify the household characteristics that make it more likely for a household to be in each of these categories. They consider two specific approaches, an ordered logit model and a multinomial logit model.[6] Whilst the ordered logit approach is good for understanding the relative influence of different household characteristics on its poverty status, the more widely used multinomial logit approach enables the identification of the characteristics that are more prevalent within each category (McCulloch and Baulch, 1999: 13). It does though suffer from the need to make the strong 'independence of irrelevant alternatives' drawback,[7] but other options such as the multinomial probit model have their own problems.[8]

A different approach is to recognise that when modelling poverty transitions poverty states are dynamic in nature. For example, households that are escaping poverty may be affected by two sets of factors: those that made them more likely to be poor in the first place, and those which enabled them to escape from poverty. One straightforward way of undertaking this sequential modelling is by means of a series of related probit models, as used for instance by Bhide and Mehta (2003) in modelling poverty transitions in rural India. The first step of the model considers whether or not a household is poor in the earlier period, and the second step models for each group separately the factors associated with the same household being poor or not in the second period.

However, when the dependent variable just distinguishes the poor from the non-poor, as in the probit model, this implies the loss of a substantial amount of information about the household's living standard which, measurement error notwithstanding, is known much more precisely than this. It may be much more promising to model the factors influencing the change in household living standards by what is essentially a micro-level growth equation (Dercon, 2003; Fields et al., 2003). In this way it is also straightforward to quantify the different factors associated with changes in living conditions and it does not lead to concerns related to the aforementioned approaches, which might be sensitive to the level at which the poverty line is set.

Estimation Results

Both the discrete and continuous dependent variable approaches outlined above are applied to the panel data set described and analysed in Section IV with a view to understanding the factors associated with a household's poverty status. Similar sets of explanatory variables are used in each case, and are almost all based on household characteristics in 1992. Additionally, a very small number of variables measuring changes over the period, each of which can reasonably be considered to be exogenous for purposes of this model. Important likely explanatory variables suggested by the descriptive analysis in Section IV include demographic variables and other characteristics of the head, education, physical of assets, location, type of work, and relevant changes in household demographic variables. Many other changes in household characteristics may be important influences of changes in poverty status, such as changing economic activity status, and are likely to be endogenous.

Discrete models of poverty status. As discussed above, household movements relative to the poverty line are considered by means of a multinomial logit model and then a sequential probit formation. In the former case the dependent variable distinguishes four cases: the never poor; those poor in both periods; those poor in 1992 and not in 1999 (escaping poverty); and those non-poor in 1992 but that were poor in 1999 (falling into poverty). The purpose of this analysis is to provide a more careful analysis of the types of households in each of these groups, though does not form a sufficient basis for drawing conclusions about the associated causes. The results are interpreted in terms of the marginal effects of each variable, in other words the marginal effect of a change in that explanatory variable on the probability that a household is in the group under consideration.

As can be seen from Table 4, this model is relatively successful in predicting the extreme cases of households that are always poor (the model predicting successfully nearly 77 per cent of the households that are in fact chronically poor) and, not surprisingly, is least successful at predicting the two intermediate categories of transitory poor.

Focusing throughout on marginal effects that are significant at the 10 per cent level at least, the most important determinants of which poverty category a given household is in include education, assets (including housing), location variables, the main economic activity, demographics, and changes in the household head or in demographic composition over the period (Table 5). Education of the head, and

Table 4. Comparisons between predicted and actual groups based on the multinominal logit model

	Predicted				
Actual	Chronic poor	Never in poverty	Moving out of poverty	Moving into poverty	Total
Chronic poor	348	25	75	6	454
Never in poverty	70	74	58	7	209
Moving out of poverty	154	39	129	6	328
Moving into poverty	55	17	26	16	114
Total	627	155	288	35	1105

Table 5. Multinomial logit marginal effects 1992/99 panel

	Poverty status						
	Not poor		Chronic poverty		Moving out of poverty		Moving into poverty	
	(1)		(2)		(3)		(4)	
Variable	Marg effect	T ratio	Marg effect	T ratio	Marg effect	T ratio	Marg effect	T ratio
Constant	0.4413	(2.224)**	−0.2972	(−1.786)*	0.1730	(0.931)	−0.3170	(−2.574)**
Age of head	−0.0058	(−0.884)	0.0023	(0.495)	0.0018	(0.298)	0.0017	(0.5)
Age of head squared	0.0000	(0.68)	0.0000	(−0.502)	0.0000	(0.022)	0.0000	(−0.65)
Female head	0.0695	(1.472)	−0.0443	(−1.383)	−0.0279	(−0.649)	0.0027	(0.11)
Dependency Ratio	−0.1215	(−1.345)	0.0863	(1.269)	0.0030	(0.036)	0.0321	(0.738)
Household size	−0.0156	(−2.042)**	0.0075	(1.575)	0.0043	(0.647)	0.0039	(0.99)
Rooms per adult equivalent	0.1549	(3.955)***	−0.1728	(−4.567)***	−0.0118	(−0.313)	0.0297	(1.642)
Education (yrs.)								
Head primary	0.0173	(2.282)**	−0.0047	(−0.955)	−0.0156	(−2.271)**	0.0030	(0.807)
Head secondary	0.0386	(2.382)**	−0.0317	(−2.27)**	0.0088	(0.56)	−0.0157	(−1.619)
Spouse primary	0.0096	(1.251)	−0.0153	(−2.816)***	0.0073	(1.027)	−0.0016	(−0.401)
Spouse secondary	0.0768	(2.131)**	0.0060	(0.224)	−0.0878	(−2.2)**	0.0049	(0.284)
Number of assets per household								
Land (rural) hectares	0.0181	(0.667)	−0.0262	(−1.165)	0.0426	(1.585)	−0.0345	(−2.131)**
Land	−0.0111	(−0.461)	0.0280	(1.34)	−0.0325	(−1.335)	0.0155	(1.028)
Chickens	−0.0017	(−0.218)	0.0083	(1.562)	0.0002	(0.032)	−0.0067	(−1.553)
Cows	0.0130	(1.517)	−0.0127	(−2.067)**	−0.0003	(−0.038)	0.0000	(−0.005)
Goats	0.0082	(1.089)	−0.0006	(−0.114)	−0.0009	(0.13)	−0.0068	(−1.654)*
Region								
Urban central	−0.0410	(−0.345)	0.0976	(0.833)	−0.1253	(−1.088)	0.0687	(0.727)
Rural central	−0.2077	(−1.659)*	0.1989	(1.635)	−0.1630	(−1.368)	0.1717	(1.786)*
Rural east	−0.3018	(−2.392)**	0.1983	(1.627)	−0.0942	(−0.793)	0.1978	(2.061)**
Urban east	−0.1070	(−0.786)	0.1083	(0.822)	−0.0845	(−0.635)	0.0831	(0.802)
Rural west	−0.1837	(−1.465)	0.2093	(1.723)*	−0.2058	(−1.72)*	0.1802	(1.876)*

(continued)

Table 5. (*Continued*)

	Poverty status							
	Not poor		Chronic poverty		Moving out of poverty		Moving into poverty	
	(1)		(2)		(3)		(4)	
Variable	Marg effect	T ratio	Marg effect	T ratio	Marg effect	T ratio	Marg effect	T ratio
Urban north	−0.2465	(−1.713)*	0.2284	(1.836)*	−0.1046	(−0.762)	0.1227	(1.201)
Rural north	−0.5213	(−3.867)***	0.4001	(3.315)***	−0.1537	(−1.234)	0.2749	(2.886)***
Type of work								
Agricultural own account	−0.0494	(−1.019)	0.0421	(1.171)	−0.0140	(−0.307)	0.0212	(0.824)
Agricultural wage	−0.0357	(−0.299)	0.0342	(0.406)	0.0882	(0.834)	−0.0867	(−0.988)
Other	−0.0162	(−0.18)	0.0716	(1.153)	−0.0688	(−0.825)	0.0134	(0.274)
Non agricultural own account	0.2154	(3.2)***	−0.0167	(−0.303)	−0.1433	(−2.042)**	−0.0555	(−1.21)
Change variables								
Change in household size	−0.0043	(−0.42)	0.0155	(2.296)**	−0.0297	(−3.125)***	0.0185	(3.568)***
Head change male–female	−0.5008	(−2.192)**	0.0403	(0.302)	0.3412	(1.922)*	0.1193	(1.572)
Head change (dummy)	0.0239	(0.342)	0.0111	(0.24)	−0.0473	(−0.748)	0.0123	(0.337)
Change in number of children less than five years old	−0.0155	(−0.993)	−0.0153	(−1.513)	0.0254	(1.771)*	0.0054	(0.695)
Change in number of children between six and 14-years-old	−0.0239	(−0.609)	0.0314	(1.303)	0.0127	(0.373)	−0.0202	(−1.026)
Change in the number of worker aged individuals	−0.0057	(−0.382)	−0.0051	(−0.529)	0.0194	(1.413)	−0.0087	(−1.17)

*Significant at 10% level, **Significant at 5% level, ***Significant at 1% level.
Number of observations 1103, Chi squared 355.7422.
Defaults: missed education (for head and spouse), urban west, non agricultural wage employment, land (urban).

spouse at secondary level, all have strong positive influences on the likelihood that a household is never poor. Where the spouse has been educated to primary level or the head to secondary level, both have strong negative influences on the likelihood that the household is chronically poor.

These results correspond strongly with prior expectations, and education is very likely to be a strong causal influence on a household's poverty status. They also correspond to the findings in the second round of UPPAP in which the communities covered primarily identified hard work and gainful employment, the productivity of which is enhanced by good health and appropriate education, as priority factors for moving out of poverty. Although completion of primary education is expected to significantly improve well-being in itself, the communities emphasised access to skill and education at higher levels as crucial for sustained poverty reduction. In our estimation, the negative effect of the head having primary education on the probability of a household escaping poverty may seem counterintuitive, but this is probably picking up the effect above – households whose head had completed primary school in 1992 were less likely to be poor to start with.

Rural residents with more land are less likely to fall into poverty, and those households that owned cattle in 1992 are significantly less likely to have been chronically poor over this period; the same variable has a quite large positive but not quite significant impact on the likelihood of a household being never poor. According to UPPAP findings, pastoral communities that were not affected by cattle rustling, drought, animal diseases and the associated low yields, reported welfare improvements. This is largely due to better marketing opportunities and access to grazing land. Households whose main economic activity is non-agricultural own account work are also significantly more likely never to have been poor over this period. By contrast there is no significant association between working in own account agriculture and poverty status, despite the high concentration of poverty evident among such households in simple bivariate analysis. The other characteristics of such households (for example low levels of education) may be more important in explaining the high incidence of poverty among this group. UPPAP results also help in understanding this, in that some communities in the second round felt that poverty among crop farmers had increased over time due to deterioration of farmland quality, coupled with an inability to purchase hybrid seeds and fertilisers. Communities also attributed low earnings among most crop farmers to taxes (which they say is the single most important impoverishing factor) and limited markets and low prices, especially for maize. The econometric results suggest though that these factors did not apply in all communities.

There are a number of strong associations between poverty status and locality of residence. In one sense such correlations are unfortunate because they mean that the model (or available data) has been unable to capture the more fundamental factors underlying, for instance, the greater poverty of the rural north. But equally they do highlight the presence of important real geographic differentials. The rural northern region is where the effects are strongest, where households are significantly less likely to be never poor, significantly more likely to be chronically poor or have moved into poverty over this period. Those in the rural eastern region are significantly less likely to be never poor, but more likely to be moving out of poverty – this being a locality where poverty fell sharply between 1992 and 1999. Those in the urban areas of the western region are significantly less likely to have been chronically poor or descending into poverty over this period, and significantly less likely to escape. Again, these patterns are consistent with the geographic pattern of poverty reduction over this period (Appleton, 2001).

As already seen in Section IV, changes in poverty status over a period may reflect changes affecting the household over this period. Many such changes are likely to be endogenous (for example accumulation of assets) and so cannot be considered as explanatory factors in models of this kind. However, for some types of changes it may be legitimate to argue that they are not endogenous, including certainly changes in the ages of household members and also perhaps changes in the household head. Only these types of change variables were included in the regression. Some turn out to be important. Most importantly, increases in household size have a significant positive influence on the likelihood that the household is chronically poor or falls into poverty (consistent with the descriptive results in Section IV), while reductions in household size have a significant positive impact of the likelihood of escaping poverty.

Given the restrictive structure imposed by the multinomial logit model (in particular the independence of irrelevant alternatives assumption, and that it may be conflating correlate of initial poverty status with correlates of change over time), we now consider the factors associated with whether a household is poor or not to start with separately from the factors associated with changes (or not) in the household's poverty status. We do this by means of three separate probit models as discussed above. The results of this model are reported in Table 6, where the dependent variable takes the value 1 if the household is poor in the relevant year and zero otherwise. The likelihood of a household being poor in 1992 is significantly negatively associated with the head having primary education or the spouse (where present) having secondary education; with the household having cattle; with the number of rooms per adult equivalent; and with being engaged in a non-farm own account activity. Regional dummy variables are not significant here.

Many more variables though are significant at the second stage. Conditional on a household having been poor in 1992, residence in any rural region is strongly positively associated with the household being in persistent poverty, with the effect being largest for the north. Households with higher levels of assets, specifically the human capital of the head or spouse; cattle; and land in rural areas are significantly more likely to escape poverty. Apparently counter intuitively ownership of land for those in urban areas is positively associated with remaining in poverty, though this is not the case in rural areas. The urban result though may be picking up those households that need to rely on agricultural activities despite living in a town. Those poor households whose head was widowed in 1992 were significantly more likely to have escaped poverty by 1999.

For those that were non-poor in 1992, descent into poverty is positively associated with residence in any rural area, with the effect again being largest in the north. Descent into poverty is also negatively associated with: land ownership in rural areas; secondary education of the head; working in a non-agricultural own account activity; and positively associated with living in the urban north and with the household head changing from being male to female. In broad terms these results are consistent with those of the multinomial logit model, but in some

Table 6. Probit regressions 1992/99 panel: marginal effects

Variable	Poor/Not Poor 1992		Poor or Not Poor in 1999 Conditional upon being poor in 1992		Poor or Not Poor in 1999 Conditional upon not being poor in 1992	
	No. of Obs: 1,103 Chi squared 150.1669		No. of Obs: 537 Chi squared 91.77121		No. of Obs: 566 Chi squared 121.7139	
	Marg effect	T ratio	Marg effect	T ratio	Marg effect	T ratio
Constant	-0.5147	(-0.957)	-1.8054	(-1.937)*	-3.6388	(-3.456)***
Age of head	0.0179	(1.158)	-0.0009	(-0.035)	0.0340	(1.151)
Age of head squared	-0.0001	(-0.671)	0.0000	(-0.158)	-0.0004	(-1.217)
Female head	-0.1045	(-0.778)	-0.0311	(-0.144)	0.0730	(0.298)
Head is widowed	0.0361	(0.2)	-0.5295	(-1.764)*	0.0252	(0.08)
Head is married	0.0934	(0.621)	-0.2586	(-1.049)	0.2202	(0.876)
Number of Males less than 5 years old	0.0769	(0.982)	-0.0748	(-0.532)	-0.2173	(-1.259)
Number of Females less than 5 years old	0.0793	(1.077)	-0.1543	(-1.112)	0.1356	(0.893)
Number of Males between 6 and 14 years old	0.0688	(1.06)	-0.0328	(-0.266)	0.0594	(0.435)
Number of Males between 6 and 14 years old	0.0383	(0.573)	-0.0087	(-0.071)	-0.0445	(-0.337)
Proportion of household are workers	0.0869	(0.37)	0.4711	(0.87)	0.6425	(1.406)
Dependency ratio	-0.0162	(-0.055)	0.3508	(0.975)	0.2816	(0.698)
Household size	0.0016	(0.046)	0.0668	(0.953)	0.0447	(0.666)
Rooms per adult equivalent	-0.3621	(-3.772)***	-0.5941	(-2.951)***	-0.0986	(-0.689)
Education (yrs.)						
Head primary	-0.0471	(-2.599)***	0.0036	(0.135)	0.0249	(0.741)
Head secondary	-0.0458	(-1.155)	-0.1641	(-2.217)**	-0.1400	(-1.88)*
Spouse primary	-0.0298	(-1.581)	-0.0485	(-1.665)*	-0.0513	(-1.523)
Spouse secondary	-0.1792	(-2.203)**	0.1374	(0.796)	0.0285	(0.226)

(continued)

Table 6. (*Continued*)

Variable	No. of Obs: 1,103		No. of Obs: 537		No. of Obs: 566	
	Chi squared 150.1669		Chi squared 91.77121		Chi squared 121.7139	
	Poor/Not Poor 1992		Poor or Not Poor in 1999 Conditional upon being poor in 1992		Poor or Not Poor in 1999 Conditional upon not being poor in 1992	
	Marg effect	T ratio	Marg effect	T ratio	Marg effect	T ratio
Number of assets per household						
Land (rural) hectares	0.0584	(0.89)	−0.2517	(−1.969)**	−0.2828	(−2.165)**
Land	−0.0194	(−0.332)	0.2197	(1.843)*	0.1512	(1.272)
Chickens	0.0240	(1.25)	0.0277	(0.984)	−0.0400	(−1.146)
Cows	−0.0355	(−1.699)*	−0.0565	(−1.762)*	−0.0192	(−0.527)
Goats	−0.0030	(−0.166)	−0.0012	(−0.045)	−0.0472	(−1.463)
Region						
Urban central	−0.0018	(−0.006)	0.8036	(1.418)	0.3930	(0.623)
Rural central	0.0317	(0.107)	1.4640	(2.405)**	1.5862	(2.343)**
Rural east	0.1903	(0.641)	1.3442	(2.222)**	1.8839	(2.723)***
Urban east	0.1063	(0.323)	1.0018	(1.508)	0.6412	(0.939)
Rural west	−0.0601	(−0.202)	1.5788	(2.608)***	1.6279	(2.387)**
Urban north	0.2935	(0.87)	1.4192	(2.355)**	1.4379	(1.939)*
Rural north	0.4717	(1.552)	2.1761	(3.596)***	2.7228	(3.902)***
Type of work						
Agricultural own account	0.0725	(0.607)	0.2366	(1.177)	0.1962	(0.977)
Agricultural wage	0.3099	(1.088)	−0.0532	(−0.126)	−0.4550	(−0.723)

(*continued*)

Table 6. (*Continued*)

	No. of Obs: 1,103		No. of Obs: 537		No. of Obs: 566	
	Chi squared 150.1669		Chi squared 91.77121		Chi squared 121.7139	
	Poor/Not Poor 1992		Poor or Not Poor in 1999 Conditional upon being poor in 1992		Poor or Not Poor in 1999 Conditional upon not being poor in 1992	
Variable	Marg effect	T ratio	Marg effect	T ratio	Marg effect	T ratio
Other	0.0628	(0.287)	0.5082	(1.484)	0.2434	(0.62)
Non-agricultural own account	−0.4367	(−2.616)***	0.2506	(0.791)	−0.5592	(−1.912)*
Change variables						
Change in household size	—	—	0.2157	(1.622)	0.0660	(0.411)
Head Change Male–Female	—	—	−0.9419	(−1.291)	2.0783	(2.611)***
Head Change (dummy)	—	—	0.0621	(0.253)	0.0251	(0.08)
Change in number of children less than five years old	—	—	−0.2299	(−1.559)	0.1019	(0.566)
Change in number of children between six and 14-years-old	—	—	−0.0568	(−0.402)	0.0556	(0.331)
Change in the number of worker aged individuals	—	—	−0.1262	(−0.959)	0.0028	(0.018)

*Significant at 10% level, **Significant at 5% level, ***Significant at 1% level.
Defaults – Missed Education (for head and spouse), Urban West, Non Agricultural Wage Employment, Land (urban).

Table 7. Factor affecting changes in household well-being

Variable	Change in log welfare	
	Coefficient	T ratio
Constant	7.5775	(23.662)***
Age of head	−0.0044	(−0.715)
Age of head squared	0.0001	(0.828)
Sex of head	−0.0044	(−0.418)
Head is widowed	0.0658	(1.015)
Head is married	−0.0679	(−0.694)
Number of males less than 5-years-old	−0.0129	(−0.315)
Number of females less than 5-years-old	−0.0147	(−0.388)
Number of males between 6- and 14-years-old	−0.0109	(−0.389)
Number of females between 6- and 14-years-old	0.0023	(0.036)
Proportion of household are workers	−0.1285	(−1.627)
Dependency ratio	−0.1920	(−1.378)
Household size	−0.0186	(−1.157)
Rooms per adult equivalent	0.0409	(1.096)
Education (yrs.)		
head primary	0.0032	(0.487)
head secondary	0.0554	(3.509)***
spouse primary	0.0099	(1.262)
spouse secondary	−0.0423	(0.731)
Number of assets per household		
Land (rural) hectares	0.0637	(2.518)**
Land	−0.0243	(−1.028)
Chickens	−0.0049	(−0.614)
Cows	0.0111	(1.402)
Goats	0.0039	(0.547)
Region		
Urban central	0.5008	(0.186)
Rural central	0.0722	(−3.703)***
Rural east	−0.0655	(−4.895)***
Urban east	0.3562	(−1.083)
Rural west	0.4775	(−4.321)***
Urban north	−0.0310	(−4.009)***
Rural north	−0.4521	(−8.23)***
Type of work		
Agricultural own account	−0.1422	(−3.079)***
Agricultural wage	−0.1604	(−1.394)
Other	−0.1355	(−1.614)
Non-agricultural own account	0.0078	(0.094)
Change variables		
Change in household size	−0.0725	(−2.069)**
Head change male–female	0.1254	(0.715)
Head change (dummy)	−0.0704	(−1.025)
Change in number of children less than five years old	0.0192	(0.512)
Change in number of children between six and 14-years-old	0.0088	(0.212)
Change in the number of worker aged individuals	0.0461	(1.321)

(*continued*)

Table 7. (*Continued*)

	Change in log welfare	
Variable	Coefficient	T ratio
Initial income	−0.7908	(−26.937)***
	No. of Obs – 1103	
	R-squared = .481,	

*Significant at 10% level, **Significant at 5% level, ***Significant at 1% level.
Defaults: Missed education (for head and spouse), urban west, non-agricultural wage employment, land (urban).

instances they are more intuitive than the latter because they impose a less restrictive structure.

Modelling continuous changes in living standards.   Finally we consider the factor changes influencing changes in household welfare of households within the panel. Regressing the change in the logarithm of the welfare measure over the period on its own initial level (similar to a growth regression equation) and many of the other explanatory variables considered in other models above identifies many of the same factors as being important, but also some additional ones (Table 7). The model has a good fit as measured by its R-squared value. The initial level of the logarithm of welfare has a strongly negative coefficient, so that ceteris paribus the growth rates of the household consumption measure are higher for households that were poorer to start with.

But there are many other important intervening factors. Growth rates of the welfare measure are significantly faster for households where the head has secondary education, or that have more land in rural areas, but they are slower for households engaged in own account agriculture, a finding which differs from those identified above and is perhaps more intuitive. Again, there are strong regional effects, with growth rates being lower in rural areas of all regions, again most strongly in the north. Growth rates are significantly lower in urban areas of the northern region. Again, this is consistent with the evidence on changing living conditions and poverty over this period (Appleton, 2001). Increases in household size over the period also have a negative influence on the growth of well-being. Many of these factors of course favour richer households relative to poorer households, so offsetting the potential convergence suggested by the negative coefficient of the initial welfare level.

Again, despite the greater flexibility this model offers, these results are broadly consistent with those identified in the other econometric models. They also confirm some of the factors identified by the qualitative studies.

VI. Conclusions

This paper represents one of the first attempts at combining qualitative and quantitative information to understand the factors underlying poverty transitions and persistence. The application to Uganda has shown that this dual approach offers a much richer understanding of these factors than using either approach in isolation.

The quantitative analysis provides a national picture, and its multivariate nature allows many factors to be considered simultaneously, and their relative importance to be assessed. It has also been more successful than the qualitative sources in identifying escapes from poverty and their main influences. But it also misses many factors, with the limited nature of a survey questionnaire inevitably restricting the range of factors that can be considered and also the understanding of them that can be obtained in a survey format (for example, gender). Put another way, well-conducted qualitative analysis provides a much richer understanding of many of the processes underlying poverty and poverty transitions. For example, the survey can measure reported purchases on alcoholic beverages and study their determinants, but is weak in being able to identify the impoverishing social and economic impacts of excessive alcohol consumption.

In the case of Uganda, in cases where the qualitative and quantitative analyses cover similar topics, their results generally confirm or complement each other. Both the qualitative and quantitative results identify ownership of, or access to, assets at individual, household and community level as being major factors influencing poverty transitions and persistence. Lack of education and lack of key physical assets such as land and cattle are clearly identified as very important factors in both qualitative and quantitative work, as are demographic factors such as high dependency rates or increasing household size. The activities people are engaged in are important drivers of poverty dynamics, with working in non-agricultural activities in rural areas often being an important escape route: but this too often depends on having a sufficient level of human capital.

It is important to have a broad interpretation of assets and of the mediating factors that influence livelihoods. Social and political capital, as well as security, is clearly an important factor, including such factors as poor governance, excessive local taxation, a culture of excessive drinking, and pervasive insecurity – especially in the north – being identified as very important factors especially in qualitative work. Indeed, in the second round of UPPAP, insecurity in the affected areas was the primary factor reported to be responsible for declines in well-being. The survey confirms that households that are persistently poor or fell into poverty were those that were more likely to purchase alcoholic drinks and to spend on them, matching the findings of qualitative work. Other important mediating factors are norms in relation to gender and other disadvantaged groups such elderly people or the disabled, with such groups often being doubly disadvantaged by having a lower levels of assets and attaining a low return on the assets they do have due to various factors, including processes of exclusion.

Results from the recent round of UPPAP reveal that communities that enjoyed welfare improvements during the 1990s associated the changes with expanded household asset bases. Although the communities appreciated increased access to health, education and safe water, they lamented the deterioration in the quality of public service delivery. The households that were reported to have enjoyed welfare growth were those with hard working and educated members and those with family assets acquired through purchases or inheritances. Conversely households that experienced declines in welfare were reported to be those that had lost productive assets (which, in some cases, were liquidated to finance other pressing needs, though as noted above, in other cases for less pressing needs). Agricultural produce marketing constraints and a feeling of exploitation of the smallholders in the context of liberalisation were also identified as influencing factors for deterioration of living standards. Furthermore, the UPPAP respondents strongly stress increased taxation, in a bid by the central authorities and local governments to increase revenue, as well as the impact of HIV/AIDS, were also considered very important factors underlying falling living conditions. The impact of HIV/AIDS is obvious, the point about taxation, widely stressed in UPPAP for different forms of taxation, seems to be related to respondents not seeing the benefits of the revenue collected.

This paper has demonstrated that there is clearly considerable value added in combining qualitative and quantitative approaches equally and in a meaningful way to understand drivers, maintainers and interrupters of poverty. This approach can equally be applied in other countries, and there is also scope to develop it further in Uganda, in providing additional understanding of key issues. Further work on gender and purchases of alcoholic drinks, for example, would seem to be two important priorities in this respect.

Acknowledgements

The support of the UK Economic and Social Research Council is gratefully acknowledged. The work was part of the programme of the ESRC Global Poverty Research Group (grant M571255001). We gratefully acknowledge constructive comments and suggestions from two anonymous referees, the editors of this special issue, Howard White, and the comments of participants at the International Conference on Chronic Poverty, University of Manchester, April 2003, where an earlier draft of this paper was presented.

Notes

1. An acceptable error range in this instance was considered $+/- 7/8$ years – in line with what appeared to be a natural structural break in a frequency distribution of age differences, between the two periods. For example in the 1992–1999 two wave panel the acceptable age range allowed for the 7/8 year gap between the panels and then allowed for an error range in age recording or $+7$ and -8 years.
2. At a 10 per cent significance level.
3. Although panel households are more likely to have latrines and flush toilets, these variables are not of interest in this analysis, and therefore of no concern.
4. Other two and three wave panels, for Uganda, covering various groupings of years between 1992 and 1995 also show substantial movements into and out of poverty.
5. This could also be considered in terms of absolute levels of expenditure on alcoholic drinks per adult (or per adult male). Here though our focus is on the relative importance of expenditure on alcoholic drinks as a share of the household budget.
6. McCulloch and Baulch (1999) argue that there is a natural ordering of the chronically, transitorily or never poor.
7. This property is a consequence of the implied assumption of no correlation between the error terms. As a consequence if, for example, an alternative choice of poverty is introduced, all the selection probabilities would be reduced proportionately.
8. For example, important difficulties include the dimensionality of the response probabilities and being computationally extremely resource intensive.

References

Alderman, H., Behrman, J., Kohler, M. J. and Cotts Watkins, S. (2000) Attrition in longitudinal household survey data: some tests for three developing – country samples, *Policy Research Working Paper 2447*, World Bank.

Appleton, S. (2001) Education, incomes and poverty in Uganda in the 1990s, *CREDIT Research Paper 01/22*, Nottingham: University of Nottingham.

Barahona, C. and Levy, S. (2003) How to generate statistics and influence policy using participatory methods in research: reflections on work in Malawi 1999–2002, paper presented at *Q–Squared in Practice: A Conference on Experiences of Combining Qualitative and Quantitative Methods in Poverty Appraisal*, University of Toronto, 15–16 May 2004.

Bhide, S. and Mehta, A. K. (2003) Chronic poverty in rural India, an analysis using panel data: issues and findings, paper presented at the *Staying Poor: Chronic Poverty and Development Policy Conference*, Chronic Poverty Research Centre, University of Manchester, April.

Bird, K. and Shinyekwa, I. (2003) Multiple shocks and downward mobility: learning from the life histories of rural Ugandans, paper presented at the *Staying Poor: Chronic Poverty and Development Policy Conference*, Chronic Poverty Research Centre, University of Manchester, April.

Davis, B. and Stampini, M. (2002) Pathways towards prosperity in rural Nicaragua: or why household drop in and out of poverty, and some policy suggestions on how to keep them out, *ESA Working Paper 10*, Rome: FAO.

Deininger, K. and Okidi, J. (2003) Growth and poverty reduction in Uganda: 1999–2000: panel data evidence, *Development Policy Review*, 21(4), pp. 481–509.

Dercon, S. (2003) *The Impact of Economic Reforms on Rural Households in Ethiopia: A Study from 1989–1995* (Washington, DC: World Bank).

Ellis, F. (2000) *Rural livelihoods and diversity in developing Countries* (Oxford: Oxford University Press).

Fields, G. S., Cichello, P. L., Freije, S., Menendez, M. and Newhouse, D. (2003) Household income dynamics: a four country story, *Journal of Development Studies*, 40(2), pp. 30–54.

Hulme, D., Moore, K. and Shepherd, A. (2001) Chronic poverty: meanings and analytic frameworks, *CPRC Working Paper 2*, Manchester: IDPM, University of Manchester.

Jalan, J. and Ravallion, M. (2000) Is transient poverty different? Evidence for rural China, *Journal of Development Studies*, 36(6), pp. 82–99.

McCulloch, N. and Baulch, B. (1999) Distinguishing the chronically from the transitory poor – evidence from Pakistan, *IDS Working Paper 97*, Institute of Development Studies, University of Sussex, UK.

Okidi, J. and McKay, A. (2003) Poverty dynamics in Uganda: 1992 to 2000, *CPRC Working Paper 27*, Manchester: IDPM, University of Manchester.

Parker B. and Kozel, V. (2004) Understanding poverty and vulnerability in India's Uttar Pradesh and Bihar: a mixed method approach, paper presented at *Q–Squared in Practice: A Conference on Experiences of Combining Qualitative and Quantitative Methods in Poverty Appraisal*, University of Toronto, May.

Ravallion, M. (1996) Issues in measuring and modelling poverty, *Economic Journal*, 106, pp. 1328–33.

Republic of Uganda (2000) *Uganda Participatory Poverty Assessment Report: Learning From the Poor* (Kampala: Ministry of Finance, Planning and Economic Development).

Republic of Uganda (2002) *Uganda Participatory Poverty Assessment Report: National Report* (Kampala: Ministry of Finance, Planning and Economic Development).

Sen, A. K. (1999) *Development as Freedom* (Oxford: Oxford University Press).

Sen, B. (2003) Drivers of escape and descent: changing household fortunes in rural Bangladesh, *World Development*, 31(3), pp. 513–34.

Wresinski, J. (1987) *Grande pauvreté et Précarité Economique et sociale* (Paris, Rapport du Conseil Economique et Social, Journal officiel de la République française). English version available as Wresinski (1994) *Chronic Poverty and Lack of Basic Security* (Landover, MA: Fourth World Publications).

Wood, G. (2003) Staying secure, staying poor: the 'Faustian bargain', *World Development*, 31(3), pp. 455–71.

Appendix

Table A1. Basic descriptive statistics of data used in econometric analysis

Variable	Mean	St. Dev
Age of head	*42.41*	*15.49*
Age of head squared	*2038.50*	*1490.50*
Female household head	*0.21*	*0.41*
Household head is widowed	*0.10*	*0.30*
Household head is married	*0.77*	*0.42*
Number of males less than 5-years-old	*0.67*	*0.84*
Number of females less than 5-years-old	*0.67*	*0.90*
Number of males between 6- and 14-years-old	*0.80*	*1.06*
Number of Females between 6- and 14-years-old	*0.80*	*1.02*
Proportion of dependants in household	*0.51*	*0.24*
Proportion of the household working	*0.53*	*0.25*
Household size	5.76	3.34
Rooms per adult equivalent	*0.74*	*0.56*
Education (yrs.)		
Head primary	*3.96*	**2.77**
Head secondary	*0.51*	**1.22**
Spouse primary	*2.07*	**2.72**
Spouse primary dummy	*0.29*	**0.45**
Number of assets per household		
Land (rural) hectares	*2.43*	*1.68*
Land area	*2.72*	*1.56*
Chickens	*1.69*	*2.16*
Cows	*0.98*	*1.99*
Goats	*1.58*	*2.33*
Region		
Urban central	*0.06*	*0.23*
Rural central	*0.26*	*0.44*
Rural east	*0.19*	*0.40*
Urban east	*0.03*	*0.17*
Urban west	*0.04*	*0.18*
Urban north	*0.03*	*0.16*
Rural north	*0.12*	*0.32*
Type of work		
Agricultural own account	*0.67*	*0.47*
Agricultural wage	*0.02*	*0.15*
Other	*0.05*	*0.22*
Non-agricultural own account	*0.10*	*0.29*
Change variables		
Change in household size	*0.30*	*3.07*
Head has change from male to female	*0.01*	*0.11*
Head change (dummy)	*0.08*	*0.27*
Change in number of children less than 5-years-old	*−0.24*	*1.44*
Change in number of children between 6- and 14-years-old	*0.49*	*1.84*
Change in the number of worker aged individuals	*−0.05*	*1.82*
Income	*8.69*	*0.59*

Defaults: Missed education (for head and spouse), urban west, non-agricultural wage employment, urban land.

Note: Land (rural) hectares is the hectares cultivated by rural based households.

Table A2. Descriptive data comparison for 1992, full panel and reduced panel after matching

	IHS sample		Full panel			Matched panel		Attrited sample		
	Mean	s.d	Mean	s.d	Diff	Mean	s.d	Mean	s.d	Diff
Change in Income	–	–	0.35	0.70	–	0.34	0.69	0.37	0.73	−0.03
Age of head	40.17	15.25	43.04	15.42	−2.86***	43.40	15.50	46.44	16.24	−3.04***
Female head	0.27	0.44	0.24	0.42	0.03	0.21	0.41	0.28	0.46	−0.07
Education										
Missed	0.28	0.45	0.20	0.40	0.07	0.25	0.43	0.33	0.49	−0.08
Primary	3.93	2.87	3.73	2.81	0.20	3.97	2.77	3.78	2.83	0.19
Secondary	0.68	1.48	0.47	1.20	−0.21*	0.51	1.22	0.35	1.10	0.16
Spouse missed	0.40	0.49	0.29	0.45	0.11	0.30	0.46	0.29	0.45	0.00
Spouse primary	3.14	2.93	1.87	2.65	1.27***	2.07	2.72	1.53	2.52	0.54
Spouse secondary	0.35	1.05	0.11	0.58	−0.24**	0.12	0.61	0.13	0.64	−0.01
Dependency ratio	0.47	0.27	0.51	0.25	−0.04	0.51	0.24	0.52	0.26	−0.02
Household size in 1992	5.07	3.39	5.62	3.29	−0.54**	5.77	3.34	5.56	3.36	0.21
Rooms per adult equivalent	0.72	0.58	0.74	0.56	−0.02	0.74	0.56	0.73	0.55	0.01
Region										
Central	0.15	0.36	0.16	0.35	−0.02	0.17	0.35	0.16	0.33	0.01
East	0.14	0.35	0.12	0.30	0.01	0.12	0.30	0.14	0.31	−0.02
West	0.08	0.28	0.03	0.18	0.046***	0.03	0.18	0.03	0.16	0.00
North	0.11	0.32	0.07	0.23	0.039**	0.08	0.25	0.09	0.23	−0.01
Type of work										
Agricultural Own Account	0.53	0.50	0.67	0.47	−0.13***	0.67	0.47	0.66	0.47	0.01
Agricultural Wage	0.03	0.18	0.02	0.15	0.01	0.02	0.15	0.03	0.17	−0.01
Other	0.06	0.24	0.06	0.23	0.01	0.05	0.22	0.09	0.29	−0.04
Non Agricultural Own Account	0.14	0.35	0.09	0.28	0.05*	0.10	0.29	0.09	0.28	0.01
Non Agricultural Wage	0.22	0.42	0.16	0.37	0.06*	0.17	0.38	0.13	0.34	0.05
Income	8.79	0.69	8.68	0.59	0.11	8.69	0.59	8.64	0.59	0.05
Household was sick in 1992	0.19	0.39	0.17	0.38	0.02	0.16	0.36	0.18	0.39	−0.02
Assets										
Land	–	–	2.56	1.65		2.72	1.56	2.11	1.77	0.62***
Chickens	–	–	1.63	2.17		1.69	2.16	1.50	2.18	0.19
Cows	–	–	0.89	1.91		0.97	1.98	0.61	1.60	0.36**

*Significant at 10% level, **Significant at 5% level, ***Significant at 1% level.

Table A3. Probit regression—whether household is in the full panel?

Variable	In full panel (no/yes)		In matched panel (no/yes) (compared with 'full' panel	
Constant	−1.6703	(−10.255)***	−0.0285	(−0.039)
Female head	−0.0578	(−0.981)	−0.1712	(−1.299)
Age of head	0.0043	(3.104)***	−0.0040	(−1.201)
Household size	0.0164	(1.357)	0.0497	(1.602)
Head is married	−0.0520	(−0.77)	−0.0754	(−0.463)
Number of Males less than 5 years old	0.0356	(1.362)	0.0070	(0.105)
Number of Females less than 5 years old	0.0378	(1.474)	−0.0838	(−1.304)
Number of Males between 6 and 14 years old	0.0043	(0.183)	−0.0664	(−1.175)
Number of Females between 6 and 14 years old	0.0357	(1.485)	−0.0308	(−0.515)
Days Ill	0.0005	(0.458)	−0.0050	(−0.647)
Sick	−0.0005	(−0.523)	0.0055	(0.714)
Household public goods				
Flush toilet	0.1723	(1.403)	0.6295	(1.768)*
Latrine toilet	0.1843	(3.531)***	0.3624	(3.134)***
Other type of toilet	0.0965	(0.588)	0.5630	(1.25)
Piped water	−0.5779	(−3.811)***	−0.2144	(−0.489)
Public tab	−0.3627	(−1.694)*	−0.1431	(−0.635)
Protected water source	−0.1340	(−0.978)	−0.2273	(−0.708)
Unprotected water source	0.0277	(0.723)	0.0750	(0.837)
Rain as water source	−0.8061	(−1.763)*	–	–
Vendor	–	–	−0.3406	(−0.7)
Education (yrs.)				
Head missed	0.0629	(0.836)	0.0484	(1.51)
Head primary	0.0082	(−0.488)	0.0305	(0.657)
Head secondary	−0.0033	(−0.199)	−1.2002	(−1.222)
Spouse missed	−0.0419	(−0.466)	0.0987	(1.39)
Spouse primary	−0.0333	−(2.529)**	0.0404	(1.481)
Spouse secondary	−0.1737	−(1.485)	–	−DEFAULT AS NO UNIV OBS
Type of work				
Agricultural own account	0.1415	(2.228)***	0.0627	(0.475)
Agricultural wage	−0.1274	(−1.07)	−0.2527	(−0.907)
Other	−0.0668	(−0.731)	−0.0248	(−0.114)
Non-agricultural own account	−0.1037	(−1.006)	−0.1661	(−0.944)
Region				
Central	−0.0114	(−0.242)	0.1397	(1.69)*
North	−0.1877	(−2.196)**	0.0705	(0.673)
East	−0.0101	(−0.199)	−0.0796	(−0.958)
Income	0.0015	(0.293)	0.0433	(0.556)

*Significant at 10% level, **Significant at 5% level, ***Significant at 1% level.
Defaults: Missed education (for head and spouse), urban west, non-agricultural wage employment, urban land.

Consumption and Welfare in Ghana in the 1990s

FRANCIS TEAL

I. Introduction

The money metric framework for the analysis of welfare has come in for some very strong criticism, most notably from Amartya Sen (for example Sen, 1987). How welfare can be measured and whether it is possible to say if welfare has changed between two points of time are at the centre of disputes both within and across disciplines. In this paper the issues posed for multidisciplinary research of differences of approach to the problem of measuring welfare will be addressed in two specific contexts. The first is the sense in which a measure of consumption expenditure can be treated as a measure of welfare. The second is whether larger households can be viewed as richer than smaller ones. These two issues are connected. As noted by White (2002) the relationship of welfare to household size is an example where different disciplines appear to be able to come up with different results. 'Much anthropological writing on Africa is unambiguous in the view that larger families are better off... but these findings are at odds with the "stylised fact" from quantitative poverty profiles that larger households are poorer' (ibid: 515).

At a conceptual level Sen's objection to approaching welfare from a utility perspective is that welfare cannot be viewed simply as the value of some bundle of consumption goods. At the level of its practical application many would argue that the focus on consumption expenditure in poverty studies, in which poverty is defined as a household falling below some critical level of consumption, is to miss many of the most important aspects of poverty. Thus one area of disagreement across disciplines is how welfare measurement should be approached and whether one of the central aspects of the household that has been measured – the household per capita consumption – is useful as an indicator of what is meant by poverty.

As already noted there is a clear difference of view across disciplines as to the relationship between welfare and household size. White (2002) discusses several possible reasons why the consumption measure may be misleading as a measure of household welfare. First, a measure of welfare that divides household consumption by household size does not allow for the existence of economies of scale in household formation. Secondly, households may choose their size for a range of reasons some to do with the value of children, some to do with the value of additional labour for farm activity. Thirdly, in a risky environment being part of a larger household may offer more security or better access to contacts for employment opportunities. Finally households may value size for reasons which are not economic, higher status may attach to individuals in larger households. One value of a multidisciplinary research program is that it allows different perspectives to be taken on similar data.

These issues, of the link from consumption to welfare and household size, will be addressed drawing on data which provides the basis for measuring changes in household consumption over time in Ghana. Two reports have presented data showing that poverty in Ghana has declined, the first compares 1987/88 with 1991/92, the second compares 1991/92 and 1998/99 (GSO, 1995, 2000). It has been argued that economic reforms in sub-Saharan Africa can lead to higher incomes and lower levels of poverty, Demery and Squire (1996). The Ghana data has been prominent in this debate as Ghana was among the first of the reforming economies in Sub-Saharan Africa and those reforms were sustained over the decade of the 1990s. The poverty measure used in the reports is based on the consumption expenditure of a household. Thus the data allows both the general questions posed above to be addressed in the specific context of Ghana.

In the next section the issues involved in measuring consumption are discussed. In Section III a distinction is drawn between an outcome and opportunity measures of welfare to clarify in what sense consumption can be treated as a welfare measure. In Section IV the data is used to show whether, on average, consumption has increased for most Ghanaians in the 1990s. In Section V the data analysis is extended to measure how growth has varied across different kinds of household and in Section VI the implications of the relationship between household size and consumption for welfare measurement are assessed. A final section concludes.

II. How Should Consumption be Measured?

The empirical question appears to be a very simple one: has poverty in Ghana declined over the decade of the 1990s? Even if we approach the concept of poverty by focusing on consumption answering this question is difficult in part because alternative data sources can give different answers to how consumption has changed.

Deaton (2003) shows that the assessment of how fast poverty is falling in the world depends on which statistical sources are used.

> Calculations using the Penn World Tables combined with inequality measures, by Surjit Bhalla (2002) by Xavier Sala-i-Martin (2002) and by Francois Bourguignon and Christian Morrisson (2002) show rapid poverty reduction in the 1980s and 1990s.... These optimistic calculations are starkly at odds with the World Bank's numbers on global poverty. The World Bank ... uses household survey data to measure directly the living standards of the poor, and their calculations show relatively little poverty reduction in the 1990s. (Deaton, 2003: 3–4)

The major source for this divergence is that the PPP macro numbers show a much faster rate of growth of average consumption than do the survey based numbers.

The measurement of poverty using the survey approach, which has been followed in the case of Ghana, is now one standard in the literature. GSO (2000) provides the P_i measures for poverty due to Foster et al. (1984) broken down by location and by main economic activity. The period covered is from the third to the fourth GLSS survey (from 1991/92 to 1998/99). The study also reports a breakdown of the sources of the decline in poverty due to the 'growth' effect and the 'redistribution' effect using the method of Datt and Ravallion (1992), which shows that by far the most important source of the decline in poverty over this period was the growth effect.

More recently the issue has arisen as to how pro-poor growth should be defined. As Kraay (2004: 3) notes:

> ... despite the widespread use of the term, there appears to be much less consensus as to what exactly pro-poor growth means, let alone what its determinants are. According to one view, growth is pro-poor if the accompanying change in income distribution by itself reduces poverty (Kakwani and Pernia, 2000). However, this definition is rather restrictive, since it implies for example, China's very rapid growth and dramatic poverty reduction during the 1980s and 1990s was not pro-poor because the poor gained relatively less than the nonpoor. A broader and more intuitive definition is that growth is pro-poor if the poverty measure of interest falls. Ravaillon and Chen (2003) propose this definition and apply it to a particular poverty measure, the Watts index. (Kraay, 2004: 3)

The welfare index which underlies the analysis of poverty in GSO (2000) is total household consumption per equivalent adult expressed in constant prices of Accra in January 1999.

This approach to poverty measurement is firmly in the 'quantitative' tradition. Money metric measures of welfare add the consumption across individuals where an allowance is made for the different prices households may face. While neither measuring consumption nor allowing for differing prices are without their problems the result is a measure of real aggregate household consumption. Those sceptical of the ability of numerical analysis to capture changes in welfare have naturally been sceptical of the argument that poverty fell in Ghana. It seems rather obvious to those familiar with the poverty of farmers in Ghana and who observe the large number of young people milling around in urban centres with little, or nothing, to do that poverty has not been falling. The numbers are thought to be either wrong or misleading.

Why might the welfare measure underlying the Ghanaian quantitative analysis of the decline in poverty be misleading?

In comparing two poverty profiles over time, in the absence of panel data, it is not possible to compare the same individuals or households. Might the poverty measure be misleading as it hides important differences across different kinds of households? One procedure which has been developed by Ravallion and Chen (2003) is to measure the 'growth incidence curve' (GIC), which shows the growth rate for each percentile of the population. Such a curve is relevant both to an assessment as to whether growth is pro-poor in the sense that the poorest percentiles of the population saw increases in their expenditures and as a valuable way of comparing welfare over time. In particular it explicitly allows for the possibility that any rise in inequality is sufficient to offset the rise in average income so the poor do not gain. Inequality matters, of course, in itself. One of the findings from the new well-being functions is that relative income is important, indeed possibly more important than the absolute level of income.

In this paper this procedure is extended by looking at the GIC for three kinds of households classified by the occupation of the household head: wage employees, non-agricultural (that is, urban) self-employed and farmers. In the absence of panel data this is a step closer to answering the question as to whether growth was pro-poor for all kinds of household. It is possible to go one step further in comparing different households if we are able to estimate a household level consumption function which shows how household size impact on consumption. Such an analysis provides a direct link between consumption per capita and household size in explaining any change in the poverty measure.

In summary there are substantive problems that need to be tackled in measuring changes over time in household consumption for different kinds of households. Even if those problems can be solved critics of the utilitarian calculus will wish to argue that it is in no sense a proper measure of welfare. It represents a measure of the opportunities open to an individual. It explicitly ignores the use to which these opportunities are put and their effects; as we will discuss in the next section it is to the outcomes that many argue the notion of welfare should be directed.

III. Is a Measure of Consumption a Welfare Measure?

Is the distrust of the money-metric due to the practical problems of measurement just raised or is the objection more fundamental: that a money metric approach cannot be used to make statements about the effects on welfare or well-being? To address that issue clarity is required as to what is meant by the terms welfare and well-being.

By an increase in welfare economists working in the tradition of money-metric have meant an increase in choice, Dinwiddy and Teal (1995). Greater choice implies more opportunities which is what is meant by an increase in welfare. Such a view on welfare is directly criticised in Sen (1987: 12):

> Choice behaviour is, of course, of much interest on its own. But as an interpretation of well-being, the binary relation underlying choice is very strained.

It confounds choosing with benefiting, and it does this by what looks like a definitional trick. The popularity of this view in economics may be due to a mixture of an obsessive concern with observability and a peculiar belief that choice (in particular, market choice) is the only human aspect that can be observed. (Sen, 1987: 12)

This distinction is clearly important. Being able to choose a greater range of goods is distinct from benefiting from such choice. The money metric measures of welfare are concerned with increases in choice not increases in welfare in the sense that Sen defines the term. The traditional view of welfare as increases in choice also contrasts with the notion of well-being which underlies the recent development of 'happiness' functions. Such functions measure outcomes while traditional welfare measures are concerned with opportunities. The term well-being is now used (see Kingdon and Knight, 2003) to mean subjective assessments of 'happiness' which is measured by means of a survey instruments which ask for an assessment of 'how happy you are' on a graduated scale. It seems clear that Sen and those estimating 'happiness' functions are in agreement that welfare measurement must be concerned with outcomes.

If the measure of consumption is only weakly correlated with well-being then the critics of money-measure metrics would appear to be correct in their view that it is not a good measure of welfare in the outcome sense of the term. However it seems rather doubtful that one would wish to infer, for example from a happiness function, that higher levels of consumption are not desirable because 'wealth does not buy happiness'. Indeed as those working on the happiness functions recognise the most likely interpretation of the results with respect to income is that individuals adapt to some 'normal' level of income. Well-being functions can be interpreted as identifying factors that determine a subjective measure of well-being in societies with given levels of income. If so they are uninformative as to how much well-being improves with rises in consumption over time. If it turns out that a rise in consumption is only weakly correlated with welfare in the outcome sense of the term then the issue becomes how the opportunities summarised in the money-metric measure of welfare can be converted into welfare in the outcome sense of the term. A measure of consumption will be a part of any assessment of the welfare of a society if greater opportunities are regarded as desirable. The fact that it is not a sufficient statistic is clear, not simply because it measures opportunities rather than outcomes but because, as was argued above, it must be relevant who benefits from an increase in opportunity and how the spread of those opportunities changes over time.

IV. The Money-Metric Measure of Consumption for Ghana

In this section the empirical, and data, issues in using a consumption measure of welfare are addressed. Ghana is used as an example where, as has already been noted, consumption data has been used to argue that poverty has declined with the clear implication that welfare has risen.

The data available for assessing changes in consumption per capita in Ghana over the 1990s is presented in Table 1. Table 1 Line 1 shows figures from GSO (1995) for household expenditure per capita in 1991/92 prices, Line 2 shows the figures from GSO (2000) for household expenditure per adult equivalent from 1991/92 to 1998/99

Table 1. Expenditures in Ghana 1987/88–1998/99: household survey and macro data

		GLSS1 1987/88	GLSS2 1988/89	GLSS3 1991/92	GLSS4 1998/99
1	HHEXP/capita ('000 cedis 1991/92 prices) (a)	198.3	187.5	215.0	
2	HHEXP/AE ('000 cedis 1998/99 prices) (b)			1130.8	1412.1
3	Index 1998/99 = 100	73.9	69.9	80.1	100
	HHEXP/Capita Weights used for GLSS 4				
4	Nominal ('000 Cedis)	87.0	107.9	208.9	1,336.3
5	CPI 1998/99 prices	6.8	8.6	15.8	88.7
6	CPI 1991/92 prices	43.3	54.6	100	561.2
7	Real ('000 Cedis 1998/99 prices)	1,283.2	1,249.1	1,326.8	1,336.3
8	Real ('000 Cedis) 1991/92 prices)	202.7	197.4	209.6	235.0
9	*HHEXP/capita* Index 1998/99 = 100	*86.5*	*85.7*	*90.5*	*100*
10	GDP per capita ('000 Cedis 1998/99)	822	842	890	992
11	Investment per capita ('000 Cedis 1998/99)	69	81	94	222
12	Consumption per capita ('000 Cedis 1998/99)	694	700	723	820
13	*Consumption per capita macro index 1998/99 = 100*	*84.6*	*85.3*	*88.2*	*100*
14	*Income in principal job ('000 Cedis 1998/99) (c)*	*1,430*	*1,537*	*1,814*	*1,990*
	Natural logs of:				
15	Real HHEXP/capita ('000 Cedis 1998/99 prices)	13.78	13.75	13.79	13.87
16	Income in principal job ('000 Cedis 1998/99)	13.30	13.20	13.55	13.41

Notes: (a) Household expenditure per capita (HHEXP/capita) is taken from GSO (1995, Table 2.1, p. 6); (b) Household expenditure per adult equivalent (HHEXP/AE) is taken from GSO (2000, Appendix 1, p. 35); (c) Income in the principal job is obtained from the employment part of the GLSS surveys.
Sources: GLSS Surveys and World Development Indicators (2004). As noted in the text the aggregate expenditure data for the third round of the survey were revised at the time the fourth round was analysed. We use throughout this study the original data so that we can compare out results with those published in GSO (1995).

in 1998/99 prices. If these figures are linked to provide an index of household expenditure per capita (thus ignoring any differences between persons and adult equivalents) a rise in per capita expenditure of 35 per cent over the decade is obtained. The index number is shown in Line 3 of Table 1.

In this paper a measure of per capita expenditures is adopted. To that end Line 4 of Table 1 shows the nominal figures for expenditure per capita over the four periods. It will be noted that the figures for 1991/922 and 1998/99 are very close, although not identical, to the relevant ones from the published reports. In the table the CPI indices used are reported so providing two series of constant price household expenditure per capita.[1] The implications of these calculations are shown in index number form in Line 9 of the table. Per capita household expenditure rises by 16 per cent, approximately half the figure in Line 3, obtained by linking the GSO studies.

Next the macro data are presented. Table 1 Lines 10–12 show per capita figures for GDP, investment and consumption taken from the World Bank Indicators Data for 2004. Line 13 shows the implied rise in consumption per capita to be 18 per cent which is higher than the figures from the surveys given in Line 9. Line 14 shows the data from the surveys for the incomes in the principal jobs of the individuals in the labour force. For reasons discussed below this income number is likely to be less reliable than the expenditure data. In the final two lines of the table the logs for the per capita household expenditure and the income data are shown. It is these which will be used as the basis for the growth rates that will be presented.

The first point to note from the table is that the three sources of information available for the rise in consumption or income per capita over the period from 1987/88 to 1998/99 – macro, individual survey income based and household survey expenditure based – show rises of 18, 12 and 11 per cent respectively. There is a remarkable concordance between the individual income based data and that derived from the household expenditure data. The macro data suggest rather higher growth. It is clear that the two surveys reports should not be linked as we have done in Table 1 Line 3 in part because the estimate of household expenditure per capita for Round 3 of the survey was substantially reduced when the fourth round was analysed.[2] The published reports do not allow comparisons to be made over the decade which is the purpose in this paper.

A second rather striking finding from Table 1 is that the estimates of consumption per capita from the surveys are almost twice the numbers reported in the GDP statistics. Deaton (2003) compares survey estimates of consumption per capita with those from the national accounts for some 127 countries. He finds that:

> ... consumption estimated from the surveys is typically lower than consumption from the national accounts; the average ratio is 0.860 with a standard error of 0.029, or 0.779 (0.072) when weighted by population. (India has particularly low ratios.) The exception is sub-Saharan Africa, where the average ratio of survey to national accounts consumption is unity in the unweighted and greater than unity in the weighted calculations. (Deaton, 2003: 7)

It appears that the Ghana data is an outlier in how high are the survey estimates relative to those in the national accounts.

Figure 1 shows a comparison of the three sources of data derived in Table 1 all of which are related to a money-metric measure of welfare change.[3] The first is a measure of household per capita consumption, the second is a measure of income— both of these drawn from the GLSS survey data. The third is the data from the macro accounts. In the creation of the fourth round of the GLSS data household weights were created to address some problems in the sample design. In Figure 1 the data is presented for weighted consumption. The weights were designed to be applied to households so they are not applied to the individual based income data. The growth of consumption from the macro data is higher than that from the survey based data. In contrast the estimates of growth based on household consumption are remarkably similar to those based on individual income.

Does this increase in average per capita consumption imply that welfare increased? It was argued above that, even within the context of a money-metric measure of

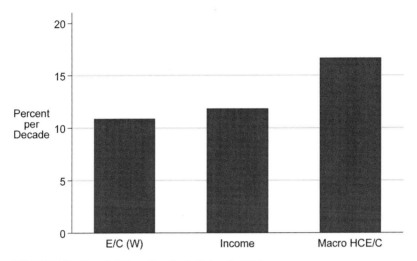

E/C (W): Weighted Household Expenditure Per Capita from the GLSS surveys.
Income: Income in the Principal Job from the GLSS surveys.
Macro HCE/C: Macro data for Household Consumption Expenditure per Capita

Figure 1. Rates of growth of expenditure and income: 1987/88–1998/99

welfare, *who* benefits is a key part of its interpretation as a welfare measure in the opportunities sense of the term. In Table 2 how the allocation of workers across types of employment has changed across the four waves of the survey is shown. The major change has been a shift from wage employment to urban self-employment. Thus it is necessary to assess how far consumption and incomes of these different workers has changed.

In Figure 2 the data for income and consumption per capita are presented. The top part of the figure presents the rates of growth of income where individuals are classified by their principal source of income, while the bottom half gives rates of growth of household expenditure per capita where households are classified by the occupation of the household head. While both income and consumption data support the view that wage employees have done much better than farmers, the perspective on the self-employed depends on whether income or expenditure is used (see Appendix Table for the data for Figure 2).

Our first problem with money metrics is apparent from this distinction between income and consumption. It is usually argued that the expenditure data is more reliable than the income, particularly for the self-employed where measurement problems are severe. If that view is accepted then it is the household expenditure data in Figure 2(b), which must be used as the basis for any welfare assessment. Adopting the household as the basis for measurement however creates the problem of how household averages can be linked to numbers in the household, the subject of Section VI.

V. Growth Incidence Curves

In the last section the average for per capita consumption by kind of household was given. In this section the procedure used by Ravallion and Chen (2003) is adopted to present 'growth incidence curves' (GIC). Figure 3(a) shows the GIC for

Table 2(a). Labour force status: percentages of individuals by category of employment

	1987/88	1988/89	1991/92	1998/99
Wage employees	17.3	18.1	15.4	12.8
Government	8.0	7.9	7.8	5.9
State enterprise	1.9	2.3	1.2	0.5
Private	7.4	7.9	6.4	6.0
Other (a)	NA	NA	NA	0.4
Farmer	58.7	54.6	56.7	54.7
Non-agricultural self-employment	19.5	24.2	23.5	28.2
Unpaid family	2.2	1.1	1.3	1.0
Unemployed	2.2	1.9	3.2	3.4
Total	100	100	100	100
Labour force participation	0.87	0.89	0.89	0.87

Table 2(b). Labour force status: sample size (number of observations)

	1987/88	1988/89	1991/92	1998/99
Wage employees	1,053	1,133	1,231	1,308
Government	485	492	627	599
State enterprise	118	142	94	55
Private	450	499	510	616
Other (a)				55
Farmer	3,567	3,420	4,548	5,579
Non-agricultural self-employment	1,185	1,513	1,885	2,875
Unpaid family	135	73	255	103
Unemployed	136	120	102	344
Total	6,076	6,259	8,021	10,209

Note: In the 1998/99 survey age workers who worked in NGOs, cooperatives or international organisations were identified separately.
Sources: GSO surveys.

the overall average of household consumption per capita. The pattern is not dissimilar to that presented by Ravallion and Chen (2003) for China in that the growth rate rises with the percentile but is positive for all. The figures, however, differ dramatically in their magnitude. While the median rate of growth in China over the period 1990–1999 was 5.5 per cent *per annum*, the median rate of growth in Ghana was 13.3 per cent *per decade*. Growth was pro-poor in the sense that Ravaillon and Chen (2003) define the term in that the growth rate was positive for the poorest percentiles.

In Figure 3(b) the next step is taken to asking if this average figure hides important differences across households by presenting the GICs for the three kinds identified in the previous section: farmers, the urban self-employed and wage employees. It is clear that the average does hide very important differences. Growth was not pro-poor among farmers. Within the farming sector growth was negative until the 64th percentile. At the median per capita consumption fell by 3 per cent over the

a)

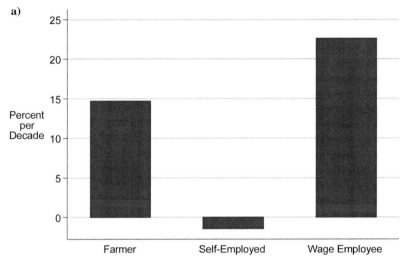

Income in the Principal Job from the GLSS surveys.

b)

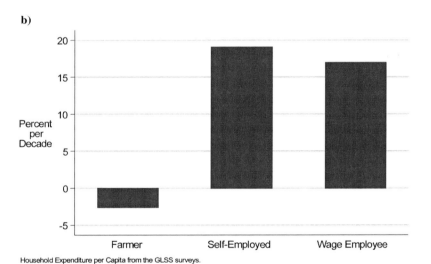

Household Expenditure per Capita from the GLSS surveys.

Figure 2. (a) Rate of growth of income by occupation: 1987/88–1998/99. (b) Rate of growth of expenditure per capita by occupation if household head: 1987/88–1998/99

decade. In contrast all percentiles of self-employed and wage employee households saw rises in their per capita consumption. At the median for the self-employed and wage employees growth was 23 and 20 per cent per decade respectively.

The GICs show clearly the nature of the growth process and the process by which average consumption per capita rose. It is of course this average figure that is being cited when it is argued that poverty fell. Among the poorest percentiles the pattern of growth was very different for farmers from either the self-employed or wage employees. Poor people in these two types of household saw relatively large rises in per capita consumption while farmers saw approximately similar size falls. The

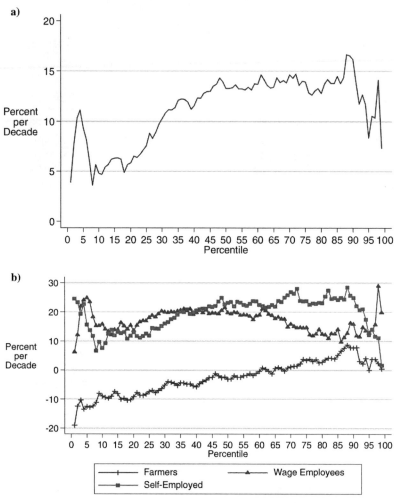

Figure 3. (a) Growth incidence curve: 1987/88–1998/99. (b) Growth incidence curves: 1987/88–1998/99. *Note*: The GICs are based on Household Expenditure per Capita from the GLSS surveys

net result was a modest rise in average consumption per capita as shown in Figure 3(a).

VI. Household Size and Welfare

We return now to an issue which has been the subject of disputes across disciplines: are larger households richer than smaller ones? Lanjouw and Ravallion (1995) note that:

> ...there is considerable evidence of a strong negative correlation between household size and consumption (or income) per person in developing countries. It is often concluded that people living in larger and (generally)

younger households are typically poorer. There has been much debate as to which is the 'cause' and which is the 'effect' in this correlation. (p. 1415)

They go on to argue that 'the existence of size economies in household consumption cautions against concluding that larger families are poorer' (ibid: 1415). This was one of the arguments discussed in the introduction as to why a simple inverse relationship between per capita consumption and household size should not lead one to conclude that larger households were poorer.

How important is understanding the relationship between household size and consumption to understanding the changes in per capita consumption in Ghana over the period that has been investigated in this paper? The answer to that question, shown in Figure 4, is that it makes a substantial difference both to the average and to the different kinds of household identified by the data. If controls for household size are used then the result is to halve the point estimate on the rise in overall consumption. The effect of these controls differs across the three types of household, reducing the change for the self-employed but increasing it for wage earners. These effects reflect the fact that, in this data as in almost all household survey data, household size is strongly negatively correlated with per capita consumption for all types of household. As household size fell for the self employed – both rural and urban – and rose for those headed by a wage employee the effects of controlling for household size on the picture of growth of consumption is not simply to change the average but to change the ranking across kinds of household.

How can these results inform the issues across disciplines as to how welfare is related to household size? Are the results misleading because there are economies of

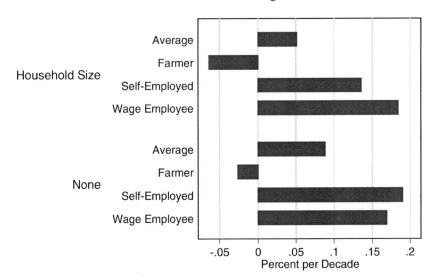

Household Expenditure per Capita from the GLSS surveys.

Figure 4. Rate of growth of expenditure per capita by occupation of household head: 1987/88–1998/99. *Notes*: The top part of the Figure shows changes with controls for household size, the bottom part of the figure has no controls. The average row is the average across the three kinds of household. Note that this differs from the average reported in Figure 1 which is for all households not simply the three kinds identified in this figure.

scale to household formation? One way that economists have approached the issues of economies of scale in household formation is to ask if the income effects from household formation can be identified. This is the approach adopted by Deaton and Paxson (1998). Their argument is that if household formation generates economies of scale then the income effect should be to increase the demand for private goods within the households providing that the own and cross-price elasticities of the good are sufficiently low. The good they focus on is food. If there are gains to increases in household size that get reflected in increased incomes they argue this should lead to an increase in household per capita consumption of food as this is a good for which it is likely that the own and cross price elasticities of demand are sufficiently low that we can be sure that if real incomes are rising then per capita food consumption should rise too. They investigate this prediction across a large number of data sets and find that it is systematically rejected. In summary they can find no evidence for the beneficial income effects that household economies of scale should generate.

In Figure 5 a similar approach to that used by Deaton and Paxson (1998) is adopted for the Ghana data to see if there is any evidence that household per capita food consumption increases with household size. In the top part of Figure 5 the food share is plotted against household size from an underlying regression which controls for total consumption per capita. As the food share is per capita food expenditure divided by total consumption per capita, if the food share falls with household size in this figure, it implies that per capita food consumption is falling with household size.

The top part of Figure 5 shows this relationship for each of the kind of households and for the total. It is apparent that the result here is the same as that obtained by Deaton and Paxson (1998). Larger households have lower per capita food consumption, exactly the opposite of what we would expect if there were economies of scale to household formation. As Deaton and Paxson (1998) acknowledge this is a very puzzling finding as there seem strong grounds to expect household economies to exist.

It was noted in the introduction that households may choose their size for a range of reasons some to do with the value of children, some to do with the value of additional labour for farm activity. This is implicitly an argument that we cannot give any causal interpretation to the result showing that as household size rises consumption per capita falls. That is clearly correct as we cannot be sure that some other factor is not jointly influencing both variables. Is it possible that the results in top part of Figure 5 can be explained by the role of children in the household or by the need for labour for farm activity? Considering first the role of children the bottom part of Figure 5 confines the sample to households with no children. The decline of the food share with household size (implying falling per capita food consumption) is almost identical to that observed for the full sample. Can the results be explained by the need for labour in the household enterprise? Again the answer appears to be no. The relationship is very similar across all three kinds of household – whether or not the sample is confined to those with no children. For households headed by a wage employee there is a similar decline to that observed for the self-employed.

Another possibility raised in the introduction was that risk might play some role in household formation. The ability of cross-section data is limited in its ability to answer such a question, although it may be noted that the variance of the per capita

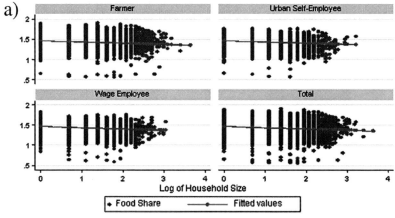

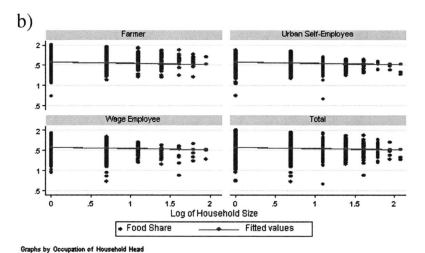

Figure 5. (a) Food share as a function of household size: all households (with controls for household per capita expenditure). (b) Food share as a function of household size: households with no children (with controls for household per capita expenditure). *Notes*: The lines shown are the predicted food share for households in which the underlying regression controls for household per capita consumption. Thus a falling food share in these figures implies that per capita food consumption falls for households with a given per capita consumption as household size increases.

consumption of farmers is lower than that of urban households. While farmers may face more risk due to the uncertainties of the harvest, urban employees can be subject to substantial uncertainty about both their ability to find employment and the returns from that employment.

The very generality of the finding that the expected increase in a private consumption good like food cannot be observed in larger households cautions against thinking of specific factors in this data set. If there are no economies of scale to household formation where does that leave the debate across disciplines as to whether larger households are poorer? It would appear we are faced with more questions than answers. There is a very strong case that they should exist but the inability to observe their consequences makes any attempt to adjust household level welfare to an individual basis deeply problematic.

What can we infer from the results? As has already been noted while they are not causal they do give us additional insights into what happened to the households over this ten year period. For households of a given size average household consumption has risen by only 5 per cent over the decade. Further, and more important from a welfare perspective, the results show that the differences across households are further accentuated by these controls. We know from the GIC of the previous section that most farmers saw falls in their expenditures. For those households who saw no change in size this fall will have been greater.

VII. Conclusions

In this paper two issues have been investigated. The first is the sense in which a measure of consumption expenditure can be treated as a measure of welfare. The second is whether larger households can be viewed as richer than smaller ones. Both these issues have been investigated drawing on data for Ghana covering the 1990s and both have been the subject of much debate across disciplines.

It has been argued that consumption can be treated as a welfare measure in an opportunity sense of that term. The data from Ghana has been used to show how a money-metric measure of consumption can be linked to welfare defined in terms of the opportunities made available to the household. Such an approach is quite different from one based on some measure of happiness (as in 'happiness' functions) or any outcome based measure of welfare (such as Sen argues should be used). A money-metric measure of consumption is explicitly concerned not with outcomes but with opportunities. In so far as greater opportunities are thought desirable then it can be argued that the money-metric can be used as a welfare measure.

The empirical analysis showed that the largest and poorest section of Ghanaians, the farmers, saw a fall in their expenditures over the decade of some 3 per cent. In contrast the urban self-employed and wage employees saw rises in excess of 15 per cent. Households headed by wage employees or those with urban self-employment have close to twice the per capita expenditure of farmers. The average consumption measure, which rose by 11 per cent, is what underlies any assertion that poverty fell. The reason the assertion has proved so contentious is clear: such averages hide falls in consumption amongst the poorest and rises for others.

One of the advantages of the money-metric measure of welfare is that it is possible to ask what happened to different kinds of household. In the paper a Growth Incidence Curve (GIC) has been presented. Calculating a GIC for Ghana over the period of the 1990s reveals that while on average per capita consumption rose across all percentiles of the distribution this was not true for farmers who are on average the poorest. While on average growth was pro-poor within the poor there were substantial gainers and losers. The controls for household size do not alter the pattern by which farmers saw falls in their average per capita consumption while other groups saw rises but they did change the magnitudes. On average there was a rise of only 5 per cent in per capita consumption for all households when there were controls for household size.

While it has proved possible to give a fairly clear answer to the question as the sense in which a measure of consumption expenditure can be treated as a measure of welfare the same is not true for the second issue posed by the paper as to whether larger households are richer or poorer than smaller ones. Here more questions were raised than answers provided. The argument has been widely advanced that economies of scale in household formation mean that the inverse correlation in the data between household per capita consumption and household size does not imply that larger households are poorer. In the Ghana data, as for other data sets investigated, it is very hard to find any evidence for such economies. How such findings affect the link from consumption per capita in the household to individual welfare is a major unanswered question in the literature at present.

Acknowledgements

This paper draws on the Ghana Living Standard Surveys (GLSS) for the periods 1987/88, 1988/89, 1991/92 and 1998/99, which are nationally representative household surveys. The CSAE is greatly indebted to the GSO for making the GLSS data available. The support of the UK Economic and Social Research Council is gratefully acknowledged. The work was part of the programme of the ESRC Global Poverty Research Group (grant no. M571255001). Thanks to GPRG colleagues from the Universities of Manchester and Oxford when this paper was presented at a GPRG Workshop.

Notes

1. For the third and four waves of data the CPI indices are the deflators used by the published reports. For the first two waves of the data we have linked these figures to a measure of the CPI derived from figures from the Ghana Statistical Office.
2. In GSO (1995, Table 2.1: 6) the figure for consumption per capita is given as Cedis 215,000, as reported in our Table 1. At the time of the analysis of the fourth round this figures was revised down to Cedis 183,000, a reduction of 15 per cent. This figure can only be obtained from the data, not from the report, which gives figures in terms of adult equivalents rather than per capita and uses 1998 prices. In GSO (2000: 3) there is a warning that 'the results reported here are not strictly comparable with the previous report'. In this paper the original data is used. A more detailed use of the data can be found in Teal (2001).
3. The growth rates used in the figure are based on the differences of logarithms.

References

Bhalla, S. (2002) *Imagine there is no country: poverty, inequality and growth in the era of globalisation* (Washington, DC: Institute for International Economics).
Bourguignon, F. and Morrisson, C. (2002) Inequality among world citizens: 1820–1992, *American Economic Review*, 92(4), pp. 727–44.
Datt, G. and Ravallion, M. (1992) Growth and redistribution components of changes in poverty measures, *Journal of Development Economics*, 82, pp. 275–95.
Deaton, A. (2003) Measuring poverty in a growing world (or measuring growth in a poor world), *NBER Working Paper 9822* (Cambridge, MA: National Bureau of Economic Research).
Deaton, A. and Paxson, C. (1998) Economies of scale, household size, and the demand for food, *Journal of Political Economy*, 106(5), 897–930.
Demery, L. and Squire, L. (1996) A macroeconomic adjustment and poverty in Africa: an emerging picture, *The World Bank Research Observer*, 11(1), pp. 39–59.

Dinwiddy, C. and Teal, F. (1995) *The Principles of Social Cost Benefit Analysis for Developing Countries* (Cambridge: Cambridge University Press).

Foster, J., Greer, J. and Thorbecke, E. (1984) A class of decomposable poverty measures, *Econometrica*, 52, pp. 761–5.

Ghana Statistical Service (GSO) (1995) *The Pattern of Poverty in Ghana: 1988–92* (Accra, GSO).

Ghana Statistical Service (GSO) (2000) *Poverty Trends in Ghana in the 1990s* (Accra, GSO).

Kakwani, N. and Pernia, E. (2000) What is pro-poor growth, *Asian Development Review*, 18(1), pp. 1–16.

Kingdon, G. and Knight, J. (2003) Well-being poverty versus income poverty and capabilities poverty? *CSAE Working Paper 2003–16* (Oxford: Centre for the Study of African Economies, University of Oxford).

Kraay, A. (2004) When is growth pro-poor? Cross-country evidence, *IMF Working Paper WP/04/47*, Washington DC: International Monetary Fund, accessed at: http://www.imf.org/external/pubs/ft/wp/2004/wp0447.pdf

Lanjouw, P. and Ravallion, M. (1995) Poverty and household size, *The Economic Journal*, 105, pp. 1415–34.

Ravallion, M. and Chen, S. (2003) Measuring pro-poor growth, *Economic Letters*, 78, pp. 93–9.

Sala-i-Martin, X. (2002) The disturbing 'rise' of global income inequality, *NBER Working Paper No. 8904* (Cambridge MA: National Bureau of Economic Research).

Sen, A. K. (1987) *The Standard of Living* (Cambridge: Cambridge University Press).

Teal, F. (2001) Education, incomes, poverty and inequality in Ghana in the 1990s, *CSAE Working Paper 2001–21* (Oxford: Centre for the Study of African Economies, University of Oxford).

White, H. (2002) Combining quantitative and qualitative approaches in poverty analysis, *World Development*, 30(3), pp. 511–22.

World Bank (2004) *World Development Indicators* (Washington, DC: World Bank).

Appendix

Table 1A. Mean household expenditure per capita (annual measures)

	1987/88	1988/89	1991/92	1998/99
Wage Employees (N) (Units)	797	896	991	1046
1998 Cedis	1,739,173	1,671,170	1,814,395	2,041,369
	(1,511,205)	(1,526,970)	(1,627,723)	(1,784,568)
Logs (1998 cedis)	14.11	14.06	14.12	14.28
	(0.70)	(0.72)	(0.77)	(0.73)
US $	659	613	707	812
	(561)	(559)	(649)	(708)
Farmers (N) (Units)	1,649	1,655	2,299	2,940
1998 Cedis	1,001,534	960,789	969,044	1,007,263
	(814,842)	(846,274)	(798,623)	(831,395
Logs (1998 cedis)	13.58	13.52	13.54	13.55
	(0.68)	(0.69)	(0.70)	(0.70)
US $	384	350	384	382
	(310)	(304)	(315)	(318)
Self employed (N) (Units)	517	720	985	797
1998 Cedis	1,487,194	1,426,714	1,592,886	1,802,173
	(1,275,218)	(1,328,677)	(1,409,819)	(1,527,338)
Logs (1998 cedis)	13.94	13.88	14.02	14.13
	(0.72)	(0.74)	(0.72)	(0.77)
US $	657	522	617	718
	(484)	(484)	(556)	(619)

(continued)

Table 1A. (*Continued*)

	1987/88	1988/89	1991/92	1998/99
All (a) (N) (Units)	2,963	3,271	4,275	5,465
1998 Cedis	1,284,687	1,257,936	1,308,746	1,454,805
	(1,172,096)	(1,219,156)	(1,246,675)	(1,348,863)
Logs (1998 cedis)	13.78	13.75	13.79	13.87
	(0.73)	(0.75)	(0.77)	(0.79)
US $	489	460	512	570
	(440)	(444)	(492)	(538)

N is the number of households, the figures in ( ) parentheses are standard errors.
(a) These figures are the totals for the three categories identified, not for all households in the survey.
Sources: GSO Surveys.

Table 1B. Mean incomes (annual measures)

	1987/88	1988/89	1991/92	1998/99
Wage Employees (N) (Units)	1,037	1,126	1,194	1,305
1998 Cedis	1,778,911	1,689,260	3,090,051	3,598,023
	(2,104,238)	(1,302,311)	(1,660,000)	(2,960,000)
Logs (1998 cedis)	14.12	14.11	14.33	14.35
	(0.73)	(0.74)	(0.84)	(0.93)
US $	680	616	1,225	1,417
	(845)	(475)	(6,899)	(11,457)
Farmers (N) (Units)	2,153	2,397	2,827	3,804
1998 Cedis	613,684	549,858	801,104	734,051
	(995,435)	(1,096,544)	(2,679,654)	(1,988,513)
Logs (1998 cedis)	12.55	12.31	12.90	12.69
	(1.27)	(1.35)	(1.11)	(1.23)
US $	241	199	316	279
	(402)	(393)	(1,109)	(766)
Self employed (N) (Units)	1,184	1,512	1,884	2,875
1998 Cedis	2,612,870	2,988,574	2,525,945	2,922,687
	(5,146,664)	(11,100,000)	(4,774,953)	(15,500,000)
Logs (1998 cedis)	13.95	13.94	14.05	13.94
	(1.28)	(1.33)	(1.15)	(1.22)
US $	982	1,099	971	1,172
	(1,899)	(4,158)	(1,814)	(6,442)
All (a) (N) (Units)	4,374	5,035	5,905	7,984
1998 Cedis	1,431,100	1,537,009	1,814,246	1,990,290
	(3,072,143)	(6,245,886)	(8,190,408)	(15,200,000)
Logs (1998 cedis)	13.30	13.20	13.56	13.41
	(1.38)	(1.50)	(1.25)	(1.37)
US $	546	563	709	786
	(1,152)	(2,337)	(3,377)	(6,074)

N is the number of individuals for which there is data on income, the figures in ( ) parentheses are standard errors.
(a) These figures are the totals for the three categories identified, not for all individuals in the survey.
Sources: GSO Surveys.

INDEX

Page numbers in *Italics* represent Tables and page numbers in **Bold** represent Figures.